Freelance Jobs for Writers

Freelance Jobs for Writers

A Complete Guide to Freelance Writing Opportunities

Edited by Kirk Polking

Cincinnati, Ohio

Second printing 1984

Library of Congress Cataloging in Publication Data
Main entry under title:

Jobs for writers.
  Bibliography: p.
  Includes index.
  1. Authorship—Vocational guidance. I. Polking, Kirk.
PN151.J6   808'.042   80-16070
ISBN 0-89879-142-1

Design by Barron Krody

Preface

Freelance writers who feel their fate is determined by the responses in their mailboxes from magazine and book editors will discover through this book a set of happy alternatives.

The forty chapters detail writing-related jobs that you can find in any community: jobs that are interesting, challenging, and flexible enough to fit a part-timer's schedule; jobs that are solid sources of spare-time income.

Each of the contributors writes from personal experience, so you can avoid the pitfalls they discovered the hard way. They offer a step-by-step outline of where to find the clients; how to handle the job in the most efficacious way; and how to get paid a fair price.

While there are some unique jobs we haven't amplified in this book — such as the partnership of writer Jules Maitland and actor Stanley Johnson, whose firm "Personal Words" writes and delivers eight-minute funeral eulogies for seventy-five dollars — we have added Editor's Notes to individual chapters wherever possible to pinpoint related ideas for the freelancer to consider.

As with any business, a good letterhead and some business cards will help establish your professionalism and are a good investment. Some freelancers design promotion packets to describe in more detail the special services they offer.

If you have dreams of becoming a full-time freelancer, there are several important guidelines to keep in mind: (1) Don't quit your regular job until you have freelanced enough on nights and weekends to already be earning a good percentage of your present income just from freelance work; (2) Try to develop as many continuing freelance assignments for local clients — such as company magazines or monthly PR retainers — as possible, so that you have a consistent income you can count on; and (3) Remember that you must charge enough for your services to cover not only an hourly rate that you think is fair, but which includes the 20 to 25 percent your employer would be paying you in fringe benefits such as medical insurance, vacation pay, etc., which you'll now have to pay yourself, in addition to your regular business overhead expense.

To most freelancers, a book on the bestseller list or a four-figure check from a major magazine are still primary goals. But in between shooting for the stars, you might try looking beyond the mailbox to the clients down the street or in the next town who need writing talent for regular or special projects.

We welcome comments from readers on their own personal experiences in each of the freelance areas covered in this edition, as well as in additional fields, for consideration in our next revision.

A companion volume on full-time career writing jobs is also in the works for those writers who want a regular weekly paycheck while they write the Great American Novel on weekends.

In either case, writing is nice work — and you can get it, by following the tips in this book!

—*Kirk Polking*

Contents

and national publications pay a modest fee. In either case, it's a chance to show editors what you could do with a larger, paid assignment; and the clips are a good addition to your portfolio when you're seeking other jobs.

Business Writing by Robert E. Heinemann 55

Companies *must* communicate today—to their customers, dealers, salesmen, shareholders, the general public. Even large firms with in-house staff and outside agencies occasionally need extra help. Learn how to find the freelance markets among businesses in your area and deliver what the client wants at the right price.

Business Writing: Anniversaries 68
by Etna M. Kelley

Department stores have sales every year to celebrate their anniversary, but what about the local manufacturer that's about to turn fifty years old, or the local bank that's seventy-five, or the company that introduces its fifteenth new product on its fifteenth birthday? It all means business for the freelance writer and PR person. Here's how to get it.

Business Writing: Meetings by DeForest Walton 74

Whether a company makes a product or provides a service, it holds some kind of sizable meetings. They may be training seminars, conferences, a sales presentation, or even a live "show." And professional writers are needed to create an effective presentation with all the collateral materials and visual aids to support it.

Column Writing by Al Eason 79

Are you an expert on a subject that would interest a lot of newspaper readers in your region? If so, smaller papers that don't have a staff writer on the subject are prospects for a freelance column of yours. If you're willing to sell your columns in person to noncompeting papers in the area, you can start a self-syndication business. Specialized national magazines may be additional markets for the same columns in an expanded form.

Comedy Writing by Eugene Perret 83

Your friends say you have a terrific sense of humor, and you've wondered how to turn that knack for a witty line or situation into freelance income. A top comedy writer shows how to get started locally before branching out into writing gags and comedy material for professional performers and TV shows.

cash in on the trend of roots-seeking. Family trees, family histories, commissioned biographies, and local history brochures are among the possibilities available in practically every community.

Government Public Information
by Ted Oglesby

Larger daily newspapers cover state and national government activities, but the working of grass roots local government is often a mystery to most citizens. Many small cities and counties welcome the offer of part-time professional help from writers who can do more in-depth explanatory features on local government, brochures on how taxes are spent, etc. Large cities may also offer part-time writing projects for regional offices of federal agencies.

Newspaper Stringing by James McLendon

When something happens in your immediate area that would interest a newspaper in another city, you can become your own personal wire service to provide that copy by collect phone call to the distant paper. That newsbreak may also be worth another assignment from the same source if the story has news follow-up or expanded feature story possibilities.

Opinion Research Interviewing
by Michael H. Ketcher

The major polling organizations like Gallup and Louis Harris, plus innumerable market research firms, need interviewers to get the public's opinion on everything from presidential candidates to the latest salad dressing. Pay is minimal but steady and the interviewing experience will enhance your writing.

Printers' Writing Jobs by C.G. Welton

Printers are usually so busy printing clients' materials that they don't have time to merchandise themselves. That makes the 26,000 commercial printers in the US likely prospects for you, the freelance writer. You can also help them get more business from existing clients, and new business from prospects they haven't called on, by creating ideas for these customers. If you have the right typewriter you may also be able to provide camera-ready copy for small customers.

company and the politician's audience, but the research and writing techniques are similar for both markets.

jobs with business, the US government, patent attorneys, publishers, and others. Beginners may find an alliance with a translation agency a good way to get established in the field.

TV Documentaries by Joseph Hanania 236
When the FCC passed the regulation in 1971 requiring each television station to set aside at least a half hour a day to non-network programming, opportunities expanded for writers who could provide worthwhile documentaries that stations could produce inexpensively and still provide a service to the community.

TV Editorials by Cookie McGee 243
Is there a station manager in your area too busy to write his own editorials? Can you present a concise case for his likely opinion on local, national, and international affairs? If so, your market is waiting.

TV News and Features by Dave Derkacy 247
You'll rarely have an exclusive spot newsbreak to sell a network, but all stations are potential markets for less timely news features that have strong local appeal—sports events they don't have enough staff to cover, festivals, personalities, etc. Here's how to get the station to provide both film and studio space for editing.

Advertising

by Linda Trainor

Breaking into advertising copywriting is comparatively simple, because there is a constant need for new pitches for familiar products and services. But, like any other profession, advertising has its drawbacks. That fact never struck me so forcefully as on the Monday morning I was asked to write two radio commercials for a Las Vegas hotel, several pieces of billboard copy for a racetrack, and a couple of ads for a liquor account, all in addition to creating bits of miscellaneous copy. Things were shaping up for an interesting week.

But there was a catch: It all had to be done by the following *day*. Being relatively inexperienced, I was overwhelmed at the prospect of trying to meet such a deadline. But I did it. I know of no better way for a writer to learn or improve his writing skills than through copywriting.

Basically, there are two kinds of copywriters: staff copywriters and freelancers. Once you develop some skill and some samples, you *can* be both if you want. But let's concentrate here on getting freelance assignments. Before anyone is going to hire you to write copy on a freelance basis, he or she wants to see some proof of performance. Finished samples are your credentials. Fiction, poetry, articles, plays, or scripts are generally not acceptable evidence of your ability to write copy that sells. In fact, advertisers and agencies are sometimes reluctant to hire poetry or fiction writers. Your freelance possibilities will be considerably narrowed if you have no solid copywriting experience.

Getting Experience

How do you get the experience? Do your homework, select your prospects, and hit the streets.

Homework. Study your local newspapers, magazines, advertising sheets, and Yellow Pages. Study the ads for several weeks. *Who* is advertising, *what* are they advertising, and *how often* do they advertise? Keep a daily list by category. You will begin to see a pattern which will tell you where the biggest demand for copywriting is. Typically, department stores, drugstores, and food markets will advertise every week, maybe every day. But there are many less obvious advertisers who can use freelance copywriting help: cleaners, auto repair shops, jewelry stores and boutiques, car washes, nursery schools.

Select prospects. Review your prospect list and pick several products or services that interest you or with which you have some familiarity. Compare this list with all providers of the same product or service in your area. For example: If Van's Cleaners advertises every Thursday, who are Van's competitors? Are they advertising like Van's? If not, they are good prospects. Try to sell them your services.

In the coming years, attorneys will become an increasingly important market for freelancers. Lawyers are now permitted to advertise. The nature of their training and practice makes it difficult for them to write simple copy, something their average clients can understand.

Local newspapers and magazines also need freelance copywriters for their smaller advertisers who do not have agencies.

Hit the streets. Make phone calls, knock on doors. Doing your homework and selecting prospects will be a waste of time unless you are willing to get out and ask for the business.

Four Major Types of Clients

An alternative to trying to crack the freelance market without samples is to look for project assignments.

Where? Just about anywhere. To simplify your search, I've classified the giant advertising field into four broad categories:

Ad agencies and other producers. A friend got her first copywriting job in a large agency without ever having written a line of copy. "I spent several weeks reading advertising trade publications and pumping a copywriter I knew," she says. "I kept asking questions like 'Why is this ad good or bad?' 'How did you figure out what to say first?' Things like that. Meanwhile, I called or wrote letters to a couple of agencies every ten days or so. Sometimes I'd just congratulate them on an award they'd won or comment on a new account they were working on. I had to be very careful, of course, so my persistence didn't become outright harassment. Finally, one of them decided to give me a try."

The smaller the agency (and some consist of one person), the fewer credits you'll need to break in. Small agencies are usually overworked and understaffed.

Some writers recommend writing sample ads to show what you can do. Creative directors of some large agencies tend to view this as proof of your inexperience, but small agencies may be more interested.

Beyond formally structured advertising agencies, there are any number of individuals and companies involved in advertising services: artists, photographers, printers, typesetters, print and audiovisual production companies, etc. All of these are potential markets for freelance copywriters because they often are called upon to provide services outside their specialty.

A partner in a commercial art studio recently showed me a list of his clients that includes some of the largest companies and advertising agencies in the country. "I work on all kinds of projects for these companies," he explained. "More often than not, I also end up hiring the writers. Of course they're hired on a freelance basis. We work by the job or project, and we can't afford staff copywriters who may have to sit around waiting for the next project."

It takes a little phone work, a little footwork, and a lot of perseverance, but you can build a good stable of these producers while holding a full-time job. Eventually, they will come to depend on you to complement their specialties. In the meantime, you will be building a portfolio.

A word about samples: *Always keep them.* No matter how bad, unimportant or distastefully designed you think they are, eventually you will find someone who wants to see a sample just like that big ugly one you wrote three years ago. What's worse, they will think it's great. Advertising is a very subjective field, so it's important never to prejudice what a potential client or employer will think is good. More than once I've found the client ignored the samples I thought were terrific and looked instead at something I hated, telling me that that was exactly what he had in mind. The first assignment I got from Walt Disney happened just that way.

The educational promotions director at the Disney studios asked me if I'd had any experience writing copy for educational films. I begged the question, because the only sample I had was an unimpressive little black-and-white catalog I'd written for an obscure company that produced and rented films about horses. I tentatively relaxed as she began leafing through a handful of flashy samples: slick four-color catalogs, ads, promotional pieces. Then she stopped at the little black-and-white catalog. I was horrified and wondered why I hadn't left it at home.

"This is exactly what we're looking for," she smiled. "Do you know much about horses?" I admitted to a slightly better than average knowledge. "We want to promote a Super 8 version of our feature on the Lippizaner Stallions, and we need someone who can write to horse people about horses," she explained. Solely on the basis of that one little catalog, I walked out of the Disney studios with an assignment to do a brochure, two consumer ads, and two news releases. You never can tell, so don't throw anything away.

Business and industrial firms. Large companies often have their own in-house advertising departments; smaller companies rely almost totally on outside agencies, freelancers, and the media (newspapers, magazines, radio and TV) to help them produce their advertising materials. Within companies, advertising efforts usually fall under the jurisdiction of departments entitled "communications," "public relations," "marketing," "sales promotion," or "advertising." They use staff and/or freelance writers, much the same as agencies and producers do. They may or may not employ an agency to supplement their in-house capability.

Business and industry generally provide a good training ground for new copywriters since there is less competition: Advertising is not their main business. They produce and sell something else. The advertising department is just that, a department—like accounting or shipping—which is only a tiny fraction of the whole business. Therefore company rates for copywriters are usually much less than what an ad agency or producer might pay because their requirements are less stringent. On the other hand, they are often willing to work with someone who has a little experience.

One of the biggest ad markets within the business and industry category is the retail department stores. They consume thousands of words of copy a day in all media—not to mention their volumes of direct-mail catalogs. Al Hampel, executive vice-president and director of creative services for Benton & Bowles, a large agency, agrees that retailing is an effective training ground for writers. In an ad he wrote for the Magazine Publishers Association, Hampel said, "If you have a son or daughter who wants to be a copywriter, encourage him or her to get a job in a department store. It's the best training they could get." And if you already have another job and want to freelance ad copywriting, retail stores are a good place to look for extra work that their regular writers are too busy to handle.

Retailers are good markets for the beginning copywriter, but they aren't the only ones in business and industry. Recently, an insurance company in my town advertised for a proofreader in its advertising department; and a magazine sought an all-round helper with some writing, some research, and some general office experience. While these ads were for full-time positions, they indicate where opportunities may also exist for freelance jobs.

Mass media. Radio and television stations, newspapers and magazines, all use copywriters. True, advertising agencies and companies themselves provide the media with much of their finished advertising material. But there are many other advertisers who have no professional advertising assistance and so the job falls to the media they use. It's one of the services the media make available to advertisers to ensure getting more of their time and space dollars.

This market is not quite so broad as the first two, but it still holds plenty of opportunities. I know one young man whose real goal was to become a radio announcer and disc jockey. He took a less than spectacular job with a small-town radio station in the Midwest. To supplement his pay, he began to sell time (commercials) for the station. As he began selling, he found that his clients often asked for his help in writing their commercials. Accidentally and incidentally he broke into advertising. [See separate chapter on radio copywriting.]

Newspapers and magazines need copywriters for the same reasons radio and television need them: to write material for smaller advertisers who have no agency.

William Kerr-Gray, former executive editor of a national fashion trade publication, told me he hired aspiring young copywriters all the time. "One of the brightest young men I've known came to me for a summer job. Before he came for the interview, he read several issues of the publication and pulled out a handful of ads. Then he typed short notes telling me how he would have made them better and stapled a note to each ad. He didn't write one thing; he just critiqued already-published ads. I hired him on the spot." This same approach could be used by a freelancer seeking assignments.

Miscellaneous. These markets are not insignificant compared to the three previous categories, despite the grab-bag heading.

Mail-order and direct-mail advertising, for example, are multimillion-dollar industries and growing every year. Your own mailbox is ample evidence of this. There are companies that specialize in catalog and mail-order advertising and produce hundreds of thousands of pages, trumpeting everything from hardware to rose bushes to sailboats to exotic animals. The list can go on and on. They all need someone to write their advertising copy. Where do you find them? Check your Yellow Pages.

An important source of information about jobs in advertising is the advertising trade journals (such as *Advertising Age* and *Broadcasting)* and your local newspaper. The classified sections of these publications offer a wealth of ideas and information. But don't just look under *Advertising* or *Copywriter.* Sometimes the fine print will reveal that you are just what employers are looking for. Here are some example headings to check: *Catalogs, Creative, Editorial, Freelance, Gal/Guy Friday, Journalism, Part Time, Promotion, Proofreader, Publications, Publicity (PR), Retail, Technical, Writer.* Reading the advertising trade journals will also keep you aware of what's happening in the industry, which will give you an edge when you're asking for that first chance.

How Much Can You Make?

Now that you know a little about where your market is, what can you expect to get paid for your efforts?

One direct-mail catalog producer I know pays new freelance writers $25 per page of catalog copy. You may have to write three to twenty blocks of copy per page. A typical catalog could be twenty-four to forty-eight pages long. As a writer proves his ability, the page rate can increase to $50 and up.

Clients sometimes prefer to pay freelance writers on an hourly basis, for assignments that are usually simple and immediate in nature: three two-column-by-six-inch ads, or a handout circular for next week's Moonlight Sale. Writers who are paid an hourly rate are usually very fast and very good. You estimate the number of hours necessary to complete the assignment, and you will be expected to be very close to the mark. Rates can range from $40-$50 an hour.

For longer or more complex assignments, daily or weekly rates can be arranged. Daily or weekly projects are common during peak periods when large advertising campaigns involving a variety of media are being mounted. Advertising agencies and larger companies have a good idea how long they will need an extra writer or two. Often you will be provided with a typewriter and desk in your client's office for the duration of the assignment. Rates will usually start at an average of $100 a day/$400 a week and go up from there.

Monthly retainer fees are a good way to provide yourself with a more dependable income. Although retainers are not common, anyone using freelance copywriting services on a regular basis might be willing to negotiate a monthly retainer. The idea behind this arrangement is simple: You charge your client a fixed monthly fee—say, $500. In return, you will write all the copy he will need for the month—whenever he needs it. Recreational-vehicle, auto, and mobile-home dealerships who advertise weekly are good prospects for retainers. The amount of the retainer is negotiated and should be reviewed periodically to be certain it is fair to both parties.

Ad agencies and company advertising departments will often negotiate rates by project. For example, if they want a full-page ad and two smaller ads featuring golf equipment on sale, a freelancer might get seventy-five dollars for writing the whole package. Fees vary, of course, in relation to where you are, how great the need is, and the amount of competition. How fast you can increase your income depends a lot on you and a little on luck.

Newspaper Ads for Small Businesses

As a writer I have learned to try many new fields, and have finally established myself in what I've found to be a specialty with very little competition.

I prepare six-to-nine-inch single-column "articles" (they're actually ads) for various businesses, such as "The Home Front" (for realtors), "Calling All Homemakers" (for furniture outlets), "Fascinating Facts" (for insurance concerns), "Your Car Needs Our Care" (for wheel-alignment specialists) and many others, including mobile-home dealers, druggists, beauty shops, service stations, and jewelers.

My copy is original—breezy, entertaining, and different from the usual advertising format. And my ads are designed to permit choice placement. For example, "Calling All Homemakers" appears on the lifestyle page, to zero in on the target audience. "Fascinating Facts" applies the analogy of sports as setting a fast pace in competition to the fast service provided by a dependable insurance company; this ad, naturally, appears on the sports page. A small photo and the byline of the operator or owner of the business almost invariably accompanies the ad/article.

This service is greatly appreciated. I receive $10 for each ad/article I write that appears in various local newspapers on the basis of a single insertion weekly. Ten such accounts in eight months netted me $100 per week.

Facts and background material are garnered from the proprietors, trade papers, sports mags, reference books, and current events. I prepare and submit two to four articles to each client for approval. Statements are mailed monthly.

Occasionally an account will require a format different from the single-column arrangement. This results from the use of "cuts" to illustrate particular types of businesses. My fee for this special service is also ten dollars per issue.

Location seems to have some bearing on my success, as I find that many small towns and cities in the 8,000 to 25,000 population bracket have limited facilities for providing my type of service.

So start with home folks—the businesses and business acquaintances in your neighborhood stores, shops, and services. Then branch out to nearby towns, or even distant ones. Be sure always to feature your clients wherever practicable as the writers of their ads. They will love you for it.

— *Fred H. Drewes*

Anthology Editing

by Lloyd Zimpel

It looks easy enough, this business of putting a group of other people's magazine articles between book covers. Write a few letters begging for permission to reprint, find the closest Xerox machine, buy a big bottle of rubber cement, dash off a clever introduction, and there you have it: a fat manuscript with your name as editor prominently thereon. What would it all take — a couple of weeks? And doesn't it beat sweating over a novel where *you* have to make up all the words?

If you have that illusion, hang on to it, for once you decide to toss off such an anthology, you'll need it to sustain you through the confusion of unanswered letters, malfunctioning photocopiers, outlandish requests from would-be contributors, and fingers always stuck together with glue.

I've edited two anthologies — or readers, collections, compilations, whatever you choose to call them—and I've also coauthored a technical book and published a novel, as well as numerous short stories and articles. Now, if you expect me to say that editing those collections was enormously harder than the other writing efforts — wrong. It was easier. But easier only in a relative way. In itself it held frustrations, as one publisher warned me when I proposed an anthology of articles on the recent change in attitudes toward work. With the myriad nonwriting details demanded by such a project, he said, the job would involve "much more tedious and annoying labor than I suspect you realize." He suspected wrong; after all, I'd already edited one such pain in the neck, and besides, I wasn't asking for a rose garden.

But as his response shows, the toughest part is convincing the publisher that he will enrich himself and the world of letters by underwriting your project. That's achieved less by magic than by sheer stubbornness — an endless persistence that eventually puts you in the right place at the right time.

The Initial Query

In assembling *Man Against Work,* brought out by Eerdmans, I'd sent out several query letters before I got a nibble. A publisher asked to see more detail. So as not to do too much work before I had a commitment, I simply photocopied the first pages of a few selections. He found these intriguing and inquired after still more, perhaps a table of contents.

This definite interest warranted more work, and I whipped together a tentative list from the great variety of pieces on the subject that I'd accumulated. *Hmm,* yes, came his response. The idea looked very good indeed, but — would I believe the coincidence? — in point of fact he had a book *very similar* to this which would be out soon . . . . So now it was my turn to utter a thoughtful *hmm.* Clearly, he'd been fishing to see how my book compared to his, and while there's nothing wrong with that, it does indicate what I mean by being in the right place at the right time. If I'd been a few months earlier with this publisher, it would have been *my* collection on his press.

With sufficient persistence, you'll hit on a publisher who has an open spot somewhere on his list. Depending on your subject, you may want to concentrate on specialty publishers — those heavy with business, sport, social science, or hobby titles. Alas, even when your subject is right up the publisher's alley and he accepts your proposal, he'll probably do so with reluctance, telling you that he'd much prefer a single-author treatment, since some publishers believe that such a book stands a better chance for big sales.

Your original query should also establish that you are wholly at ease with, if not expert in, the subject of your collection. Indeed, if you're not already knee-deep in the field, this is not the time to start wading. Ideally, for this kind of anthology (presumably a sideline to your main interest) you will have amassed much material over the years, perhaps in support of some obscure enthusiasm — famous sumo matches, say; or conflicting opinions on the Common Market; or history-making backgammon games; or the theory and practice of contemporary swineherding — the possibilities are endless.

Whatever it is, you undoubtedly already have a drawerful of clippings, tearsheets, offprints, and photocopies which you never knew quite how to use, except possibly someday as background for a novel or a full-scale nonfiction work. For my anthology *The Disadvantaged Worker,* published by Addison-Wesley, I'd accumulated such material during two years of part-time reading on the problems of employment for minority workers, partly as a result of my nine-to-five job, and partly as fallout from coauthoring an earlier book on training the hardcore unemployed. It's certain that without more than a nodding acquaintance with your subject you'll have difficulty pulling together enough relevant material in a reasonable amount of time. (It goes without saying that the problems of compiling a book of original material, for which you must seek out authors and assign each a topic, are far more difficult.)

Your Authoritative Background

Besides demonstrating *your* familiarity with your subject, you must make the publisher understand that you also know what everyone else has written about it, and thus you've come to see the void that your proposed collection will fill. If you've worked personally in the field, all the better, because frequently not only must you sell the publisher on your ability but convince him as well of the importance of, say, swineherding, perhaps even persuade him that swineherds actually do exist. For however close to your heart your subject might be, it probably means nothing to the publisher. All he wants to know is whether it's important enough for five thousand people Out There to buy a book about it. No matter how obvious you think that is, you'll have to muster enough evidence to satisfy him.

Take a moment to consider the poor publisher. There he sits, mothering a neat list of movie-star reminiscences, revelations of unidentified flying objects, and novels exposing the Mafia—all subjects he is comfortable with, having put out similar books last year, and the year before. He knows how many copies they'll sell. But here you come trumpeting your outlandish swineherding proposal. Swineherding? Such oddities make him nervous; he's leery that a smart-aleck author is trying to put something over on him. To assuage his fears and assure him that the world needs such a book, you'll have to exert your best efforts. Here enters the truly creative aspect of anthology compilation, in those first exchanges with a prospective publisher.

Of course, in being creative you still have to be honest. At this stage of the relationship the publisher won't necessarily take your word anyhow, and he'll do as he does with other specialized book subjects: farm out the proposal to a couple of people in the swineherding field for independent evaluations of your idea and its market possibilities. The completed manuscript might also get an outside reading. In some cases a big publisher will conduct his own research on your proposal. One large house turned down my proposal for *The Disadvantaged Worker* because "our research indicates that most people wanting this information find it located in a number of noncommercial publications such as government publications, magazine articles, journal articles, etc." But it was for exactly that reason—to bundle the materials into one handy source—that I'd proposed the book. In the end I found a publisher who did his research with a number of personnel officers in large corporations; they thought such a book would be valuable for staff training, and the promise of multiple-copy sales swung the deal.

Once a perceptive publisher approves your proposal, he'll send along the contract. In the case of anthologies, it sets forth not only who gets what but—because of permission fees—also who pays for what and how much. Sometimes the writer can negotiate a favorable deal wherein the publisher agrees to pay not only a cash advance (usually small), but also to foot the entire cost of reprint fees. On one of my collections, permission fees were taken care of in that way; on the other, the publisher and I split payment of the fees down the middle, with the publisher paying my half for me out of an advance, as well as granting me an additional cash advance. Both are standard practice, as is an alternative method where the writer pays the entire reprint tab, although even then the publisher handles the physical business of making fee payments out of a hypothetical advance against royalties, so that nothing comes out of your pocket.

Royalties and Reprint Rights

The royalty schedule on anthologies varies wildly. Much depends on whether the book is hardbound or paperback, on its retail price, and on what part of the reprint fee the publisher will pay. Both of my collections came out in paper, which meant a reduced rate. Where the publisher paid the full fee, the rate was 5 percent of the retail price per copy of the first 5,000 sold, and $7^1/2$ percent for all copies after that.

A more likely and more lucrative arrangement, with you and the publisher splitting reprint fees, would be 10 percent for the first 5,000 copies and 15 percent thereafter, as was the agreement with my first collection (although here a reduced rate applied to copies the publisher sold by direct mail). In any case, the usual $10-12^1/2-15$ percent schedule commonly paid for hardbound novels doesn't apply to anthologies. In some cases, I'm told, the rate on college-text anthologies sinks to a dismal 3 to 5 percent. Still, most publishers won't undertake a collection unless it promises several years of sales, and those will add up nicely.

Once it's settled who pays the fees—and the publisher will settle that unilaterally unless you get your oar in early—then you face the task of getting permission to use the articles you want. Doubtless the publisher has already insisted on a firm estimate of the total fees. To arrive at this, write to a few of the copyright holders and see what they are asking. One of my collections cost only about $300 in fees, the other some $900. Obviously, the reprint fee for an individual article depends upon both the reputation of the author and the source of original publication. A trade journal, for example, may ask for no fee or a nominal $10; the *Harvard Business Review* asks a standard $250, others ask even more. Certain material, such as that published in noncopyrighted US government journals, of which there are many, is available for reprint without cost. When the magazine has assigned copyright to the individual author or his agent, matters get more complicated, frequently more expensive, and may require considerable negotiation.

Prior to the recent new Copyright Law, most copyrights were held by the magazines. Put your case to them in a letter along these lines:

Dear Magazine Editor:

I am editing a yet-untitled reader for the Hoggee Publishing Company on the theories of swineherding, to appear in spring 1985 in a trade paperback edition of about 250 pages to be priced at approximately $6 retail. For this edition I would like permission to reprint the article "Soo-wee, Soo-wee," by Alan Author, which appeared in your magazine for September 1976. Full credit will be given. Would you please sign the authorization below and return it as soon as possible in the enclosed envelope. A duplicate of this request is enclosed for your files.

. . . . .

Permission is given to reprint the above-described material:
By _____Title _____Date _____

This form may come back to you with no request for permission payment. Fine. Other times, if the fee asked seems too grand for your budget, so inform the magazine. On several occasions magazines lowered their fees to what I could afford; they recognized that the reprint itself was of some credit to the magazine. But in other cases the magazine held out for an extra $50—not always with the author's prior knowledge—and so I passed up their piece. With both collections the highest fee paid for a single article was $100, twice, for essential pieces that could not be replaced with lower-cost substitutes.

Cutting Remarks

Now, as the permission letters come in (you're keeping meticulous files of all correspondence), you can start putting the articles together on paper in that perfect form you've carried only in your head thus far. At this point there may be problems. How, for example, to resolve those startling repetitions in different pieces? (Why, it's almost as if some writers were *copying* each other—preposterous!) But mostly you'll have to standardize capitalization, punctuation, spelling, and see that space breaks and the like conform throughout [see separate chapter on copyediting]. Much of this, predictably, you'll miss until the last proof, when panic sets in.

You will also have to decide early on a consistent means of showing copyrights. This is usually done with a note at the foot of the first page of each piece, or by relegating all notices to a page at the front of the book. But if a copyright holder *specifies* that his copyright must appear in a certain place and in a certain form, you'll save yourself trouble by printing all notices similarly.

Some pieces you'll have to cut for space. Here you are absolute monarch, so take it easy. If more than a few sentences have to go, get permission by sending the copyright holder a copy of the piece showing what you propose to trim. Some magazines and authors forbid cuts out of hand, but with most material you'll be permitted to pick and choose—after all, you're paying—with the assumption that you know best what will make a successful book.

One tricky aspect of anthologizing magazine pieces is that they frequently contain time references that would look foolish in the context of a book's greater permanence. Watch for such things as "when the issue was voted on last month." Often such casual time pegs can be painlessly excised so long as you don't fool with the author's meaning. Cutting "last month" from that phrase probably won't alter the sense. But when a time reference is important, changes are called for. If, for example, an article writer described a factory strike "of two years ago" to distinguish it from other strikes, but four years had passed since the article first appeared, and it would be another year before the anthology was published, that reference then would have to be changed to "the strike of 1980" (or whenever). Another article might mention legislation "recently sponsored by the Administration." The meaning was obvious when the article appeared in 1982, but a different administration might be in Washington when readers come upon the book, so the phrase becomes "sponsored by the Reagan Administration in 1984."

Introductions and the Foreword

How about an introduction, to get in your own two cents' worth? For my anthologies I wrote introductions and, for one, a lead-in to each of ten sections as well. If you don't really need an extensive introduction beyond a few notes about the purpose of the collection, don't insist on one. On the other hand, if you need a lengthy, authoritative examination of the swineherd's role in history to provide a necessary focus for the book, and if it's good enough and sufficiently independent of the pieces in the book, you may be able to publish it as a magazine article and thus garner some prepublication notice for the book. This occurred with my introduction to *Man Against Work*. (To complicate matters, I then had to secure a release from the magazine publishing my article to use the piece as introduction for my book.) Or, conceivably, your collection might be enhanced by a foreword from a world-renowned expert in swineherding, in which case you'd best arrange for it beforehand—and add his fee to your original cost-of-permissions estimate.

As things start to take shape, inquire of your publisher if he can make do with a pasted-up manuscript of photocopied articles instead of a freshly typed one, thus saving time, money, and errors for everyone. Some publishers will agree, but so as not to arouse the printer's ire you'll have to paste it up in a certain form: a single column of print affixed to each sheet of typing paper, with titles, subheads, footnotes, and additional matter typed in place as they are to appear in final form.

Even with a completed manuscript, whether pasted up or typed, your work as editor may not be done. Unless your publisher is one of the giants with a high-powered staff of marketing experts, he'll probably look to you for assistance in reaching the special audience which, as you'll recall, you promised would leap at the book. Now you must deliver, and this means more than sending in the addresses of your relatives and insisting on a half-page ad in the *New York Times Book Review*.

What the publisher needs is a careful list of all magazines, journals, obscure newsletters, tipsheets, and the like that swineherds rely on for news of the trade; many will carry surprisingly extensive notices of your book. On top of this, you should contrive to get the mailing lists of all the top swineherding associations so that your publisher can circularize them with direct-mail advertisements of your book. Since these lists usually aren't easily available, you'll have to use your connections in the field. You would do well, too, to get the book into the hands of anyone who might provide a usable advertising blurb or help get the book noticed in the right circles by displaying it in a booth at the next swineherds' convention. If you have a slight bent for self-promotion and aren't easily embarrassed, you'll find this sort of thing can be fun and that you don't mind serving as the unpaid—and, it may seem to you, sole—promoter of your book. Besides, there is always the possibility that you'll do such a good job that the book will make a pile of money.

But even if it doesn't, you'll very likely find that compiling an anthology has its own rewards, particularly if it's done between jobs, without displacing work you'd feel guilty about putting off. Ideally, you're working with material built around an old, familiar enthusiasm, and that in itself can be fun. Even if the money doesn't spark retirement plans, it may exceed expenses. And then, too, as you pick and choose, cut and edit, wheel and deal for permission rights, there arises a minuscule but delicious sense of power. Not much, not enough to corrupt, but, as a hapless novelist and short story writer, I can tell you I savored that very little very, very much.

Arts Reviewing

by James Boeringer

As a devotee of the art of writing, you may also be interested and informed in the fields of drama, music, or the visual arts as well. Why not combine your writing skill with another artistic field you also know, and market your critiques? New plays, musicals, concerts, lectures, exhibits — all provide material for you.

Your own qualifications, besides your ability to write, are (1) enough knowledge of your subject to earn the respect of your peers, and (2) enough genuine enthusiasm to ensure a lively and personable reaction to what you see and hear.

Have a Main Idea

A measure of basic journalism enters into critical writing. Most editors will insist that paragraphs be short and that the standard who-what-when-where questions be covered in the lead. You should also make the main idea of your review immediately clear. This main idea should summarize the succession of aesthetic experiences the event offered.

For example, a recital offering music by C.P.E. Bach, Mozart, Beethoven, and Brahms could be conventionally reviewed according to how well each piece was played. A more perceptive critic would notice that four kinds of classicism were involved.

This central idea allows the writer to move logically and pointedly through his descriptions and evaluations, pulling them together. If his lead paragraph has stated the idea in an arresting way, his chain of supporting observations can hold the reader all the way to the end.

Be Brief

If your job is that of criticizing staged events for a daily paper, there is another practical advantage to the "main idea" approach, inherent in the fact that your night editor will hold a limited amount of space open for you until a specific deadline time.

This usually gives you about twelve column inches or 350 words, and anywhere from thirty minutes to an hour in which to compose them.

It would probably be easier to write a thousand words in that time, because anybody can write a lot of bad material fast. The main idea helps you to keep your material short and to the point, and filling unused space is easy. If the editor does have to cut without consulting you, he will prune subsidiary material instead of your main criticisms.

Still another advantage is the fact that you will get better headlines. You do not get to write your own heads; this is done by the night editor or by a head writer who has been trained to distill his words from your opening paragraph. So get right to the point.

If you ramble at the beginning, you may wind up with a head like "New Play Fails" for a review that later on expresses the opposite idea. Your readers always think you wrote the head, even though you have no control over it; so main-idea criticism is a good way to avoid embarrassment.

A detail of format: your review is always the last thing to come in, and if you have left no space for the head, then the editor, who is probably harried by that time, has to paste half a sheet at the top of your page. So start halfway down, and triple-space. [At newspapers that use computerized typesetting systems, reviewers may be asked to learn to type their copy on a video display terminal (VDT).]

Maintain Your Own Viewpoint

Just as in fiction a clear and fixed viewpoint must be maintained, so in a review it is your own ideas that you must put across, not the general reaction of the audience, or what you overhear intelligent-sounding people saying in the lobby.

By all means report an audience reaction if it is a striking one, like a standing ovation or twenty curtain calls, but if you are convinced that such a reaction was only misdirected mob impulsiveness, say so, and give your reasons. By the same token, never be afraid to be enthusiastic about an event that seemed to leave everybody cold, if you really felt that way.

Be Clear

Never assume your reader has been there. It is up to you to re-create the event and to put your own interpretation across with absolute clarity.

The reason for this is that criticism must be readable and meaningful in the complete absence of the event being discussed. The arts supply the springboard, but the criticism must acquire an independent existence and an importance all its own. What it has to say must be permanently valid and interesting.

This is why the writings of really great critics like Max Beerbohm and George Bernard Shaw are republished to be read and reread long after the events they discussed have faded away.

How to Sell

Let's suppose you have done some practice reviewing, and you have sharpened your skill in grasping and expressing a main idea briefly, clearly, and from your own interesting viewpoint. Now how do you sell your material?

You might start with a weekly paper. Reviewable events tend to occur on weekends, and weeklies tend to come out on Thursdays. That fact eliminates the rush of the dailies.

Go to the editor and talk over the project with him. Chances are he has to do almost everything by himself. He has probably been pestered by the local Artists' Series committee to give them more coverage, and will be glad to pay anywhere from $15-$25 for your work, to which you can add the value of the brace of free tickets you'll get, which are always for excellent seats.

Working as a correspondent for a national trade magazine in the arts is much like working for a weekly newspaper, in that there is no pressure. In this case, you write a sample summary review of a month's important arts events in your area and submit it with a query. It's difficult for a New York or Chicago trade magazine to maintain a corps of writers all over the country, and there is sometimes an opening. Such magazines pay as little as they can, say $35-$50 a release to start, but as you prove your own value, you can earn up to $75-$150 or more per summary.

After apprenticeship on weeklies or as a trade magazine correspondent, you can move on to a daily. Read the local papers carefully, and ascertain which are not covering arts events at all or are sending unwilling news reporters to cover them. Then submit your query and sample to the editor or publisher.

You can also work through the ordinary personnel office. I secured an excellent series of assignments on the *Daily Oklahoman* simply by going to the personnel office and filling out the usual forms, putting down "music critic" in the blank for "type of position desired." The mere fact that there was no established file of such applications may have brought mine to the attention of the editor.

Dailies pay better than weeklies. The lowest figure you should take would be $20-$35 per review, and you can get up to $50 or more. Beyond higher figures, one moves into a salaried position.

Related Opportunities

Another, related job with daily newspapers — less creative but nonetheless necessary and remunerative — is that of compiling and summarizing local calendars of arts events and editing accumulations of wire-service releases. This is on small newspapers—a segment of the work carried out by regular full-time editorial employees. Occasional part-time specialized work can be negotiated.

Freelancing arts-related *features* to national magazines is easy if you are alert to good subjects, which are, chiefly, world premieres, arts festivals, significant revivals, local-color events, and celebrity interviews. The pattern of these articles is somewhat different from simple criticism, since you must intersperse lively, revealing anecdotes among your discussion and comments.

A world premiere is, of course, the first time some artistic creation is revealed to the public. It may be commissioned music, a new mural or monument, or the first performance of a drama that has some connection with your locale.

A festival is a complicated, cooperative venture usually devoted to a specific area of the arts. For freelancing purposes, the more unusual and fresh the area, the better — and the more marketable.

I happened to be in South Dakota during the revival of the first opera ever written west of the Mississippi (it was by General Custer's bandmaster); the uniqueness of the work and the odd combination of opera and frontier life sold it to the Sunday *New York Times*.

Local color sold another of my arts-related articles to the *Times*. This time it was about an avant-garde theater in Oklahoma, a state more likely to be associated with the oil wells that stand on its capitol grounds.

Keep in mind that interviews with visiting artists are salable. Every new article about a celebrity helps his career. He knows this, and will be willing to take time to talk to you. Take some photos, or get them from the artist's agent.

Photographs should accompany *all* these freelance features since they increase the value of your pieces, which could range from $75 to $250 upwards, depending upon the scope and significance of your material.

Tips and Warnings

Stick to professional events. In reviewing amateur work, you have the unpleasant choice of compromising your standards or infuriating a segment of your public, which is bound to have a rosy view of local "talent."

Be prepared to be criticized yourself. Your well-wishers will keep quiet; so most of your mail will be fairly virulent. Respond patiently and open-mindedly to all letters: Everyone is capable of error, including you.

Don't become intoxicated with your own power. Coming out in print repeatedly with your opinions can give you a rather heady view of your own sagacity, which can spoil your writing with smugness, sarcasm, or condescension. Your job is to seek out and express aesthetic truth, not to inflate your own ego.

Be positive of your facts. You're safe if you say "Madame Tessitura sounded as if she had a cold." But if you say "Madame Tessitura certainly had a bad cold," she can sue you, and only a doctor's certification will get you out of it.

Keep up your sense of humor. Enjoy the funny things that keep happening in the arts. Recognize the importance of what you are doing, but don't take yourself or your job too seriously. Besides being profitable, criticism should provide the healthy, enjoyable satisfaction that any other kind of real creative writing provides.

Editor's Note: If you live in Nashville, New York, Los Angeles, or any other city with music recording companies, there may be additional freelance opportunities writing liner notes for record albums. You'll need familiarity with the artist's background and style and access to the A&R (Artists and Repertoire) person at the record company. Fees are negotiable, but the average is $100-$175. And no matter where you live, there are possibilities with some national magazines and local papers for freelance record reviews.

Associations

by Mary A. DeVries

Associations need writers and editors, and they have room for both beginners and professionals. Considering that a new association springs up somewhere almost every day, the market is likely to continue expanding in the foreseeable future.

What type of work is available? Writing, editing, and other. The "other" is many things, but in preparing copy for publication, it often involves design, layout, production supervision, printing arrangements, or possibly some related administration.

As a former editor of publications for a national professional society, I have written and edited a typical variety of association literature. The society I worked for had a membership of about 2,000 and was growing steadily. You might use this size and the projects I describe as a relative guide in evaluating opportunities with other associations.

The Market

The Chamber of Commerce of the United States describes associations thus:

By custom and practice, trade associations are generally defined as voluntarily joined, non-profit organizations of competing or related business units. Professional associations may be defined as voluntarily joined, non-profit organizations of individuals in the same or related professions and semi-professions. In the former case, memberships usually are corporate or company units, whereas in the latter, they are on an individual basis.

The association market is distinct and immediately recognizable: The word "association" or "society" almost always appears in the organization's name. The market, which includes local, state, regional, and national groups, is much larger than is generally recognized. The latest edition of Gale's *Encyclopedia of Associations* lists some 17,750 organizations, and current estimates far exceed that number.

Although general references to the *association* field include both *trade associations* and *professional societies,* in specific instances it is more important to keep in mind that a society is often concerned with an educational function, while a trade association may be more concerned with product or industry promotion.

The importance of *any* association to the freelance writer is that it makes extensive use of the written word. It's the only way an association can regularly unite its geographically scattered membership. True, it may have monthly meetings, annual conferences, or occasional workshops, but the day will never come when *all* members of an association attend such events.

Every association, then, is really a little publishing house, with one difference: The small and moderate-sized groups rarely have an editor or writer on the staff full time. Often they rely on their business manager or a harried volunteer to handle their publications, and would gratefully welcome a freelancer's offer of help.

Among typical association projects are newsletters, information bulletins, speeches [see separate chapter on speechwriting], reports, form letters, brochures and programs, booklets and manuals, news releases, directories, and books. Nearly all require both writing and editing, and often production work and distribution as well.

Don't be overwhelmed by the many things you suddenly realize you aren't familiar with. You can learn what you need to know in the library and through conversations with local printers. You don't even need a college degree—just the desire to learn and the willingness to work hard.

After you have looked through some books [see this book's bibliography], you should write letters—lots of letters— to set up a file of sample association literature. Consult a directory of associations for names and addresses.

The largest is Gale's, in three volumes. Volume I is arranged by category (business, educational, cultural, medical, religious, etc.).

Volume II is a geographic index (check this one for organizations in your area), and Volume III lists newly formed associations. It's available in most large libraries.

Somewhat smaller is the directory of *National Trade and Professional Associations of the United States,* listing around 6,000 associations and their publications. It is available from Columbia Books, Inc., 777 14th St., NW, Washington DC 20005. The American Society of Association Executives, 1575 Eye St., NW, Washington DC 20005, annually publishes a *Who's Who in Association Management,* listing about 7,000 member associations. Remember, too, to check the Yellow Pages for associations nearby. Usually they are listed under Business and Professional Associations or Clubs and Associations.

Writing the Association Newsletter

Most associations have at least one newsletter, and you should have no trouble collecting samples. They will not necessarily be good examples, so if you think you can do a better job, you already have a prospect.

Could you write the nontechnical items you see in a newsletter? Could you solicit and edit the articles purchased from other freelancers or written by association members? Could you lay out each issue? Could you work with the typesetter and printer in production? Could you make arrangements with the printer or a mailing house to maintain the organization's mailing list and to provide address labels each month? If so, association newsletters may be what you should pursue. If you find an association that doesn't have a newsletter, so much the better—you can offer to start one.

Preparing Booklets and Manuals

What types of booklets do associations publish? You name it. A booklet may be anything from a history of the industry to a description of a career-guidance program. It is the publication editor's job to discuss the project with the association manager, do the necessary research, conduct interviews, and write the copy. After the copy satisfies the association manager, it's on to the production phase.

You will have to mark the copy for the typesetter (using standard editorial marks, which your printer can provide); select typefaces for the text and for heads, subheads, and captions; proofread galleys, and approve corrected galleys and press proofs; select paper for the body and for the cover; and if the association wants to protect its materials, copyright the finished products. (Write to the Copyright Office, Library of Congress, Washington DC 20559, for forms and instructions.) Unless your printer has a graphic artist handy, you may even end up having to design the cover as well, or at least roughly sketch an idea for an artist.

If you have never done any of this before, it is crucial that you choose an obliging printer and seek all the help you can get in selecting typefaces and paper, in estimating size, and so forth. If the association has a tight budget for production, you will have to work closely with the printer in keeping costs in line.

Have him point out the differences in paper quality and cost, and the difference between using one color or two or simply screening one color to give the impression of two. Ask him to explain copyestimating and copyfitting to you. If he can't do this, he may not be the best printer for you while you are in the learning stages.

Manuals are frequently needed for chapter operations and publicity. A chapter operating guide can be prepared only in cooperation with chapter officers, who can fill you in nicely on how to establish and run a chapter. The association manager will be able to provide related information about national regulations and influences.

A publicity manual might instruct a chapter or regional office in setting up a public relations program, detailing how to write press releases, how to get them printed, where to mail them, and when to mail them.

Samples of most of these manuals are scarce, I'm afraid, except for one. A membership promotion manual is an important tool that many associations need but don't have, and you're in luck here. The American Society of Association Executives has an excellent example: *The Membership Director's Manual.*

The Prospects

You will need a 3x5 card file of the associations you select as prospects. Definitely include those close to home and close to your heart, but don't stop there.

As you make your contacts, be aware of certain occupational hazards. You could be unlucky enough to reach an association manager who does the writing and editing himself and wants to keep it that way, even though it's clear to you that he is an enemy of the English language!

You may reach associations that survive, barely, with volunteer assistance only. Do not write them off too quickly. Recently I spoke with the executive director of a national communications association and remarked that they were fortunate to have enough volunteer assistance not to need freelancers. He quickly replied, "I guess you haven't had to work with volunteer assistants, or you wouldn't call us fortunate!"

But once you have a job, you must still proceed with caution. You may have to deal with publications-committee volunteers who cannot resist playing editor or writer. They will do things you will have to undo, and will offer dangerous suggestions you will have to ignore, gently, without losing your job in the process.

Don't despair. The best advice I can give is to have confidence in yourself and in what you have learned is professionally proper and correct. Fortunately, you are likely to meet helpful individuals who will be glad to bequeath to you the headaches of the writer and editor.

The Proposal

After you have done your background research, collected your samples, and set up a file of prospects, you may need one final thing: proposals. These should be brief, well-written offers to lend your experience and talent to the prospective association's publishing program. If you want to do certain things only, you should make that clear. Mention any applicable education, training, and experience.

Show them the economy of work done on a freelance or job basis: You do much of the work at home, so they don't even have to provide a typewriter or office for you; you handle your own payroll taxes; and as a professional, you have the necessary reference materials, the tools of the trade, and the required printing contacts.

Emphasize that you are available for occasional freelance assignments, should they already have a staff editor for regular activity. After all, that editor may have more than he can handle at times.

Always leave something in writing, even if you visit the association in person. Business cards or printed stationery make a good impression.

How to Calculate Fees

Except for very small associations or those that seem to have definite budget problems, most will pay $5 to $10 an hour, depending on the project and your experience; or a flat per-project fee. Larger associations will pay $10 to $25 per hour. If you're just getting started, it wouldn't hurt to consider lower rates while building some credits.

Top writers and editors may receive more than the standard fee, especially if they have substantial association experience. Newsletter writers and editors charge per issue anywhere from $100 for a two-sided $8^{1}/_{2}$ x 11 sheet to $500 and up for a larger publication. If the association is agreeable, however, you are much better off working by the hour until you are able to judge how long it takes to do different things.

Associations expect a lot from writers and editors today, but they are a very friendly lot, and best of all, they need you!

Audiovisual Writing

by Allan Amenta

Several years ago, as a freelance audiovisual writer new to California, I sent a brief direct-mail letter to a random scattering of industrial companies, business firms, and AV producers within a fifteen-mile radius of my typewriter. I had written a fair amount of sales copy for clients over the years, but this was the first such letter I had ever composed in my own behalf. Within ten days, I had earned $1,000 from a client who needed both a concept and a script in a hurry. The script was for a short motion picture about a new product his company was going to introduce at a national trade show. Since that time I have never been without clients.

Now let's dissolve, film fashion, to a day a few months later. Before the clock struck noon, I had signed two contracts totaling $7,000 for my services. It was the most money I had ever contracted for in one day, or even one month. (And I include payment for a TV episode I once collaborated on.) The first contract was for $1,000, to write an annual report for a local corporation. The second was for $6,000, to develop and write scripts for several instructional filmstrips. Quite a difference.

That lucrative day confirmed something I had known for a long time: The AV market pays well, extremely well—much better than many print markets. And the pay is getting better all the time.

The audience for AV productions is pretty much invisible, largely unpolled by the experts and virtually unnoticed by the Hollywood studios.

But the audience is there, a many-faceted mosaic of large and small groups—employees, students, nurses, teachers, physicians, secretaries, managers, salespeople, farmers, voters, consumers, ethnic minorities.

And the programs they watch? The sheer variety of titles is staggering. They cram hundreds of catalogs describing motion pictures, videotapes, filmstrips, and slide films on more subjects than you or I ever dreamed of: technical films on how to fix or mix things; motivational programs on how to cope, win, succeed, interact, adjust, manage, and supervise; training programs that tell you which button to push, lever to raise, or dial to twist; and educational films that visualize the microcosm of bacteria and the macrocosm of planets and galaxies.

Who sponsors and produces these programs, and why? Just about any company, organization, or group with a mission, motive, and the money to reach the right audience with the right message at the right time. They include sponsors in business, industry, education, medicine, religion, government, foundations, and in military, social, and political organizations. More and more, these sponsors are turning from the rhetoric of print to the imagery of film and video.

The Other Movies

If you think Hollywood creates most of the films Americans watch, you're wrong. The movie capital produces only about 20 percent of all AV programs. An astonishing 80 percent originates outside of feature films and commercial television. This non-Hollywood world of special-purpose films for special audiences goes by a number of names: *non-theatrical, informational, sponsored,* or *client* films. Educators prefer *instructional media, nonprint materials,* and *software.*

But whatever the label, it's a sweet market for writers—a market now approaching three billion dollars for production, according to Tom Hope, editor-publisher of *Hope Reports* (1600 Lyell Ave., Rochester NY 14606), the most comprehensive research and informational service in the AV industry. As Hope sees it, the AV market is on an upward curve in production and distribution that will extend far into the future. The need for new programs of every kind has never been greater, nor the AV market better, as sponsors, educators, and producers seek more effective, efficient, and economical ways to communicate.

Writers are vastly outnumbered by other specialists in the AV field. Most people involved in AV don't really know how to put a complete script together. To be sure, in the teamwork process of programming, producers, directors, photographers, cinematographers, and others sometimes make valuable contributions to a script—a word here, an idea there. But most seem to lack the ability or the discipline to go from scratch to script, unless they started out as writers.

The Other Language

There's a reason for the scarcity of good writers in the nontheatrical field. Many clients, educators, and even some professional print writers think an AV program is just another format for stringing words together. It's as though AV stood for Abominable Verbosity.

History confirms this: Print people usually turned out scripts that were talky, unimaginative, pedantic, uninspired, and soporific. Happily, pedagese and prolixity aren't good enough any more, even though they still contaminate too many programs.

Communicators and educators also recognize that fancy thingamabobs and expensive thingamajigs do not a program make, either. It takes imagination, ideas, concepts, and scripts. Without them, cameras and projectors, no matter how sophisticated, are little more than hollow containers.

But you've got to know the language.

As an AV writer and consultant for many years, I've found the hardest thing to overcome is the client's conditioning to print and talk. And in my AV scriptwriting classes, the biggest obstacle is the same thing—the students' Gutenberg hang-up. Most students, in the belief that a script is an extension of literature, just can't wait to write all those beautiful words. One night after class, early in the semester, a student zoomed toward me with unexpected velocity and unmistakable ferocity. "When the hell are we going to stop this rigamarole and start writing scripts?" he growled.

Rigamarole? With what facility some novices will reduce years of experience to nothingness. And with what chutzpah they seek to start at the top, without benefit of apprenticeship and discipline, putting carts before horses, diplomas before education, and words before thought. For the first few weeks, I had been screening films and videotapes so that students could see what was good, then discussing concept, structure, purpose, and AV principles and techniques. Even Orson Welles didn't plunge into writing and filmmaking until he had viewed *Stagecoach* scores of times. And young Rob Thompson, who wrote *Hearts of the West* after scripting documentary films, urges beginning AV writers to "watch good stuff" rather than depend on how-to books. By viewing a variety of films over and over, "things just sink in, sort of by osmosis," says Thompson.

But what was good enough for Welles and Thompson wasn't nearly good enough for my very impatient and impassioned student. He was hell-bent on saddling up his typewriter pronto and riding into the glorious sunset of scriptwriting success. I headed him off at the pass and gave him the only sensible reply I knew.

"You're not ready to write scripts. You don't know the language yet. It's still foreign to you and most of the other students. And you have to learn to think it and speak it like any other language."

By foreign language, I don't mean just those sometimes bewildering AV terms you can find in almost any media or film glossary. Knowing the terminology won't make you an AV writer any more than a barroom knowledge of Freud will make you a psychoanalyst. More accurately, perhaps, AV communication is polyglot, embracing many "tongues"— images, words, music, sound effects, lighting, camera angles, optical and special effects, even silence. And they all seem to have their own grammar, syntax, vocabulary, idioms, and semantics. Without knowing the language, you are merely a stranger in forbidding territory.

And that's no wild metaphor, either. For in AV writing, you not only speak and use a different language, you also create your own geography and chronology. With images and effects, you can create a room, a community, or a town that does not exist in the real world. You can make time plunge forward, leap backward, or stand still. You can expand it, compress it, or freeze it. Of course, like the novelist and playwright, you must be able to start a story, develop it, build it, and dramatize it. But, unlike them, you are not shackled to nouns, pronouns, and verbs. You are more like the painter using a multicolored palette. And, like the composer, you have a wide range of tones, sounds, and dynamics, either to create simple melodies or orchestrate symphonic tapestries.

To do all these things is to think audiovisually—what I call *script-think*. It's having a strong sense of simultaneity for what's happening on the screen at any given moment. You think only of what the audience sees in the frame and hears on the soundtrack. "I do not follow the geography of a set," said Alfred Hitchcock. "I follow the geography of the screen. I can only think of the screen."

In his book *The Writer and the Screen,* Wolf Rilla calls the screenplay "the one nonverbal form of writing," and the writer is "not carrying on a literary activity at all. In fact, he needs to jettison much of his professional stock-in-trade and acquire disciplines that may be foreign to him." There's that word again—*foreign.* Rilla also coins the word *screenwright,* substituting it for the more common *screenwriter* and *scriptwriter.* He says: "The screenwright's language is that of images, not of words."

An AV writer, then, is not primarily a wordsmith. He's a designer, a master-planner, a visualizer, an image maker. Above all, he's a synthesizer who fuses, blends, and harmonizes many elements into a new whole—something usually greater than all the parts.

I've spent about half of my career in print—as a newspaper reporter, publishing-house editor, PR director, advertising copywriter, and magazine writer. I've accumulated many bylines and have several cartons of booklets, brochures, ad copy, house organs, newsletters, speeches, flyers, articles, box-top copy—you name it. Although I know something about printing and graphics, I could have written most of these materials with hardly more than a rudimentary knowledge of the printing process. If you write for the AV media, however, you cannot afford to be ignorant of AV production and equipment. You should know as much as possible about cameras, lenses, sound recording, optical effects, graphics, animation, and even music. You don't have to have the technical skill of a cinematographer or sound engineer, but you *should* know how their tools can be used creatively—and economically. You should know, for example, that a dolly shot, with the camera moving down a long corridor, unless absolutely vital to your film, will increase production time and cost, expand the film's running time, and slow up the action.

Scriptwriting Strictures

In his excellent book *Audiovisual Script Writing,* Norton S. Parker says: "A shooting script or scenario is the blueprint of the picture prepared by the writer, the architect of the picture. The director becomes the builder when he converts the script to action on film." Audiovisual writing is "lean writing," says Parker. "In scene description, do not indulge in the use of words and phrases which make beautiful reading but do not describe action and cannot be photographed." Write, he admonishes, so that "the film can be photographed efficiently and economically."

When you write for the AV media, keep these thoughts in mind:

An effective AV script is designed to *make a point.*

An effective script *avoids abstract language.* You don't talk freedom, liberty, equality. You visualize them with specifics.

An effective script is primarily *nonverbal* and largely *emotional* in its appeal. If you want to get a message across to viewers, aim for the heart first. It's the shortest distance to the head.

An effective script is *highly selective.* You can easily add pages to a book, but try adding them to a script without regard for the visuals.

Since most AV programs have voice-over narration, a simple two-column script format has evolved over the years. It is usually an 8½ x 11 page divided vertically into two columns, one side—commonly the left—for *Picture,* the other for *Sound.* In the *Picture* column, you include all visual content, scene description, and camera directions; and under *Sound,* you set down narration, music, sound effects, and any dialogue. In television, *Video* and *Audio* are the usual column headings, but I prefer *Picture* and *Sound* and have used them on scripts for all AV media. They are simple generic words and are all-inclusive. For a fuller discussion of script formats and AV terms, consult Parker's book and other references listed in the bibliography at the end of this book.

So Who's It For?

The best way to begin a script is not to begin with the script. That's starting at the wrong end. Your finished script, you'll discover, is only the tip of the iceberg: the rest of your work is submerged in conferences, research, interviews, telephone calls, and perhaps travel. This is the planning stage, sometimes called preproduction. It's the most important stage in the entire AV process, and it may last from weeks to many months.

To begin a script, you start with the client, the person sponsoring, underwriting, or supervising the project. He or she may come to you directly, or, as frequently happens, indirectly, as one of the clients of an AV producer who hires you.

The agenda rarely changes, whether the client is selling acreage at beautiful Lake Pocowootchi or trying to light a fire under lethargic managers, malingering employees, or disenchanted customers. Your job is to find out exactly what he wants to say, when he wants to say it, where, to whom, why, and through what AV medium. If you're working directly with the client and not through a producer, find out how much he can afford to spend. That may be the most significant question of all.

Even though clients are your prime source of information, don't expect all of them to be articulate, well-organized, or completely knowledgeable about the subject. A client may feel intimidated if it's his first AV project. Nevertheless, pin him down. Don't let him go until he has made everything crystal clear, provided you with all relevant literature, and put you in touch with experts and specialists in his organization.

Make sure he defines his target audience. Find out why he wants to do the project. What's his purpose? Is the company in trouble? Does he have to woo new markets? Does he have a high employee turnover? Are sales falling off—or employees asleep? Is his organization losing good will and trying to improve its image? Will the AV program be part of a larger communication package—printed materials, orientation, workshops and seminars? Or will the program alone carry the burden of the message and details?

I usually ask the client, "Assuming your audience forgets most of the commentary and details, what is it you want them to remember most of all?" Then I ask for a laundry list of these points. Sometimes a client's key message is brief enough to jot down on your shirt cuff.

Conveying the Message

I build a script around the client's key message or essential points, knowing that I can select concrete details and examples for reinforcement. Once I am thoroughly grounded in his subject, I look for a concept, device, or theme to make it work as an AV program. I do much more thinking than writing at this stage. In a medical script about pleural drainage, I emphasized ordinary, day-to-day human breathing to dramatize the traumatic effects resulting from an accident or violence. In a motion picture on team teaching that called for contrasting the old and new, I used old black-and-white still photos of the one-teacher, one-classroom practice. These stills conveyed the idea of rigidity and sameness, and because they were in black and white, they had an old-time, scrapbook flavor that conjured up the past. At a key point, I dissolved to color motion-picture footage of two teachers as a team in a modern elementary school, as music punctuated the soundtrack for the first time. Color, motion, and music said much more than words. This visual and aural variety immediately conveyed the classroom variety and teacher diversity the client wanted to communicate.

Concepts for AV programs can be similar to those used in books and stories. You can pose a problem, then solve it. Ask a question, then answer it. Use case histories, flashbacks, and so on. The big difference is that you rely on AV imagery and techniques, not words, to tell your story. You speak in audiovisual language.

After selecting a concept or theme I think may work, I create a structure of major sequences, making sure that all the sequences are progressively linked. Then I write each sequence separately and include all the shots and scenes to visualize the client's main points. At all times, I think only of what's on the screen and the soundtrack—what the audience sees and hears. I don't think in literary terms, in words and verbal felicities. In writing narration, I try to achieve a conversational flavor that is intelligent, civilized, and nonpatronizing.

Some people have the notion that informational, factual, functional films should not entertain audiences—only deliver messages. Hollywood films, on the other hand, are made to entertain, and that's all. You know the old quip, attributed to a Hollywood producer: "If I want to send a message, I'll call Western Union."

If some Hollywood producers fear that writers may sneak a message into a picture, AV clients fear just the opposite: that writers will ignore their message for the sake of entertaining the audience. And so clients are likely to scrutinize scripts in search of lost content and information. The mistake they make is to think that 100 percent of the message is in the narration. It isn't. Or it shouldn't be. In a good script, much of the message—perhaps most—is in the images.

In the classroom, where talk and chalk are still the two mighty pillars of learning, some educators fear that an AV program may be too affective, that is, capable of exciting the emotions. Therefore, if it's emotional, it may be too entertaining. And if you're entertaining, the usual assumption is that you have omitted the "cognitive" values—the content, the information, the subject, or the message. But whether your audience is composed of students or executives, housewives or longshoremen, a surefire way to lose their interest—and your client a lot of money—is to write a script devoid of feeling and showmanship. By all means, edify your audience, educate them and instruct them. But make sure you entertain them, too.

Payment Plans

The Writers Guild of America has established minimum rates for theatrical and TV material. No member works for less than these minimum amounts. In the nontheatrical field, however, no standard rates have as yet been established. Most AV producers set their own rates for scripts. A few insist on writers submitting bids, a practice I find questionable. In my experience as both writer and producer, I've been at both ends of three modes of payment for motion picture and video programs: a certain rate per reel (ten minutes); a flat fee for the entire project; and 10 percent of the total production cost. (Fees are quoted now more often as $/minute of finished film, usually $125./min. Range = $75-$200 per minute.)

For ten minutes of motion picture, I've been averaging $1,000, although I've contracted for much more, as well as slightly less. It all depends on the project's matter, production cost, complexity, and lead time. Established writers, of course, get top fees, and often they can negotiate for payment well above the unofficial averages and minimums.

When you work directly with corporate clients, it's best to quote the going rates for scripts and to explain current modes of payment. I have found that it's always safe with business clients unfamiliar with AV programming and scriptwriting rates to quote my hourly fee for any kind of creative work, then multiply this fee by the number of estimated hours for developing and writing a complete script. The arithmetic almost always favors the going per-reel rate, and the client is usually more receptive, since working by the hour would result in an astronomical cost to him.

For original ideas and scripts, many AV companies pay royalties, just like the publishing industry. Usually there's no money up front, but if the producer successfully markets your program or series, you can do quite well.

Other AV Media

The *sound/slide film,* or *slide/tape,* with its newfound voice (i.e. the accompanying tape recording) and classy look, has graduated from the ho-hum school of "Next slide, please" to take its place alongside the motion picture and videotape. When more and more audiences are saying things like "I forgot it *wasn't* a movie," it's a sure sign that the slide/tape program has arrived.

With the slide film and its companion format, the *filmstrip*, just about everything is cheaper—hardware and production. And it's much more available—35mm cameras and Kodak Carousel projectors exist almost everywhere.

Once the marriage of slide and sound took place, perceptive producers, clients, and sponsors began to take notice, especially those with big imaginations and small purses. And with an assist from technology, slide/tapes came into their own. Besides being less costly than the other major AV media, they can often be produced a lot faster. And there's another advantage to clients: Unlike motion pictures and even video, slides allow you to update a program easily by substituting new images for old. Re-editing the sound can usually be done with less anguish than in motion pictures, where the images are eternally locked in and to reshoot, re-edit, and remix is prohibitively expensive.

What about fees? According to producer-photographer Bill Wittich, president of Corporate Image Productions in Newport Beach, California, "They range from $1,200-$1,500 for a ten-minute program, and will increase for those that are longer or unusual in nature."

Wittich's figures confirm my recent experience as both producer and writer of slide/tape programs. Virtually all the productions ranged in total cost from $7,500-$12,000, and with only one exception, the very minimum fee I received was $500. The exception was a project with a tight budget but a very appealing subject and a wonderful client. I wrote the script for $300 because I believed in the program's message.

Because the production costs of slide/tapes are lower than those for other AV media, Wittich prefers a per-minute fee for writers to the 10 percent of the production budget fairly common in motion pictures. After using several fee formulas over the years for motion pictures, video, slide/tape, and filmstrip, I have come to favor the per-minute writing fee myself. It's simpler, it's fair, and in the case of slide/tapes, it helps to equalize the possible discrepancy between their rates and those for motion picture writing. There is virtually no difference in the work required—research, writing, etc.—for any of the media, so the rates of pay should be similar.

My minimum rate for scripting any slide film or filmstrip now is $1,000, and for motion pictures and video, $1,200-$1,500 for a ten-minute program. (Translated into per-minute rates, my fee for slide and filmstrip, for motion picture and video, is now $125 per minute.)

Many people confuse slide films with filmstrips, and use the terms interchangeably. They *are* cousins, sharing the same family tree—35mm film—but splitting off into separate branches. A filmstrip is just that—a continuous strip or ribbon of 35mm film; and that's the way it's projected, a strip of film moving vertically from one still image to another.

A filmstrip starts out as a slide film. It is not *shot* as a filmstrip; it's *made* into a filmstrip from the final selection of separate slides. This entails extra post-production stages, so the production costs are higher than for slide film. But the writing fee is the same, since the extra production work imposes no additional labor on the writer.

Opportunities for New Writers

Because of the increasing demand for AV programming and the relatively low cost and availability of 35mm slide/tape equipment, it is usually quicker and easier for imaginative writers without AV experience to break into that end of the field rather than film. But remember, just as with film and video, you must be able to visualize, to combine images, words, music, and other effects into something that really communicates within the context of the medium. I repeat: The AV media are not primarily vehicles for words. Few people want to hear a lecture via

THE TOWN WITH
THE BUILT-IN
HIT PARADE
  (An original script)

Developer: Allan Amenta

Producer: Allan Amenta

Final draft date: 2/26/77

PICTURE	SOUND
FADE IN Graphic and Title Card: Know Your Country's Songs Graphic and Title Card: And You Will Know Its History Series of Civil War photos: slaves on plantation; Union and Confederate soldiers; Generals Lee and Grant; President Lincoln. Bride and groom at wedding ceremony. Follow with more photos, as though from wedding album. Series of photos of women attired in red.	MUSIC (Kingdom Coming) NARRATOR (Over music) Kingdom Coming. . an early freedom song of the Civil War. . Introduced by the Christy Minstrels in 1862, it was an immediate success, and one of the most popular ballads to come out of that conflict. MUSIC (Oh Promise Me) NARRATOR (Over Music) A wedding without someone warbling Oh Promise Me is like New Year's Eve without Auld Lang Syne. MUSIC (The Lady in Red) NARRATOR (Over music) The Lady in Red. . In the Thirties, its Latin-American beat launched a thousand hips.

Most AV scripts in the nontheatrical field—whether they are for film, video, slide films or filmstrip—use this kind of split-page script format. Video people usually prefer the terms "Video" and "Audio" to "Picture" and "Sound."

film or videotape or slide/tape. True, there is a place for the "talking head," the all-verbal program, but, in my estimation and that of most professional scriptwriters and producers, it is a very small place. (Technical training films, for example, sometimes must rely heavily on words—but there are still ways to make them imaginative.)

Getting Your Bearings

If you want to learn the language of AV programming, if you want to break into the field, here are some things you should be doing: Steep yourself in film and video. Borrow films from your library and from a local or regional branch of a major distributor of sponsored films, such as Modern Talking Picture Service. Analyze their concepts, structure, techniques.

When you watch TV, pay attention to how shows and commercials are put together. Visit school and college media libraries, instructional media departments, and learning resources centers. View their slide films, filmstrips, videotapes, and motion pictures. Study their media catalogs, and ask questions. Find out who's screening AV programs in your town or city—church, school, company, etc. Sit in the audience and gauge the response. Talk to AV equipment dealers, training directors, media specialists, and AV coordinators.

Attend all the film festivals, workshops, and seminars you can afford. Talk to producers, directors, filmmakers, and distributors, and watch their films. If they are close at hand, call on AV producers and production-house people. If not, write to those that have catalogs, and in particular, guidelines for writers. In addition to viewing all the films and TV you can, read AV books, journals, and magazines.

Finally, keep tabs on any production activity in your territory. Get acquainted with PR and advertising agencies that handle AV programs. Find out whether a local school, college, church, or other organization plans to make a low-budget film—perhaps a Super 8 or slide-film program. Offer to write the script, for a modest fee, or whatever the traffic will bear. If you work for a company, volunteer to script a training or orientation program. Even if you don't get paid, do it anyway. The experience and prestige will be worth it.

Recently, two other AV writers and I polled 300 producers to find out just how important the writer was to the success of AV programs. We heard from nearly a hundred of them—a fantastic return. Are they interested in new writers, fresh ideas, imaginative scripts? You bet they are.

So what are you waiting for?

Book Publishing Jobs: Copyediting and Proofreading

by Elizabeth L. Dugger

Would you enjoy working with other writers' copy as a freelance supplement to your own writing career? If you have mastered grammar, spelling, usage, and punctuation, plus editorial and proofreader's marks; if you have an eye for consistency and detail, and can tell a logical statement from a fuzzy one, you should consider selling your skills to book publishers, as a copyeditor, proofreader, and, eventually, a content editor.

Copyediting, the careful preparation of a manuscript immediately prior to typesetting, lets you share the editor's point of view; pays fairly well; focuses your critical faculties; and may even bring you a publishing break for your own writing.

Dozens of publishers need freelance copyeditors. Before they can publish a book they have to find someone capable of making sure the text makes sense and reads well; seeing that the parts are all there (you'd be surprised how often a table is missing); verifying proper names and fishy-sounding statements of fact; determining whether references are cited correctly; fixing any flaws in syntax and spelling; maintaining consistency in the treatment of numbers (numerals vs. written out); and generally bringing the prospective book into agreement with the publishing house's own style.

All this takes time, a commodity as precious to publishing houses as to any other nine-to-five operation. That's where you come in. Many publishers simply haven't the staff to handle the volume of work.

But this kind of close editing can't be palmed off on just anyone. The fiction copyeditor must be a person who has read widely, who has an ear for language in many forms — expository, colloquial, idiosyncratic — and is sensitive to individual style. Nonfiction manuscripts require an understanding of the text materials and often considerable background knowledge. Certain how-to books are dotted with technical or otherwise arcane references. So, for example, if an author has written "Use a caping saw," the copyeditor should recognize the spelling error and change it to "coping."

There are plenty of fields where any special knowledge you have acquired along the road to writing — culinary skills, geography as a hobby, crafts, or professions like accounting or teaching — can make you an especially attractive choice to an editor in need of freelance assistance.

Would you catch the mistake in this sentence? "DNA was discovered by Watson and Crick in 1853." If you know the date is about a century off, you probably have a good enough grounding in biological science to be fairly uncommon. Hundreds of bio texts are printed each year, and each needs to be scrutinized for just that sort of slip.

So combined with a general, up-to-date, college-level background in any special field (for example, history, chemistry, math, geology, sociology, psychology, linguistics), your editing and error-spotting skills will be very much in demand.

Copyediting pays six to nine dollars per hour, or sometimes a per-page rate is used; still another possibility is a flat rate for the job. You keep your own log of hours (honor system), although the editor has an estimate of how long it should take you. (I aim for ten pages an hour if the typescript is very clean and reads easily, or a hundred pages a week if it takes a lot of thinking.)

Proofreading is the painstaking, word-for-word, character-for-character comparison of typeset galley proofs against the original manuscript to see that nothing was omitted, added, or changed by the compositor, that words have been divided correctly at the ends of lines, and that the type specifications (specs) regarding typeface, style, and margins were followed. The proofreader must also be on the lookout for errors in the original manuscript: This aspect of proofreading is excellent training for copyediting. The rate of pay is around five to seven dollars an hour. Be sure you understand in advance how long the editor expects the job to take. Speed and care have to be balanced here, and it does take practice. In the beginning, go slowly, spot all the mistakes, and dock your time sheet a bit for the warm-up time. Then go a bit more quickly, so long as you still catch all errors. It's like being "a little bit pregnant": A page that's a little bit wrong might as well be all wrong.

That First Job

How do you break in and become a regular copyeditor or proofreader for a publishing house? One way is to try your hand first at proofreading *locally*. That does more than teach you techniques: It adds valuable evidence of experience to your résumé.

I started proofreading as a part-timer in a small composition firm, a company staffed by a handful of typesetters producing computer-aligned cold type. Before the galleys are sent back to the compositor's customers they are proofread in-house, to minimize the number of PEs (printer's errors) the customer's proofreader will find. (That's assuming the customer *has* a proofreader — if it's not a publishing company, it might not, so the compositor's proofreader is the last line of defense against errors.)

It turned out that the day shift, where I started working, did the typesetting for books and magazines, while the evening shift did the type for advertisements. (Think of all the ads in local papers that have to be set up fresh each day.) I tried both ends of the business, which in turn gave me the credits to snag a position at a larger firm, which in turn gave me the courage (and substance) for approaching big-name publishers.

To find small firms that often need part-time help on the spur of the moment (hard work required, but they take the time to teach you), try your Yellow Pages under Typesetting. If there are no listings (as is the case in my present, very rural locale), look under Printing for the firms that advertise typesetting services.

Next, take a close look at yourself, and apply that writing knack to a beefy résumé. List a few examples that show you have the necessary skills — published articles, or consulting work, or manuscript editing for a friend, or courses taken — and then note the fields in which you are especially qualified to check someone else's writing. One part-time writer friend, for instance, is a manager in a lighting firm; he'd be great at editing texts on engineering, management, and interior design. Another's knitting and crocheting experience (thirty years' worth) would help in reading through needlework texts, as well as general fabric crafts books. Get the idea?

Now, take a look at some of your favorite books (I picked my most interesting college chemistry texts); choose several publishers from among them; and address a letter to their editors, along the lines of this note that opened the door for me with Harper & Row:

It's not easy to find competent scientists who understand good writing — maybe that's why seeing a science text through the stages of copyediting is such a difficult process. However, there are a few scientifically trained copyeditors around. I'm one of them. I have a bachelor of science degree in chemistry and a background in industrial chemistry and biochemistry.

Three years ago I began to write professionally, and soon learned to proofread and edit material for a small composition firm. In the past year, McGraw-Hill, Latham Publishing, and Lawrence Erlbaum Associates have used my science copyediting skills. The enclosed résumé provides details of this period, as well as indicating work in rewriting chemistry, botany, biology, psychology, and engineering copy, all at high school or college levels.

Do you have any similar skill requirements for this fall and winter? I am setting up my schedule for the next few months, and so far it's wide open. I am available for New York conferences (I try to visit the metropolitan area at least once a month), but have found that most such work can be carried out effectively using the mail and telephone. I have a small personal research library and access to the state library facilities here, as well as to the libraries of several colleges.

Please let me know whether we can arrange an easier way for you to schedule your fall text work this year!

Of course, if this is your first time trying out such skills, you'll reach for other qualifications to mention, like having regularly reviewed papers in your field, or having taken a short course in proofreading. I got my first assignment on the basis of past manuscript editing — but I never had to explain that it was a fellow writer's manuscript that I'd edited, as a favor!

Of course, one letter didn't put me on the "must list" with most publishers. What I often *did* get in response was a standard editing test, with a friendly invitation to try it. (This is one of the few fields where showing your skills is possible by mail — a big plus for freelancers living in the hinterlands.)

Such tests measure background knowledge, ability to catch specific errors of fact and language, and familiarity with editing marks, which appear in most writing reference texts and in many dictionaries (something you can bone up on while waiting for a reply to your letters).

Other aspects of editing that these tests examine include willingness to leave a writer's style alone if that style doesn't garble the message, the

Due to the nature of the work at Writers Digest
Books which is mostly insturctional books for writers, the copy editor must be more then some
what profficient in spelling, punctuation and
grammer. Not to be able to catch the mispellings
of the author is quiet a handycap since are books
are read very closely by professional writers.

The copyeditor should bring to the job an
understanding of some of the basic spelling rules.
For example the ie-ei rule is a "must" if one is
to know which of the following words are spelled
correctly; conceive, relieve, liesure, kaleida-
scope, neighbor, foreign, sieve, seige, and sieze.

Also the ible-able rule. The copyeditor must
know which of the flowing words should end in able:
accessible, compatible, convertible deductible,
formidible, interuptible etc.

The copyediotr should be aware too, of the
differences among American and British Spelling:
center-centre, labour-labor, judgment-judgement,
for example. (This is truely necessary because

*Try out your copyediting skills on this test, adapted from one used by
Writer's Digest Books.*

sometimes we recieve manuscrips from English authors that prefer they're own spellings to ours:
and we do'nt recommend biting the hands that fed
us.

If you haven't panicked all ready, and are
still baring with us, it behaves us to say that
a perspective copyeditor should know the seed
rule. We trust that you know how to spell exceed,
procede, succeed, superceed, acceed, consede?

The forgoing rule effects spelling only. The
copy editor should also be able to punctuate correctly. Of course their are fourty schools of
thought about how to punctuate and a rule of
thumb compromise has got to be worked out. It
would be an exageration to claim that this is easy but we think we have been able to work out a
feasable scheme which meets msot contingencies.

Handwriting , too is important; an eligible
hand is to be deplored, and is the bain of com-
positors who set the type. Incidently, it is said,
that the principle cause of drunkeness in compos-
itors is due to indecipherible editing.

ability to follow the editor's instructions *to the letter,* and the knack for catching every goof, even the misplaced apostrophes and the references that were cited in the text but omitted from the bibliography.

Content editing. The pearl of editing services, this won't come your way immediately, as most publishers prefer to first get you used to their style and break you in. It takes a lot of trust on a staff editor's part to give a freelancer the job of analyzing, shaping, and organizing a manuscript. And that trust is built gradually. The pay is princely compared to that given for copyediting and proofreading — seven to fifteen dollars an hour and up.

Why put so much hard work into someone else's writing when you could be doing your own? For these benefits: to give you a more critical attitude toward your own work; to polish your style; to brush up your special knowledge; and to get to read new material free, before it ever hits the bookstores.

And there's one more big plus. That editor you work with could be a valuable contact in getting your own book published. I happen to have a collection of chemistry-related articles I'd like to get published, so a few months ago I asked my editor at McGraw-Hill, "Who would I send my own stuff to for consideration?"

"Send it to me," he replied promptly. "I'll look it over and make sure it gets to the right person."

What better help could a freelancer receive?

Book Publishing: Indexing

by Gloria Emison

Looking up a specific item of information in a book—whether for the first or second time—can be approached in one of two ways. One kind of looker-upper will leaf through the pages, muttering "I know it's here somewhere." Another will turn to the index. If you tend toward the latter, you probably have been frustrated by inadequate indexes, or sometimes no index at all. Moreover, as a freelance writer, you are in a position to appreciate what a poor or absent index can do to a good book. Perhaps you've said to yourself, "I could do better than that!"

Indeed you could. As a habitual looker-upper, a freelance writer is especially qualified to become a member of that rare breed, the professional indexer. Freelance opportunities for indexers include book and periodical publishers, and business, government, and university publications. Qualified freelance indexers are listed free of charge in the *Literary Market Place* (205 East 42nd St., New York NY 10017) and in the *National Writer's Club Report on Competent Literary Services* (1450 S. Havana, Suite 620, Aurora CO 80012).

Landing assignments, however, requires experience. An editorial or library background helps. Lacking these, you can get experience indexing your own published work, or a friend's. If such works are not available, you might volunteer your services for a nonprofit venture. Another possible approach involves finding an inadequate index, working up a sample of how you would handle it, and sending this to the publisher. Of course, once you have experience, you can begin sending résumés to prospective publishers, and have yourself listed in the previously mentioned publications.

A newsletter of interest to indexers is published by Editorial Experts, Inc., 4600 Duke St., Alexandria VA 22304, which also operates an employment service for part-time or full-time indexers. Membership in the American Society of Indexers, 235 Park Ave. S., New York NY 10003 is also helpful.

Ideally, all indexes would be prepared by experts on the subject, as when indexes are handled by the authors themselves. However, indexing is a specific skill that many authors do not care to acquire. The professional indexer, who may not be an expert in the subject, might have to do a bit of research while preparing an index. Biographical, geographical, and historical dictionaries, a set of encyclopedias, an almanac, atlas, and thesaurus are usually all that are needed to clear up any confusion. Technical subjects may require additional, specialized reference sources.

Basic Indexing Techniques

The fundamentals of indexing are covered in varying detail in several books [see this book's bibliography]. Basically, indexes are made up of individual entries, each of which consists of a heading, its possible modifications, and the appropriate page numbers. After you read the page proof and mark it for entries, you copy the entries and page numbers onto index cards, one entry per card. These cards are then proofread against the page proof. After you alphabetize the cards, all entries are analyzed for possible consolidation of duplicates, for needed cross references, and for handling of subentries or modifications. After a final check of alphabetical order against a commonly used dictionary, the index is ready for typing, or, in some instances, for typesetting directly from the cards. There are two basic kinds of index: the keyword index and the fully analyzed index. A particular index may be a compromise between the two.

I would like to add one oft-repeated plea from frustrated looker-uppers: Please do not index a chicken recipe, for instance, solely under its official cookbook name, "Grandma's Glazed Chicken": include a cross reference under "Chicken." Please bear this in mind as a specific example of a universal principle, covering everything indexable.

When you receive an indexing assignment, do determine from the client in advance how detailed an index is expected. A key-word index obviously will be completed more quickly and result in a shorter index than one in which entries are fully analyzed. Ideally, the complexity of an index is determined by the requirements of the text. In fact, deadline, space, and budget considerations may play a large part in such decisions.

Indexing rates range from six dollars an hour and up, depending on the degree of difficulty, as well as the indexer's experience and geographical location. Although the publisher often negotiates the fee with the indexer, the cost of a book's index is usually charged against the author's royalties. Some publishers will agree to an hourly rate, while others may use a flat fee such as $1.50 per printed book page. By keeping track of time spent on flat-fee jobs, you will be able to estimate better when quoting flat fees. The American Society of Indexers also offers advice to members on the subject of fees.

Book Publishing: Additional Opportunities

by Anne Montague

Research

Individual authors and, occasionally, publishing houses assign to qualified freelancers what's inelegantly but accurately termed spade-work—digging up information. Authors will generally engage you for *original* research: unearthing and organizing all relevant data on the subject of their book or special project. Publishers will ask you to do *fact checking:* verifying and updating existing copy, e.g. for a revised edition. A letter and résumé to a publisher (followed up by a phone call) is the first step in seeking such jobs. Getting in touch with prospective authors may require more ingenuity. Check the help-wanted ads in the trade publications such as *Publishers Weekly* and in the *New York Times Book Review.* Send feelers out to the local university, too. Does Professor Weltschmerz need help compiling quotations and anecdotes for his study of nineteenth-century American journalists? (Universities abound with cheap student labor, it's true, but your experience and reliability are in your favor.) Advertising yourself is another possibility. *Literary Market Place* (205 East 42nd St., New York NY 10017), the comprehensive annual directory of the book business, lists qualified editorial free-lancers free of charge. An ad in the "Positions Wanted" column of the *Publisher's Weekly* classifieds might get results, too.

Research requires a familiarity with and an affinity for libraries; dogged persistence; a knack for locating unusual sources; and the ability to extract a gem from junk. The pay ranges from $5-$20 an hour and up, depending on the complexity of the project.

Manuscript Reading

Traditionally a full-time job given to recently graduated lit. majors, manuscript reading is increasingly being farmed out to freelancers as budget-conscious publishers make staff cutbacks.

Manuscript reading is a highly subjective undertaking. There are no rules as there are with copyediting, proofreading, and indexing—it's a matter of instinct and market awareness.

Specialized nonfiction manuscripts are usually assigned to experts in the subject, but fiction and nonesoteric nonfiction (did you know that humor is considered nonfiction?) are open to what Virginia Woolf termed, not at all pejoratively, "the common reader." A critical eye, a broad reading background, and a sense of publishing trends are the necessary qualifications. The procedure itself is simple: You read the manuscript, then write out a brief synopsis and a recommendation. Sometimes the latter can be a single sentence. "Decline with all possible speed" is how the autobiographical narrator of William Styron's *Sophie's Choice* ended some of his reports when he was a full-time reader at McGraw-Hill.

The pay is on the meager side—$25-$30 for a report on a two-hundred-page manuscript—but the experience could prove invaluable: You'll learn what *not* to do in your own writing.

Writing Jacket Copy

Those titillating phrases emblazoned on a book's covers and first couple of pages are fashioned, not by the author, but by a blurb writer. This job is not so widely available to freelancers as the others discussed here—at many publishing houses it's handled by a full-time staff—but if you're the kind of reader who can extract the essence of a book quickly and the kind of writer who can express that essence in a few riveting words, your blurb-writing talents are likely to find an outlet. Paperback houses are better prospects, and their rate of pay is the same as hardcover publishers': $60-$100. (One cautionary note: New York houses deal almost exclusively with New York writers.)

Book Reviewing

by Robert Cassidy

Ten years ago, after many disappointments, I published my first professional article—a book review in the *Washington Post*. Since then I have
written dozens more, but I'll always remember that first review (and the $50
check). That's why I'd like to suggest book reviewing as an excellent way to
break into print. It worked for me and it can work for you.

Many book review editors welcome new writers. When he was book
review editor of the *Chicago Sun-Times,* Herman Kogan says, he rarely
turned down a new reviewer. Marshall Hayes, Editor of *Book Forum* says
"Writers who want to contribute book reviews should send a book review
sample, published or not, of the kind of title we are likely to review—literary, social, biographical, art." Two other publications which solicit book
reviews are the *National Review* and *Technology Review* published by the
Alumni Association of M.I.T.

Eight Tips for Reviewers

Find your niche. What are your strong areas? Fiction? What kind?
Mysteries? French literature? Do you have a nonfiction specialty? Don't
try to be an expert in too many things. "A certain amount of humility is
helpful," says Doris Grumbach, former literary editor of the *New Republic* and now a columnist for *Saturday Review* and the *New York Times
Book Review.*

Find your book. Usually editors want reviews of new books. Keep up on books to be published in two, three, even four months. Look up the "announcements" issues of *Publishers Weekly* at your library. Several months before the spring and fall lists come out, *PW* runs special issues telling which books are about to be published. Also, each *PW* issue contains advertisements for forthcoming books. Find one for a book you're interested in, and jot down the author, the publisher, and the projected publication date.

Find your market. Know who you want to write for. Don't ask a zoology magazine if it's interested in a review of Doris Lessing's poetry.

Cultivate your local garden before searching out foreign fields. "I receive a fair number of letters from people all over the country asking to do reviews," says one Florida newspaper book editor, "and I have to send out a form letter telling them that we prefer to concentrate on Florida writers."

So start with your hometown paper. Does it have a book section? If not, does it have an arts page which might include a book review?

Look, too, through such specialty publications as technical journals and house organs.

Check *Literary Market Place* or *Editor & Publisher International Year Book* for the name and address of the appropriate editor at the target publication. If you haven't seen the publication recently, write for a sample copy.

Send your query. Write the editor a brief letter asking for permission to review the book you've picked. If you don't know the editor's name, write "Dear Book Review Editor," to avoid the sir-or-madam awkwardness. Give the title, author, publisher, and publication date. Tell the editor why you'd be a good reviewer for this book. For example, if you want to review a book on politics, and you once worked in a political campaign, mention it. Include your address, phone number, and an SASE. Also ask the editor how long he wants the review to be.

The editor should be able to get you a review copy from the publisher, or he may already have uncorrected galleys of the book in his office. In almost all cases, he should be the one contacting the book's publisher. Should the editor ask you to handle this, however, just contact the publicity department of the publishing company, say you've been assigned to review the book for such and such a newspaper, and ask for the galleys or a review copy. (By the way, if you are sent galleys, you may not get a later copy of the hardbound book, unless you have a conscientious editor.)

Most important, include samples in your query—clippings, a college essay, anything that's good. "Clippings are always impressive," says

Lewis Segal, assistant to book editor Art Seidenbaum at the *Los Angeles Times*. If you've never been published, write a sample review of a book the editor would be familiar with.

Don't send a résumé. One aspirant sent a review editor a four-page, single-spaced letter with all his qualifications and his philosophy of life. "He didn't want to do a review," says the editor. "He wanted my job."

If the review editor says yes, shout hurrah! And when you receive the book, write the editor a note of thanks, and say when you'll get the review in (if you haven't been given a deadline).

Follow the publication's style. Make the editor's job a little easier. Does your publication put the bibliographical information at the head of the review? Must you repeat the author's full name and the title in the review? Are titles italicized or not?

Keep it short. If the editor orders 800 words, don't write 1,000. An amateur is a writer who can't come in under the limit.

Beat your deadline. Get your review in a little early the first time. Editors appreciate that. If you mail the review, make sure it arrived on time by sending a return-receipt-requested card from the postal service or by including an SASE and a note that the editor can check off: "Book review received_____(date)."

Some magazines will send you galleys for correction. Proofread and return them immediately. If you're on deadline, phone in corrections.

Most newspapers don't pay for book reviews, though you do get the book and all the copies of the review you can eat. The top money is at the *New York Times Book Review*—the starting rate is $100 for 300 word mini-reviews and $150 and up for regular reviews. The *Chicago Tribune* pays $100. Most smaller papers fork out $25 to $50. Highbrow magazines, such as the *New Republic,* the *Nation* and *Commonweal,* pay modestly on a column-inch basis. You won't get rich writing reviews.

That's one *won't.* Now here are a few *don't's.*

What Not to Do in a Review

Don't aim over the average reader's head. If I heard one common complaint from review editors, it was against professorial types: "The main problem with academics is that they're writing for their peers, rather than for their newspaper audience," says Clarence Olson of the *St. Louis Post-Dispatch.* Such writing tends to be flowery, pompous, and unreadable. Avoid it.

Don't write for two competing newspapers, unless both review editors approve.

Don't write a book report—write a review. Anyone can recite the action of a novel, or the main points of a nonfiction work. Your job as a reviewer is to comment upon the book.

Your job is *not* to give it away. For example, don't reveal the ending of a mystery. Whet the reader's appetite, but don't feed him the plot.

You should also put the book in the context of other, similar books. Graham Greene's new novel should be stacked up against *The Power and the Glory;* a book of investigative journalism in Washington might be compared to *All the President's Men.* Read around the book you're reviewing. When I was asked to review Wilfrid Sheed's biography of Muhammad Ali, I also made sure to read Norman Mailer's *The Fight,* which had just been published. By "surrounding" your subject, you can assure yourself (and your editor) that you know what you're talking about.

In your review, describe how you, as a critical and informed reader, were moved, informed, made better—or worse—by the book. Explain why the book might or might not be worth buying (particularly if it's an expensive book). Is it a first novel that shows great promise? Is it the most comprehensive guide in print to keeping your plants green?

Assess the book fairly. But don't write a review that says *nothing* good about the book. Such a review is read only by the author and his editor, and it's a disservice to your readers. After all, if the book had no redeeming value, it probably should not have been reviewed.

Of course, your review should have all the elements of a good news feature: a strong lead to entice the reader, a clincher at the end that summarizes and satisfies, and supportive material in between.

Finally, be prepared for setbacks. Some editors who use new writers find it such a time-consuming process that they soon give up the practice.

But don't despair: Several editors report that their first-time reviewers have turned out well, indeed. Kogan points with pride to a then-junior at the University of Illinois who asked to review for him. That young man, Roger Ebert, went on to win the Pulitzer Prize in criticism.

Even if you don't win the Pulitzer, you can get much satisfaction—and even a little cash—from reviewing. I know that my record of freelance reviewing helped me get my present job. And, like the space program, I've had some spin-offs; editors see my reviews, then ask me to write for them. One such instance led to a contract to write a major series for the Field Newspaper Syndicate. I was paid $2,000.

Does that sound like a rave review for book reviewing? Well, judge the craft for yourself!

Business Writing

by Robert E. Heinemann

On a Saturday afternoon a few years ago I received a $1,200 payment for some writing I'd done. It arrived without ceremony or celebration. My wife continued with her reading, my children with their play. The bottle of extra-dry champagne I keep around for special occasions remained in the wine rack, unchilled and unopened. Since the banks were closed, there was little else to do but put the check in a safe place, file the stub, and return to my typewriter.

I earned the $1,200 for producing about 3,000 words. No, they never appeared in *Esquire,* the *Atlantic Monthly,* or, for that matter, in any of the slicks to which most writers aspire. The only formal acknowledgment of my authorship that was ever made was my name on that check. But then, the project — a sixteen-page corporate sales brochure — took only eight days to complete. A week before the payment in question arrived, I billed the same company another $1,000 for a follow-up project. All told, that relatively small corporation paid me something in excess of $6,000 that year, and it was just one of the several clients I served on a regular basis.

If this is starting to sound like one of those testimonial advertisements you see so often — "Send me ten bucks and I'll show you how to become as fabulously rich as I am" — let me assure you that there's no coupon at the end of this chapter. Yes, Corporate America runs a very active, lucrative writing market. From the freelance standpoint, however, it's not all that different from the traditional markets. Breaking in, then *staying* in, takes the same measure of talent, tenacity, training, and luck. Those of us who have made a living at it have walked miles of pavement, knocked on thousands of doors, sweated out recessions, and learned early to think of success in terms of dollars, not bylines.

Happily, there are plenty of dollars to go around. The capable writer who's willing to take as active an interest in the business world as he or she might in the more fashionable or exotic strata of society stands a good chance of sharing in that world's considerable wealth.

Companies *Must* Communicate

Before going any further, let's look at the reasons why this corporate communications market exists.

Today, more than ever before, a company's survival depends on the good will of its publics; that is, its shareholders, customers, employees, creditors, regulators, and the like. Their good will is essential to the company's performance. In the most basic sense, then, the purpose of a company's communications is to tell its publics about its performance. The more persuasively, the more credibly, the more completely it does this, the better its chances of survival.

These requirements all translate to an annual outpouring of billions upon billions of words — in speeches [see separate chapter on speech-writing], position papers, new-product literature, annual reports, house organs, articles, press releases, corporate histories and profiles, fact books, catalogs, and pamphlets and brochures of every description.

The implications for the writer are obvious, and while many companies, especially the larger ones, employ full-time staffs to produce such materials, most of it is purchased on the outside, from advertising agencies, public relations firms, and independents — freelancers just like you and me. In fact, when business is brisk, or when there's a special project, the PR and ad agencies will go outside, too, giving the free-lancer a secondary market.

But, before you go barreling off to your friendly neighborhood corporate entity, let's back up for a moment. One of the reasons I was prompted to write about this market was to dispel some of the popular misconceptions about it, the worst of which is that one needn't know or care very much about business to write sound business copy. While I was working on the inside, I was amazed at how many applicants for staff writing positions had no business education or training, expressed no real desire to gain such a background, and, if that weren't enough, also openly characterized themselves as "anti-business."

A similar attitude prevailed among the freelance writers who approached me with offers to "do some writing." As much as I may have empathized with their need and desire to work, I always found it difficult to take them seriously. Would these same people, knowing nothing about automobiles, and caring less, even consider wasting their energies trying to sell to *Motor Trend?* And, by the same token, would the editors of *Motor Trend* waste any of their time with these writers' submissions? In both cases, I think not.

This is not to say you have to be in total accord with the methods and practices of the business community to provide a worthy service. But you *do* have to be open-minded and willing to listen. Nor do you need a graduate degree in business administration. There are scores of easily digested books on business and its subdisciplines. A small investment in a few of the books in the Barnes & Noble College Outline Series will do for starters. You might also look into one of the inexpensive elementary business courses offered by many community colleges and adult education programs.

Moving Toward the Millions

Given these few prerequisites, you can now consider actively pursuing the market. What I offer is an orderly approach to your campaign. Call it . . . businesslike.

I once dropped in to see the PR director of a company I'd worked for on occasion. "You unnerve me," he said. "A half hour ago I got this request from the *Times,* and I can't possibly do it myself. Are you always lucky enough to be in the right place at the right time?"

The answer is, unfortunately, no. On the other hand, it isn't always *luck,* this knowing where to be and when to be there. I knew a special newspaper section was being prepared and that most local companies were being asked to make editorial contributions. I called on the people I knew were usually pressed for time. In a few hours I'd landed three assignments and over $700 in fees.

This is all by way of underscoring the importance of knowing everything there is to know about your market: how it operates, who's buying, and what they're apt to be looking for at any particular time. As with many rejection slips, most business failures can be traced to a lack of accurate market information, a result of inadequate market research. In your business venture, the need for such research is no less crucial. Not that you'll be able to amass a body of precise data. What you're looking for are a few facts to put alongside your wishful thinking.

Marketing theory says that a sale opportunity exists when recognized needs are not being met by products or services currently available. Translated, this means you'll be able to sell something if (1) someone wants to buy it, and (2) there's not enough of it, or of a suitable substitute, to go around. The objective of your market research is to estimate these levels of demand and supply in your local area, with the hope that the former outweighs the latter.

Common sense tells us that if there aren't any buyers, there won't be any demand. The first step, then, is to determine the number of potential buyers. The simplest source of this information is the white pages of your phone book, where a boldface entry ordinarily indicates a commercial establishment of some sort. Better, though, is something on the order of a Dun & Bradstreet directory. The *Million Dollar Directory,* for example, lists all US companies with $1,000,000 or more in sales, alphabetically and by location. If your public library doesn't have a copy, a local college or company library will.

Don't be fooled or intimidated by "a million dollars in sales." You'll be amazed at how many auto dealerships, insurance agencies, and real estate brokers meet that criterion. On the other hand, there are many small, aggressive companies which haven't yet reached that sales milestone, but which recognize they'll need help in doing so. If you can get in on the ground floor, and you do a good job for them, they'll remember. They might not have a lot of money to spend right now, but as they grow, so will your fees. This size firm will be listed in Volumes 2 and 3 of the *Million Dollar Directory*.

If, after consulting all these sources, you can't list at least a dozen or so companies within, say, a hundred miles of your home base, I think you'll find that the demand is too thin. But this should be the case in only a few scattered locales. The desire of many businesses to escape the high cost and complexity of the major metropolitan areas has caused them to move to what were once this country's least developed areas.

Pal Around With the Printers

The longer your list, the better your chances. Even so, knowing the number of prospective buyers answers only part of the question. What has to be determined next is whether these buyers are inclined to buy your product and how many other folks are running around trying to sell the same thing. Unfortunately, a meaningful evaluation of both sides of the market requires a more sophisticated process than counting entries in a directory. The ideal source would be a disinterested third party, one who deals simultaneously with all the buyers and sellers. If only ...

Surprise! There's probably one or more right in your hometown.

They're called printers. That's right, printers — and if there are more reliable sources of the information a freelancer needs, I've not run across them. Collectively, the printers in your area will have had some contact with everyone involved in the local corporate communications industry: the companies, the agencies, and the independents. The volume of printing sales is an accurate barometer of market activity.

Best of all, because the written word is a printer's stock-in-trade, too, he's a writer's natural ally, one who can be of great assistance over the years. I still get some of my best leads (not to mention stationery, calendars, calling cards, and other niceties) from my friends in the printing business. And, believe me, I work hard at maintaining their friendship.

If you know someone in the business, great! Start there. If not, go to the Yellow Pages. Pick out a few names, set aside a morning, and go visiting. You'll find most printers and print salespeople informal and friendly. A call I once made illustrates how I'd suggest you approach the visit.

I drove to a printshop in a part of the state where I'd never gotten much business. I walked in and was confronted by a burly pressman (I'd used the wrong door, it seems), and I asked where I might find the office. I followed his directions—not too difficult to do, since the areas in which one's supposed to walk are usually lined off in a printery, apparently to prevent people like me from falling into the collating machine—and was greeted with "What can I do for ya?" I responded, "I guess I'd just like a little information. I'm a business writer, and I've been told you people handle most of the good accounts around here."

"What kind of things ya do?" he asked.

"Well, right now I'm trying to fill out my annual report schedule. I do six or seven calendar-year reports, usually . . . ." whereupon I handed him a few I'd done for some well-known clients.

His eyes brightened — annual reports are the cream of the business for writers and printers alike — and suddenly I had a friend.

Now, at this point you may not have my kind of samples. So how do you develop this kind of instant rapport? Be honest. Explain that you're looking into the business, and you need some help. More often than not, you'll get it.

To finish the episode: It wasn't long before my new friend and I were sipping coffee, and he was rattling off the names of the companies and people he dealt with, noting those likely to be in the market for what I do and those he suspected were not. I also found out which agencies and independents worked the area, as well as the names of local artists and designers.

Coexisting With the Agencies

I did not — arfd neither should you — ask if I could use him as a reference. Until they get to know you and your work, most people in the business will be cautious about even intimating a recommendation. Such a request will make you appear both naive and opportunistic.

I don't want you to think, either, that these people are all going to be sources of instant encouragement or assignments. I got two appointments out of the described visit, but no sales. Much of what I was told I already knew.

Still, I did get new information, a few new names, and a better feel for the market. When you're starting out, *all* information is useful. If you see several printers, then call on the artists and designers they refer you to; you'll get a variety of viewpoints and a storehouse of data. Don't count on getting assignments at this point. Your goal is education. More than anything else, a good canvass will tell you whether or not you'll be wasting time pursuing the market any further.

Perhaps the most prevalent stumbling block is oversupply. In some areas, agencies have the market in a full nelson. If this is your situation, you might consider offering your services to the agencies. I refer here to advertising agencies, which ordinarily employ very few straight writers (as opposed to ad copywriters). In fact, if you don't want to get into this business with both feet, you'll be better off confining yourself to this kind of relationship. You won't make as much money, but eventually, if you're any good, you'll have steady work.

If it appears you can coexist with the agencies, stay away from them at the start. I maintained many an active client that retained a PR agency and an advertising agency. Had they known what I was up to in the beginning, they'd have done everything they could to box me out. If you're lucky enough to develop something of a reputation, eventually they'll come to you.

If your research into the market is not totally discouraging, it's time to start selling. Using the information you've gathered, the contacts you've made, and factors like size and product line, you'll begin to develop a prospect list. This really entails nothing more than writing down all your potential customers, listing the most promising at the top. For example, if you know a lot about beer, but nothing about debits and credits, a brewery is a better prospect than a bank.

The Referral Routine

Some advice on size: I was always lucky with companies in the $30- to $60-million sales bracket. With smaller firms it's difficult to identify the right person to see, and when you do, he or she is usually the busiest executive in the company. Larger firms can ordinarily afford a full-time staff or an agency. I've worked for companies of all sizes, and so will you. But, from a calling standpoint, my best reception has always come from this middle segment.

And speaking of calling, that's what the business is all about: in-person queries, one right after another.

Though I can't claim any expertise in direct salesmanship, allow me to make a few suggestions.

The prospect list gives you the *where*. Figuring out *who* is often a little tricky. You probably want to see the person who's in charge of corporate communications. Unfortunately, that listing is usually not found in the phone book. It might be the advertising manager, the public relations director, vice-president of marketing, secretary-treasurer, or assistant to the president. In smaller companies, it could literally be anyone. Sometimes the best you can do is guess. You'll find out soon enough if you're wrong.

Of course, it won't make much difference if you can't get an appointment. The most straightforward method is simply to knock on the door, walk purposefully in, and do whatever it takes to get on the docket. To my way of thinking, though, the best way is by referral. I must confess I still tremble at the prospect of a totally cold call, so getting referrals has been, is, and always shall be a way of life for me.

A referral is, simply, a third-party introduction. I want to meet Mr. X, who doesn't know me from Adam Smith. But I do know Mr. Y, who just happens to know Mr. X. If he thinks well of me there's a good chance he'll let me use his name when I call on Mr. X.

It works in reverse, too. Mr. X needs someone to do something, and he mentions it to Mr. Y, who suggests that he knows just the right person: me. I recently got such a referral from my banker. A good friend of mine who's in the executive-search business has given me several. The business editors and reporters on the local newspapers are not only excellent sources of general information (as in the case, previously noted, of the special newspaper section) but are also in a position to know every business leader in the community. And, naturally, the most desirable referral of all comes from the satisfied customer.

Happily, referrals can come from anywhere, at anytime, and from anyone, so you have to be conscientious about cultivating all your Mr. (and Ms.) Y's. I keep a careful record of everyone I meet in my travels: people who might be sources of assignments, and, if not, who probably know other people who are. On a routine basis, without being over-solicitous, I'll remind a few of them that I'm alive. Just Hello, what's new, so long.

Cold Calls, Cold Feet

If you're as squeamish about cold calling as I am, but there's no other way to approach a certain company, you might try a technique I've used on occasion. It's simple, if slightly devious, and it's never failed to get me in the door. Identify who you think you want to see. Call up, and explain that you're writing an article in which you're thinking of including some mention of the firm. You'll get an appointment, I promise. And next time, it's not a cold call at all.

One caution, though: This is not a gambit suited for every personality. It can backfire, and when it does, you'll have to be pretty quick on your feet. For example, I once tried it on what turned out to be a pretty crafty young executive. Not thirty seconds into my spiel she interrupted: "You're not here to interview me for an article. Just what do you want?"

Undaunted (and not knowing what else to say), I replied, "To meet you, actually, so that if you ever need some particularly good copy, you'll think of me."

It didn't work, and she hasn't called.

One final word on cold calls: I can list only a few times when a purely cold call has gotten me anything for my effort. I think it's an attitudinal problem. I don't like them. They take too much time. The percentages are low. And, I'm not very good at them. However, I have a friend who operates solely in this manner. She visits industrial parks, shopping centers, car dealers, small companies, and just knocks on the door. She doesn't land many large jobs, but she gets a load of the $100- to-$250 assignments.

It really doesn't matter how you get them — the appointments will come. But what do you do when you get there? First, think of all first calls as introductory. You might prepare a simple résumé that lists your qualifications, educational background, the companies you've done work for, and pertinent work experience. Unless your portfolio is crammed with relevant business-writing samples, or, at the very least, some articles that have a business slant, leave it at home. If your only qualification is that you're a freelance writer, admit it up front and explain that you're interested in doing some business writing. Lacking anything else to demonstrate your talents, suggest that you'll be happy to work on speculation in the beginning. Why not? You'd do it for a publisher or periodical.

Rules of the Game

About the worst thing you can do is suggest an assignment. There's nothing wrong with asking if a project is coming up to which you might contribute. But companies run on carefully controlled and prepared budgets, and there's no surer way to show your ignorance than to suggest that a budget be changed to accommodate your idea.

Suggesting assignments can result in a short interview. I'm reminded of the fellow who approached me with the idea that he write a history of the corporation for which I then worked. It was so easy to say no: I already had one.

Most important, adopt the philosophy that every call paves the way for the next call. Be courteous, and don't overstay your welcome. This is not a hard-sell business. The product is too subjective; the buyers are slow to act. Plant a lot of seeds and tend to them. Don't let your prospects forget you, but don't push too hard.

With the proper mix of patience and persistence, assignments will happen. Remember, though, that with the sale comes a responsibility to produce a worthy product. If the customer isn't satisfied with what he's bought, he'll shop elsewhere next time.

This applies especially to first assignments. These will ordinarily be routine projects — a simple brochure, a non-VIP speech, a rewrite of existing literature — for which the writer might expect to earn $100 to $200. But even though it represents an inexpensive way for the client to assess your ability and test the relationship, that first job is the most important one you'll ever do. Approach it accordingly.

There are so many projects available in this market that it's not possible to suggest here how to handle this or that particular one. By way of general technique, though, here are a few reminders:

Be economical. The president of a company I once worked for called me to his office after reading a draft of a speech I'd written for him. "I may not be a good writer," he began, "but I understand economics. I think you might brush up on the subject yourself, especially as it applies to waste." The moral of the story: You won't be criticized for tight, terse prose, as long as you cover all the points. But fluffy writing will rarely be tolerated.

Be clear. For some reason, young writers — I was no different — spend much of their time concocting clever phrases. Communication works best when the construction is uncomplicated and the language is direct.

Be accurate. Know the facts, and write factually. If a misstatement slips by the client's eye, it can prove very embarrassing. I should know. I once represented a company as the top exporter of a certain product. It wasn't, but no one caught me out. The real Number One demanded an apology. I didn't get a chance to make one.

Be ready to rewrite. An artist friend of mind always billed me as "the best second-draft man in the business." Overstatement, to be sure, but a nice compliment. Not that first drafts don't deserve your best effort, but very few survive intact. Business people are notorious editors. Unless there are severe time constraints, they don't usually care how many drafts it takes you to get it right. What's "right" is what pleases them. As someone once said, business people are so hard to please that if the Declaration of Independence had been submitted to a corporate executive as a draft, we'd still be a British colony.

Where the Limits Are

The idea is to get it right as early as possible. This means pinning down most of the client's objections at the first-draft stage. Don't leave the room without clearing up such nebulous comments as "This isn't precisely what I was looking for," or "The tone is wrong," or "It's not our style." Ask for specifics. Insist on examples. If you don't press for these, you'll be no closer on the fifth or sixth draft than you were on the first. Remember, you're paid for the hit, not the number of swings.

There are also some important rules about the client relationship:

Honor your client. The client is always right. Forget pride of authorship. Take criticism with a smile, even when it seems totally unjustified. Yes, it's tough. The client isn't simply a name on a masthead — you'll be sitting right next to this "editor" who's carving up your best efforts, impugning your abilities, and questioning the marital status of your parents. But turn the other cheek. If you swing back, you'll only do it once.

Honoring your client also means maintaining the confidentiality of inside information. It's not unusual to be given confidential or advance information about a new product, financial results, merger plans, a major reorganization, etc. Should the information get out sooner than intended, it might ruin an expensive, well-planned corporate strategy. Worse, the early or improper release of material information could represent a violation of the Securities Exchange Acts. It takes only one such slip to put you out of business permanently.

Finally, honoring the client means not broadcasting what you've written and for whom. Several years ago I knew a young man, a member of an agency staff, who was prone to boast that he'd written every speech that a particular corporate VIP had ever given. The VIP happened to pride himself on his own writing abilities, and when the fellow's statements got back to him it caused enough resentment for the agency to lose the account, and the staffer his job.

I could relate several similar tales, all of which had unfortunate outcomes. Remember, dollars instead of bylines. What you write for a client belongs to him. Cash your checks, and keep your mouth shut.

Know your objectives. Before taking on any assignment, I always ask two questions: What are the objectives? and Who is the audience? You have to know these things to communicate effectively. If the client hasn't arrived at the answers, don't start writing. I assure you it will be a waste of time. And don't try to answer them yourself. You'll probably be wrong.

Know your capabilities. I learned the punishment for violating this one early in my career. In an effort to impress a client, I took on a project — one of the quick-turnaround variety — that required more background in data processing than I possessed. I thought I could fake it. The client saw right through the attempt. "Why didn't you just say you couldn't pull this off?" he asked. "Now it has to be done overnight. And I'm the one who's going to have to do it!"

That had to be one of the most embarrassing moments I've ever lived through. What could I say? I didn't dream of billing the job, and I was certain I would never get another.

The whole thing could have been avoided. Admitting your limitations is far better than demonstrating that you don't know what they are. If there's enough time to do the proper research, or to get help from an expert, you can usually do a decent job with any subject, even if it's highly technical. If there's not sufficient time, you'll only be fooling yourself.

Of course, it's essential to meet all your deadlines. You should know just about how long it will take you to complete any particular kind of assignment. To that, add a fudge factor of at least a day, maybe two. If you're given a deadline that falls outside the brackets, do all your hedging in the beginning. After that, excuses or complaints will make you appear unreliable. The business is tough enough without that kind of reputation.

Know production processes. At some point, your words will usually have to find their way to the printed page, and if you haven't the foggiest notion how that's accomplished, you'll be writing in a partial vacuum. In our business, the writer is expected to be conversant with the processes of layout, photography, typography, and printing. So often there's an important relationship between the copy and the graphics, which means you'll have to work closely with designers, photographers, and printers, and learn to deal with their constraints.

You could just read a few books. In this case, though, it's much more desirable to learn the processes first hand — to see how type is specified and set, how mechanicals are made, how photographic images are reproduced, how the presses operate. We spoke earlier about the benefits of befriending the local printers and graphics professionals. Here's another.

Financial Rewards

Finally, a word on pay. The best criterion for compensation is time. Freelance business writers command anywhere from ten to fifty dollars an hour, depending on experience, past performance, and the significance of the project. I operate on the theory that I can produce about fifty "finished" words per hour, thirty to thirty-five if there's a lot of legwork or research involved. But I use this formula only as a guide. The client usually has a price in mind, and unless it's absurd, I never haggle. It turns out that they're often more generous than the formula. But if you're asked to quote a price before you've had a chance to consider the project in detail, beg off as politely as you can. Then go back to your desk, make a reasonable estimate, and put it in written form.

One last thought: Earlier, I expressed the fear that you might envision

---

Business Writing Fees

As always, the market determines the money. But business writer Robert E. Heinemann suggests the following fee guideline. The prices are for copywriting only.

Annual report	(to 3,000 words)	$2,500-$12,000
Corporate history	(to 5,000 words)	$1,000-$3,000
Corporate profile	(to 3,000 words)	$2,000-$4,000
Facilities brochure	(12-16 pages)	$1,500-$3,000
Financial presentation	(20-30 minutes)	$2,500-$7,500
House organ	(per 12-page issue)	$1,500-$2,000
Press release	(1-2 pages)	$100-$150
Product literature	(per page)	$250-$300
Recruiting brochure	(8-12 pages)	$1,500-$3,000
Sales brochure	(12-16 pages)	$2,500-$4,000
Services brochure	(12-18 pages)	$1,500-$3,000
Special news article	(per 1,000 words)	$300-$1,000
Speech	(10-15 minutes)	$500-$1,500

this market as some quick route to riches. So let me remind you that making it in this market is not an easy task, that it takes a lot of hard work, and that it's as frustrating and humbling an experience as pursuing the traditional markets.

But the business world *is* where the money is, and I'll even confess that the half-dozen or so writers I know working this side of the street make a decent living. The market is there. Go after it!

Editor's Note: In addition to the jobs described in this chapter, keep in mind, too, the opportunities with customer newsletters for retailers such as pharmacies, automobile dealers, sporting goods stores, and the like. One such writer, Charles Levin, creates four- and six-page issues in stock page sizes of 8½x5½ or 9x12 and charges $125 to $200 per issue to write and paste up for delivery to a small offset printer. He quotes a package price to the client if they want him to handle the entire production. That total cost ranges from $270 to $800 a month, depending on pressruns, which range from 1,500 to 8,000 copies. The client gets one bill.

Business Writing: Anniversaries

by Etna M. Kelley

Each year millions of dollars are spent by organizations celebrating their anniversaries. A typical celebration may include special advertising; festive functions (parties, banquets, receptions); a commemorative film; exhibits; distribution of gifts, novelties, and souvenirs. But no matter what else is done, *the printed word is usually the major tool used in commemorating the milestone.* Very often there is a company history, in hard or soft covers, or in the form of brochures, folders, booklets. The firm's management sends out releases to the press and to radio and television stations. The company magazine may appear as a special issue, or it may carry a series of articles tied to the birthday. There may be a special anniversary edition of the annual report to shareholders, or a special anniversary booklet may be distributed separately to them.

But even though the volume of anniversary printing is large, it is not nearly so large as it might be if writers would take the initiative of volunteering their services to the celebrating organizations. Much of what appears is handled by the companies' own staffs, or the staffs of their advertising agencies or public relations counsel, who are hard pressed to perform the extra duties related to the milestone, without the additional burden of turning out the writing required.

Finding Prospects

To get ideas, start by checking the ages of local firms. There are more large and successful seventy-five-year-old firms than twenty-five-year-olds. I made a study of the ages of the companies on the 1979 *Fortune* 500 list—the nation's largest industrial corporations ranked by sales. I found that the median age of the top 100 of that group was 79.5 years and the average age was 80.16. Oldest of the twenty-two that were 100 years or older was Du Pont, founded in 1802. There were forty-one in the 75-to-100-year-old group, and twenty-nine in the 50-to-75 group; and only two less than 25 years old.

Since World War II vast numbers of businesses have been started each year, but relatively few survive a decade. Yet if you think about the ages of banks, department stores, insurance companies, food firms, seed houses, and funeral establishments in your town, the chances are you will find that most of them are well past the quarter-century mark.

The *Business Founding Date Directory,* compiled by me and published in 1954, listed almost 10,000 firms founded between 1687 and 1915—118 of them in the 1700s. The oldest, Perot Malting Company, ceased operations a few years ago, but the runner-up, J.E. Rhoads & Sons, a large leather firm formerly in Philadelphia, now in Wilmington, Delaware, founded in 1702, is still operating with a member of the founding family at the helm. A high percentage of the founded-in-the-1700s firms listed in my book in 1954 are still flourishing.

The local chamber of commerce's research department will probably have dates of establishment for member companies in their cities. Consider, too, age in relation to the age of the community. In relatively young communities, or even in old ones which were late in becoming industrialized, a fifty-year-old firm might be of more interest than one a century old in Boston, Philadelphia, Baltimore, or New York.

When I compiled my *Business Founding Date Directory,* I added parenthetical comments about distinctive features, such as: oldest department store in America (this refers to Gladding's, in Providence, R.I., founded in 1766); oldest magic store on North American continent—owned by Houdini at one time; oldest real estate firm in America—operated by fourth- and fifth-generation descendants of founder; oldest flag makers in America—descendants of founder still associated with firm; America's oldest paint manufacturer; oldest newspaper of continuous publication in America; oldest auger works in world—it is believed that the holes bored in the wood of the support of the Liberty Bell were made with company's bits. A similar list could be prepared for almost any community and could be the basis of possible feature articles for local newspapers. Then there are the industrial firsts: first maker of packaged pancake flour; first to make ice cream commercially; first to develop the screw micrometer. In the fields of radio, television, even aviation, the pioneers may be relatively young—and quite proud of their firsts.

Anniversary PR

Because of my long experience as a business writer, I tend to think chiefly of the opportunities in selling anniversary articles to trade magazines, but obviously there are many other public relations job possibilities.

As a hypothetical example, let us suppose that I were a writer needing assignments in a small or medium-size city with several large industrial firms. I'd start a card file on these companies, putting down their founding years, what they produced, and anything else of interest I could learn about them. If they held open houses at any time, I'd attend them. I'd try to get literature about them—their "Welcome Booklets" for new employees, their annual reports, their company magazines. When one of them approached an anniversary year, I'd be particularly alert to its activities. (There would be greater likelihood of observance of the multiple-of-twenty-five birthdays, but I would not discount the possibility of observance of the fortieth, sixtieth, eightieth, etc.) Well in advance of the anniversary year, I'd try to interview the firm's president, public relations director, or other executive who might have some knowledge of the forthcoming anniversary program. Human nature being what it is, I might be told "We haven't made any plans as yet." That would not discourage me from inquiring again a few weeks, or a few months, later.

In my own case, the purpose of the interviews was to show my freelance writing credits and to ask for cooperation in keeping informed of the anniversary program. But on many occasions, you might get a better response if you approached the firm with "Do you need help with the research on the early days of your company? Will you commission me to write an article, or series of articles, about your history for your company magazine(s)? May I help with other special writing: releases to the press and to radio and television stations? How about special articles for the publications in your field, or related fields?" In other words, I'd be asking the company to subsidize my writing. I'd be very sure, though, to make it clear that I wanted to work *with* the company's public relations staff, or outside public relations agency, if it had these—and that I had no desire to supplant them.

Articles that I was commissioned to write for the company's own publications were paid for by the company; but articles I sold to trade magazines were paid for by those editors and I did not accept additional payment from the company—except in the form of lunches during my research with the firm. If I handled additional PR work for them in relation to their anniversary events, my fee varied with the job, but $200 a day would be the minimum.

Anniversary Articles

Trade magazine editors would like to have, and are willing to pay for, the how-to-do-it articles that recount the preparations for the various anniversary-related events, how they were conducted, and their effect—in other words, case histories. These are clipped and treasured by other companies facing their own anniversary celebrations, by libraries, and by public relations organizations.

In asking an editor for an assignment to do an article about an old company, a writer should be able to say that he has access to material about its history. If old records, ledgers, catalogs, advertisements, clippings, and photographs of founders, early employees, original products, and original buildings have been preserved by the management, the task of the researcher is easier. If the company is still in the hands of the founding family, so much the better. Interviews with long-term employees or those who have retired are often rewarding. But even without these assets, it is often possible to unearth material about the early days of an organization which can be turned into an interesting article.

Another trade magazine article for which there is considerable demand is the "What-Anniversaries-Mean-to-Your-Industry" type. Photographers, printers, display specialists, souvenir and gift vendors—all want to know how they can sell their products or services to anniversary celebrants, and they should be able to get this information from magazines in their field.

Probably the most valuable type of anniversary article is the case history. Comparatively few are published, because their preparation requires in-depth interviewing, time-consuming both for the writer and the company's management. In the preparation of such articles, I have sometimes talked to as many as five company representatives, with top management invariably represented. Sometimes I have attended several events of the anniversary program. There's quite a bit of work entailed, not only for the writer, but for the company's staff, which must furnish pictures (and captions), literature, answers to questions, information about planning—and an appraisal: "Was it worthwhile? If you had it to do again, would you do it in exactly the same way?" Sometimes it is hard to get a truthful answer, but there is usually some such admission as, "Well, we would not again schedule two important events so close together," or "We would have spent more money on souvenirs and less on refreshments."

Getting a specific answer is important, because those planning anniversaries want to know not just generalities ("It was wonderful"), but such information as "We got hundreds of unsolicited thank-you letters"; "It built morale; our employees felt that they were the hosts at the open house and took great pains to make the affair a success." Best of all, "Our sales increased sharply because of the promotions tied to the birthday."

Even though the research for a comprehensive article on a business anniversary may take quite a bit of time, the silver lining to the cloud is that you can often sell several articles about it. I ask editors to return photographs and printed literature, and I use them again and again.

To answer the question "Should I try my hand at writing about business anniversaries?" consider whether you are willing to do the thorough research required. Do you like business history: looking at old advertisements, catalogs, ledgers, and even old products and packages? Can you relate these to the present and to the future? If you can, you have in your favor the fact that the field is not overcrowded, and that it is usually easy to get a hearing from those responsible for a company's anniversary program. If you write an interesting, comprehensive article, it should have a long life. I have known people to travel great distances, even across the continent, to talk to those who have conducted successful anniversary programs. A well-written article can serve the same purpose as this kind of a journey.

Other Job Prospects

In addition to business anniversaries, consider the milestones of colleges, hospitals, charitable institutions, clubs, communities—all can be prospects for articles or public relations freelancing opportunities.

The anniversaries of inventions (such as the electric light, the radio, the airplane, the telephone) are likely to be celebrated, sometimes by entire industries. At first glance, you might conclude, "If the whole nation celebrates the invention of the electric light, the public relations people will send out reams of material; who would want anything from me?" *If your particular community does something just a bit out of the ordinary, someone will pay you for telling about it.*

I have a slogan, "Any year can be an anniversary year." By this I mean that a company need not wait for a multiple-of-twenty-five birthday, but can celebrate the in-between ones. *Seventeen* magazine made quite a thing out of its own seventeenth birthday. Heinz called attention to their reputation as the "57 Varieties" people by staging a promotion in 1957. In any given year, there are pioneers, inventors, and heroes to whom anniversary programs can be tied. Some companies celebrate not only their own birthdays, but those of their brands ("We're 86, but our best-selling brand is 50").

Procter and Gamble lets its own birthdays go by almost unheralded, but celebrates with great fanfare the anniversaries of its favorite brand, Ivory Soap. Some manufacturers celebrate the production of the umpteenth car, or can of dog food, or toaster.

Since writing about anniversaries is my specialty, it might seem odd that I should say "Come on in; the water's fine." But the field is so big, there's room for all. And no one knows better than you what the special opportunities are in *your* own town.

Business Writing: Meetings

by DeForest Walton

I am a freelance writer in a field that employs thousands of writers on salary and hundreds on a freelance basis. It is a flourishing and growing market. A good writer can enjoy a comfortable living in this field. Many of the more prolific and talented among us make thirty or forty grand a year.

My writing and that of other freelancers like me stems from the fact that practically all businesses, whether they make a product or provide a service, hold meetings. A meeting can take the form of a training session, a conference, a seminar, a school, a sales presentation, or even a live show. Call it what you will, the purpose is the same: to train, inform, stimulate a group of people. These people are employees of the company in most cases, although one company may also hold a meeting for employees of another company, or for the public.

Professional writers who know how to put together an effective presentation and all the necessary visual aids and collateral materials are paid to provide most of the material for these meetings.

One of the real pleasures of writing this type of material is the variety of the projects. Obviously, with thousands of different businesses, each with a different story to be communicated, and communicated in one of hundreds of ways, my writing assignments are always new, always challenging.

What I Write

It is rumored that Caesar said to Cleopatra, "I didn't come here to make a speech." Except in the most formal situation, no modern business meeting can be expected to be effective if it simply consists of a speaker talking *at* people. We have all been conditioned by TV commercials, which, good or bad, use visual elements to support what is said. We see charts and films, hand props and skits, cartoon characters, and even demonstrations where small pills slide through soda straws, proving, I suppose, that even exceedingly thin people can swallow them. So today it is even more important that a meeting create an atmosphere of "I didn't come here to make a speech." As a writer, my function is to develop a framework for a meeting and then to inject all the elements that will help communicate with the audience effectively.

In brief, here are some of the elements frequently written:

The framework. A guide for the meeting leader, this can be an outline he follows or even a complete running script that tells him what to do and what to say. In the case of a live show this might be like a musical comedy "book."

Supporting graphic materials. These printed materials usually are tied in closely with the meeting, but sometimes are prepared for later use by the audience members.

Handout pieces. These review, in printed form, the material presented in the meeting. Brochures, pamphlets, and booklets of every description.

Notebooks and workbooks. Used by meeting participants during or after the meeting.

Invitations, programs, letters. To promote a meeting or, in the case of live business or industrial shows, as typical theater programs.

In addition to all of these elements that are so closely associated with meetings, I frequently find myself writing materials that overlap into that gray area of promotion and point-of-sale. The reason for this is logical. If I write a meeting for the Bojax Car Company to help their field men conduct presentations to dealership salesmen on "Demonstrating the Krackerjax 6," I write a meeting guide, a film, and a handout piece on the subject. In creating these, I am in a good position to develop some related showroom comparative charts or displays recommending demonstration of the Krackerjax, or a reminder card to put on the visor inside a demonstrator.

Supporting Visual Elements

These are of infinite variety, but are in general the visual aids used in the meeting to emphasize, simplify, point up, give change of pace. They often take the form of:

Chart presentations. Prepared easel charts, flannelboard charts with symbols that can be mounted, or blackboards to be written on.

Banners and signs. Used to reveal or emphasize major concepts.

Films. Motion pictures, slide films, filmstrips. [See chapter on Audiovisual Writing for an in-depth discussion of this specialty.]

Other picture projections. Overhead types, opaque projections, table-top, continuous-operating.

Special props. Every imaginable device that a meeting leader might use to make a point.

The Market

When I talk about the market for this kind of writing, I am considering where a freelancer would sell. I am not going to discuss the salaried writer or contract writer, for that is a different story.

There are three primary markets: producers of meeting materials, advertising agencies, and the companies that hold the meetings.

Producers of meeting materials provide the best market for freelance work. They specialize in the business of providing every imaginable type of meeting and promotion material for their clients in industry. Many producers have staff writers. Many do not. Nearly all producers buy freelance work.

Your Yellow Pages will tell you who the producers are in your local area. To give you an idea of the size of this market, the Detroit phone book lists thirty companies under "Sales Counselors and Promotions."

If I were new to this kind of writing and wanted to get information about it, I'd go to one of the producers in my city and discuss the business with him. Because the only thing they really have to sell their clients is creativity, they are constantly searching for good writing talent.

Another market is the advertising agencies. Only the largest have staff writers capable of developing meetings, so agencies do use freelancers to write meetings for them. And frequently an agency client will demand this service. Again your telephone directory is your guide.

The third market is the companies that hold meetings. Now, that statement sounds absurdly obvious. But the point is worth emphasizing. Any business that holds meetings is a potential buyer of freelance writing. Of course, the big companies—Ford, GM, Dow, Standard Oil, etc.—will have a producer or an agency develop their training and promotion materials. But there are thousands of smaller companies that develop their own meetings. Some do a good job, but most of these efforts end up looking like they came straight out of the Flintstones. They need help.

If I were freelancing in a smaller city, I would make small businesses a prime target for my services.

Necessary Qualifications

The backgrounds of people writing in this field are so varied that it is difficult to discern a pattern that makes any sense. But certain attributes seem more important than others.

You must be a reasonably good writer. Much of what you write will be straightforward factual material. But you must also be able to write the language "as she is spoke." As you construct a meeting, you'll frequently write what a meeting leader will say informally.

You must have a better than average ability to visualize. In writing meetings you see them as dramatic situations, little plays in which, through your writing, you make things happen.

You must know the business world and approach it realistically. That means knowing how things get done in business. It also means being able to work closely with business people and recognizing them as, for the most part, fine and intelligent people.

You must have a good understanding of the kind of writing you are doing. It is not literary. It *is* literate. You must do the best writing you can in this specialized form.

Naturally, there are special techniques involved, so it is extremely helpful to a freelancer to have been a staff writer for one of the producers. On the other hand, those techniques are not so complicated that a newcomer who makes a sincere effort to master them can't pick them up in short order.

It will be an advantage to you if you have been a teacher, or have studied speech or dramatics. It will help you to have had a brush with advertising or marketing or public relations, or to have worked in any business that has to do with graphic arts.

A college education is helpful, because you will work with college-trained people, but it isn't really essential.

You must be located close to the businesses you write for because you will have many conferences. You can't hole up in a cabin and submit by mail. And you have to look presentable when you meet clients. They'll tolerate a few screws loose here and there, but you can't be a nut.

What Are the Price Tags?

I do not write on speculation. I do not write on a covering retainer fee. Some freelancers will do both, but I feel that these are poor business practices.

I have a verbal agreement with a client for each separate writing assignment before I begin the job. It is understood, of course, that the writing must meet the client's approval.

Time is the important factor in establishing a fee for a writing job. And it is the complexity of a writing assignment, plus the degree of client cooperation you get, that determines how long it will take to write it.

Here are some guidelines to consider when setting fees for business clients. Meeting guides and brochures: (depending on client) four pages from $250-$750; eight to twelve pages from $500-$1,500. Business slide films or motion pictures: $100-$150 per script page (one page equals approximately one minute playing time) or $1,000-$1,500 for a ten minute film.

Now, as you work with clients and develop a relationship of mutual trust, you'll find that if your writing assignment takes a lot longer to complete than expected, and if the extra time taken is the client's fault, they will invariably raise your fee.

The Rewards

It may sound Pollyanna, but I find this kind of writing rewarding beyond the fact that it provides me with a living. Besides being an outlet for a curious and inquiring mind, it allows me to *see* the results of my work. Much of the material I write has as its objective the training or education of people—helping them do their jobs a little better, helping them understand their function in a complex business and social structure a little better, helping them see a little more clearly what they can do to act constructively. What more reward could I ask?

Column Writing

by Al Eason

At forty-five years of age, my credentials for becoming a writer were practically nil. Having written nothing more complicated than a personal letter, and with only a high school education, I had never considered writing professionally. Now, some five years later, I'm a full-time freelancer. Self-syndicated newspaper columns and contract columns to magazines have furnished a stable financial base for writing endeavors in other fields.

Any writer who is oriented to column-length copy, has a fresh approach, and can consistently come up with material that will interest newspaper readers can do the same. All that's required is a bit of ego, knowledge of a particular subject, and the guts to stay when the going is rough.

Giveaway to Start

I have often been asked: "How do you begin selling a column to newspapers?" Quite frankly, I began by *giving* it away. This is often necessary for the unknown beginner so both he and the publisher can evaluate reader interest. If the column doesn't generate enough interest for a few letters, phone calls, or at least word-of-mouth comment, few publishers will allot space for it in their paper. And none will pay for it. In the beginning, the important thing is to get your copy in print. Those tearsheets with your byline are the samples used to sell the next publisher your columns.

At the end of six months, you should have a fair evaluation of your ability to continue writing a column indefinitely, and you will know what the readers think of your efforts. If the situation is still "go," grab a handful of tearsheets and hit the road!

Selling a Column

I've found there is only one way to sell a newspaper column—eyeball to eyeball with the publisher. Sending promotional material and tearsheets by mail is a waste of time and money. Most wind up in the nearest wastebasket.

Unless you have an in with another member of the staff, always try to see the publisher. *Then,* if he indicates his interest in your feature, try to get the editor who will use your material into the conference. There is a good reason for this: The final decision in buying is usually the publisher's, and few editors will disagree with his or her opinion. But having the editor present is important, too. It precludes jealousy, and makes for better relations later.

When presenting sample tearsheets to a prospective publisher, carefully choose your best efforts covering a wide range of subjects. Once the publisher has indicated his interest, the question of price arises. Many factors are involved here. Is interest local or general? Does the publisher desire an exclusive for his circulation area? Most important: What is the circulation of the newspaper?

In my particular area, where cost of living is somewhat low, rates range from five dollars per column for a small weekly to twenty or thirty dollars for stringer material I send to metropolitan dailies. The following schedule can be used as a rough guide for pricing columns of about 500 words: Charge all weeklies a flat rate of five dollars per column. For dailies with a circulation of 4,000 to 6,000, charge at least $7.50. In the 7,000 to 10,000 circulation range the price should be at least $10 to $12.50, and 11,000 to 25,000 should range from $15 to $20, *per column.*

These figures are only a guide. In some areas publishers will pay more; in some, less. *Your* price must always be worked out between you and the first publisher sold. Use this price as a base when contacting other markets.

Rates for newspaper columns are low. The freelancer must concentrate his efforts, and exhaust all conceivable markets for his copy. Sell as many columns per week as possible to each paper, and with the use of a copying machine, send *all* papers the same copy for a particular publication date. Explore the market in specialty papers that cater to a sectional or regional audience. Contact large metropolitan newspapers for a stringer agreement. (Remember, of course, that if a large metropolitan daily with which you have a stringer agreement covers some of the same circulation area as your small weeklies, material submitted to the daily has to be different from that sent to the weeklies.) Often, all columns for a single week can be written at one time and mailed in a single envelope. This saves postage, as well as concentrating the work schedule.

How to Bill

Billing is simple. When columns are sent out for the last week of a month, slip a statement in the envelope for all copy furnished in that particular month. Checks can be expected from the tenth to the fifteenth of the following month.

There are certain questions a person should ask when considering writing a newspaper column. "What subject do I know best? Do I know as much, or more, about this subject than the average person in this area?" If the answer is clear-cut and affirmative, you can probably write a column. But—can you *sell* it? The question which will determine this is: "Is the subject of prime interest to a large group of readers?" If it is not, no publisher will take a second look.

Obviously a column devoted to collectors of mustache cups would not fill the bill; whereas a health, travel, or child care column would. If you can't come up with a subject of wide appeal to the masses—forget it.

My topic, outdoor activities (hunting, fishing, camping), is a burgeoning field, and not too difficult to enter, but the freelancer should be aware of the limitations involved. "Local coverage" is the first stricture. Each paper wants coverage of local events, local people, and local recreational areas. Unless the columnist is constantly in the field, the number of papers he can satisfy soon reaches an absolute maximum.

When the writer of the outdoor column tries to expand, he finds the second joker in the deck. This is the "outdoor editor." Most newspapers of over 50,000 circulation have 'em. Trying to sell a paper copy on a subject normally covered by their staff is much like trying to peddle homemade money to the US Mint.

This is enough to drive a writer to writing columns for magazines. If he has earned prestige as a newspaper columnist, it is often not too difficult to sell a magazine publisher on an expanded version of the newspaper column. A magazine column must be longer and aimed at a much larger audience, but the columnist can recycle much of the material gathered for newspapers in his magazine columns. A column in a magazine should add at least a hundred dollars to your monthly income.

Writing assignments resulting from exposure gained in newspapers and magazines are another fringe benefit for the freelancer. Last year, for instance, I did assignments for a national dog magazine, a national fishing magazine, and an assignment that covered 2,000 miles for a regional chamber of commerce. Two of the assignments paid travel expenses, and the third was written from my files and memory. All paid well, and were welcome additions to the income from newspaper and magazine columns.

Although it is difficult to make a living from self-syndicated newspaper columns alone, they provide an excellent financial *base* for the aspiring writer. I spend only two days a week writing and processing columns. The remaining days are devoted to hunting and fishing, and writing stories and articles for magazines in four different fields.

The modest writing career which began with the purchase of a twenty-five-dollar second-hand typewriter, and with an unbelievable amount of blissful ignorance, is beginning to pay off. For over two years now, I've paid the bills, kept the family's needs reasonably satisfied, and have been happier than ever before. Who could ask more?

Editor's Note: Freelancers who have a column idea they think has national syndication possibilities will find useful the *Editor & Publisher Syndicate Directory*, 575 Lexington Ave., New York NY 10022. In addition to the names and addresses of all US syndicates, it also shows the number and titles of columns currently being distributed on individual subjects such as Antiques, Consumerism, Health, etc., and which syndicates are handling them. Usually the freelancer must show some local and regional acceptance of his column idea before being able to interest a national syndicate. If the syndicate takes on the column, it bears the entire promotion cost to sell the column to newspapers and splits the fees collected with the author.

Comedy Writing

by Eugene Perret

If a comedy writer were allowed to learn only one lesson at the beginning of his career, it should be that the gag writer is the servant of the audience and not the other way around. When I first became a television writer, I was shocked at how easily staff writers tried to escape blame by condemning the viewers. One evening while our show was being taped the writers watched on closed-circuit TV. When one of the amusing sketches we wrote proved not to be so amusing, writer John Doe screamed, "When are those fools going to laugh?" The answer is, they'll laugh as soon as they see something they think is funny.

Today's audiences are especially challenging. Because television is such a great disseminator of news, the public is much more sophisticated today than it was years ago. News items are not only telecast the minute they happen, they are also dissected by experts. The viewers know not only what is going on, but all the ramifications, too. This much knowledge offers the writer a much broader base to work with. Each little piece of general knowledge becomes raw material for the gag writer to twist and reword into a joke. Basically, a joke is two facts combined into a funny idea. The more facts that people are aware of, the more combinations the writer has to work with.

However, this same knowledge also works against the gag writer. It's very difficult to joke about something that a particular audience may take seriously. To give you an example, I was going to give a talk in front of a group of nuns. I thought a relevant topic would be the changing of the nuns' habits. There was quite a bit of publicity about the shortening of the skirt, the style of the shoes, and so on. But before I went on, one of the nuns warned me that there was in this particular community some internal controversy over this, and that feelings were running pretty high. I cut it from the speech. Much the same thing is happening in the world at large. People are becoming more aware of issues and consequently are taking a strong stand on them. When people get involved with a subject, either for or against, it can become too dangerous for humor.

Television has also made audiences much more difficult to entertain—there's hardly an old joke anymore that hasn't been done on TV or turned into a half-hour situation comedy premise. Some of the top name comics refuse to do monologues on television, because the exposure kills the good material for their nightclub appearances.

All of this has made life a little bit more difficult for the professional television writer, but it has made things easier for the beginning writer. Why? Because the beginning writer generally writes to a much smaller audience. The one thing that the beginning writer can offer to an audience that a professional television writer can't is localized humor.

I recently talked in front of a group of insurance men at a business meeting. My opening remark was "It's going to be difficult for me to give this talk. Standing in front of this many insurance salesmen, my natural tendency is just to keep saying no." I followed by saying "You insurance men have really taken over this hotel. My wife and I were on our way here and we asked a man in the lobby how to get to Room 14C. He said, 'Follow this corridor and then turn left, but God forbid if anything should happen to you, how's the little woman going to get there?' "

These jokes worked because they hit that audience right where they lived. There may be better jokes floating around, but not for that audience. That is where the beginning writer has the advantage over the professional. He can do his research at a local level. The more localized a gag is, the funnier it will be.

Early in my comedy-writing career, I performed as emcee at many banquets at the company where I worked. I knew all the people and was familiar with office events. The audience enjoyed jokes about these things.

I once tried to tape one of these shows and sell it as a comedy album. The recording was flawless, but the show was a terrible flop. Because I wanted to sell the album, I had to exclude any inside jokes. I talked about the weather, television, mothers-in-law, and so on. The new audience didn't buy the material and I didn't sell the album.

I chalked this up as just a bad show, but a few weeks later the truth was forced upon me. A group of contractors asked me to speak at a dinner dance. The first part of my routine was about them and their work. It was very successful. The second half was about me and my work. I lost that audience but learned an invaluable lesson: *The comedy has to fit the audience,* and the better the writer does his homework, the funnier his material is going to be.

How Do You Do Your Homework?

Well, you do it simply by asking some questions. If you are working locally, there is generally someone that you can contact to find out about the group.

Get a general description of most of the audience. Are there any issues that are very topical within that group? What are the general topics of conversation? Are there any expressions or sayings that have a special meaning to this group? What do they kid each other about? If you're working for a specific person—a testimonial dinner, perhaps—find out all you can about the guest of honor: his hobbies, children, etc.

Let me give you some examples of the kinds of jokes I've come up with by following these techniques.

General description of the audience. In the show I mentioned earlier that I did for contractors, the organizer told me they were all laborers but they were also very wealthy and liked to dress to show their wealth. My opening line was "It was easy to find this place. I just looked for a bunch of men in three-hundred-dollar silk suits with cement cuffs."

Finding out about a specific person. I did one show for a gentleman who was retiring. Through questioning I found out that he had three children and they were all highly respected musicians. This joke worked beautifully: "One day John said he wanted a piano player, so they had a little boy. Then he said he wanted a trumpet player, so they had another little boy. He told his wife he wanted a violin player, so they had a little girl. You should have seen the look on his wife's face one day when he came home singing '76 Trombones.' "

Expressions or sayings that have a special meaning. One show I did at an industrial plant was almost canceled because there was a small dispute going on between the company and some laborers who were known as 39-16s. This was the number used in the union contract to explain the duties that the striking workers performed. The situation was so touchy that the company executives asked me to stay away from the issue in my talk. My opening remark was "Many people have asked me about the 39-16 situation. Well, all I know about a 39-16 is that it is one-half of a really built girl." As I left the plant less than one hour later, I heard the joke quoted by a worker who wasn't at the dinner. It had traveled around the plant that fast. Why? Because it hit that group of people.

You get the idea. Find out as much about a particular audience as you can and then gear your material specifically to them.

How to Kid the Audience

There's another lesson in that last example. Kid an audience and joke with them and about them, but don't offend them. The 39-16 joke touched on a topic that was the talk of the entire plant, but it said nothing at all about the situation. That show would have been disastrous if I had done jokes about strikes or if I had taken the side of either union or management. Either way, half the audience would have been mad at me, and the others would have been uneasy.

How can you kid people without offending them? Try these approaches. Kid them about:

Things that are fabricated, or obviously not true. One fellow at our plant used to brag about his imagined drinking prowess, so I went along with him. At his twenty-five-year party, I said "The company is going to light a perpetual flame in his honor. They're going to set fire to his breath." I wouldn't dare use that line about a guy who had a *real* drinking problem—only a manufactured one.

Things they kid themselves about. I remember one gentleman who was not the most fashionable of dressers, and he was always the first to admit it. So a line we did on him was "He'd give you the shirt off his back . . . for spite." Do that same line about someone who *thought* he dressed like David Niven and you've got trouble.

Things that are of no consequence. An engineer where I worked had a very powerful telephone voice. Anytime you saw someone talking on the phone and holding it three or four inches away from their head, you knew who it was they were talking to. At one party I commented that "he was the only person in the world that you could hang up on without losing volume." To say a person has a loud or a soft telephone voice is not insulting him in any way. I would never, though, comment on whether a worker was slow or fast, good or bad, lazy or ambitious.

Beginners' Problems in Comedy Writing

Most novices *quit too soon on each gag.* This accounts for more "corny" jokes than does lack of talent. A joke is basically an association of two or more ideas expressed in a clever way. A "corny" joke—the kind that gets a groan instead of a laugh—generally has the seed of a good joke. The association is there; the fault is that it hasn't been expressed cleverly enough.

Another tendency of young writers is to *underestimate themselves*. You must remember that each half hour of comedy you see on television has been created by a staff of at least four writers. Many of these writers have staffs of their own creating material. These people work full time each week to come up with the half hour of comedy that you watch on your TV. Do you expect to sit down some evening and equal this?

Bob Hope has eight full-time gag writers, and spends about half a million dollars a year for funny lines. Would you like to guess how much hits the air waves and how much hits the trash basket?

You see bright comics take the country by storm—someone like Bob Newhart. Their nightclub routines are almost flawless. Each line is a surefire laugh. But it wasn't always that way. Newhart claims he worked on his original material for almost four years before it acquired that polish. Phyllis Diller takes great pride in the fact that she worked on her act every day for nine years.

You won't write stuff that professional in one night. However, if you can write even one good line in a night's work, you have talent. The buyers want material—they don't care how much you write and then throw away.

Another fault of beginners is that they *overestimate themselves*. Let's assume that you do write fairly professional-looking material, and you know it's professional. You type it up, mail it out to the comedian you tailored it for, and wait in confidence. If it's as good as you think it is, you'll get a check in the mail. Unfortunately, though, a prosperous comedian won't beg you to sever all local ties and move to Hollywood with him as his private gagster. I'll admit this is what we dream as we put the special-delivery stamp on the envelope, but it doesn't often happen.

The important thing to realize is that no matter how talented you might be, it takes time for others to recognize talent.

Another fault of young writers is to *give up too soon on each topic*. "There's just nothing else funny I can say about this." It's after you reach this point that your best jokes begin. I find that my strongest gags are my first and my eighth—very rarely in between. The first is often the result of inspiration, and the eighth is the result of hard concentration. The ones in between are generally the obvious ones that must be gotten out of the way before the solid ones can find their way into my mind. If you give up too soon, you rob your mind of its most creative hours.

Probably the most common fault of beginning writers is *excess verbiage—too many words*. As a gag writer, you are writing for an audience.

They won't allow you too much time between gags. To a comedian, words are a precious commodity. The more laugh lines he can get per word, the stronger his routine will be. Get your meaning across, but do it as economically as possible.

Watch out for these errors, but get writing now. The sweet part of comedy writing is that the training ground is available to anyone. You need no experience, no connections. All you need is a sense of humor and a willingness to do some work.

You can find an audience for your words tomorrow. Write some material about the place you work, about your family . . . then show it to friends. You'll get a reaction and you'll learn from it.

Working with Local Performers

If you want more of a lesson, find a banquet or a party that would be glad to have an emcee. Volunteer. If you can't stand in front of an audience, write the jokes for the guy who is ham enough to. Either way, you'll get an audience reaction. (Incidentally, performing your own material is one of the quickest ways to sharpen your gag-writing talents. You'll work harder on the gags when you're the one who has to stand up there and deliver them.)

As you gain a little confidence in your material, offer it to one of the local comics. Most of those comics will be glad to try out some of your lines for nothing, and they may even pay you.

Build a file of your material and show it to comics. You might begin with your hometown's most popular comic. Let your friends and your associates know that you have a script and you're trying to contact this person. Chances are you'll run across someone who may know his home address or his phone number. (The chances aren't that slim. That's how it happened to me.) At the same time, keep an eye on the theatrical section of the local paper. Sooner or later, you'll find he's appearing at one of the clubs in town. Call the club and ask for him. The front desk will generally connect you with the backstage phone. If he's not there, find a convenient time to call back.

If for some reason you can't contact the comedian by phone, try sending a special-delivery letter addressed to him at the club asking him to contact you.

Perhaps the simplest method is to go to the club, catch his act, and then send a message to him backstage, via your waiter, that you are a comedy writer and would like to talk to him.

Always mention that you have some comedy material. This is the key that opens the door.

Certainly people in show business guard their privacy, and it's easy to understand why. For this reason it is sometimes difficult to contact them. However, if you try often enough and always with courtesy, you should succeed.

Suppose your town has no Mr. Show Business, or at least none that you know of. What then? Keep an eye on the local papers again for news that some comedian will be appearing in your area. Make a note of it and begin a campaign to contact him and meet him while he's in town. Exhaust every angle until you come up with something definite. You might begin by calling the person who wrote the column.

Finally, become a regular reader of *Variety*. The vaudeville section lists the nightclubs of the major cities and who is appearing where. When you run across the name you're looking for, send a special-delivery letter right away or place a person-to-person call. Directory assistance will gladly supply the phone number of the club you're after.

How About Fees?

If you keep writing and improving your style and keep contacting comics, sooner or later you're going to make your first sale. Once that happens, you generally go from comic to comic and continue to build your career on your reputation. Selling gags individually can bring $3-$25. Routines can bring $100-$500 per minute.

Other pay scales can be arranged by the comic and the writer. Naturally, the comic will try to pay less and the writer earn more. But a monthly retainer is a valid form of payment, and a percentage of the comic's fee is also workable.

Commercial Reports

by Arnall Mohre

The people of the business world make millions of decisions daily. Very often, they make these decisions based on little or no direct knowledge of the specific situation at hand. So they rely a great deal upon reports from others. Sometimes these reports are supplied by employees of the same firm. But many times outsiders are the source. In about 10 percent of the cases, a freelance "reporter" provides the basic information.

What Is a Commercial Report?

Essentially, commercial reporting is a low-key form of investigative work which deals not with spies, sports cars, or sexy women, but with the humdrum, everyday business world.

A commercial report is business information, used by a business person to help him to evaluate the prospects of a given business endeavor. The two most frequently used types of commercial reports are those used for credit purposes and those used for insurance purposes. Credit reports on individuals are not relevant for present consideration, as they are handled by highly specialized credit bureaus. But credit reports on businesses (such as those compiled and published by Dun & Bradstreet) are derived from reports submitted by a certain percentage of freelancers, as well as from salaried employees. This can be a good source of revenue.

Insurance reports, however, constitute the biggest income potential for independent reporters. This does *not* involve investigating accidents to determine loss or fault. That is the job of the insurance *adjuster.* As an insurance *reporter,* the freelancer is concerned with gathering information requested, without editorial comment. An insurance company that could lose many thousands of dollars in the event of loss of someone's life, or home, or car, wants to know a little about the person, or his home, or his car, before maintaining the risk.

A report for an insurance company gives details on the subject's health, business, personal finances, character, avocations, and living conditions—all areas for concern that will affect insurability. (Any adverse information must be confirmed through additional sources before it can be included in a report.)

Insurance companies do not use freelance reporters directly. An insurance company makes a specific request for a report on an individual to an inspection company with whom they have a service agreement. The inspection company has a list of the company's requirements according to the type of report requested. The request, along with the proper client requirements, is then given to an inspector to be worked.

Requirements and Rewards

If you are able to make even a reasonable attempt at writing seriously, you have the intelligence, awareness, and curiosity to become a good commercial reporter. You must also be aware of the importance of both accuracy and confidentiality in the reports you write.

What are the rewards? Money is the immediate one. A reporter usually gets from $3-$7, with some higher fees, each time he completes a report on a given situation. This small fee should not be discouraging, as this is a volume business, and an experienced reporter averages four reports an hour. A few hours a day making reports would yield adequate pocket money and still leave time free for other writing.

There are also secondary rewards. Because the freelancer is paid in direct proportion to the volume of reports finished, he learns a quick, concise style. Because his reports are of little value if he leaves key points vague or ambiguous, he develops clarity. If he gives his work careful, critical attention, he will develop a taut, sequential, comprehensive style useful to his writing career. Another reward: The reporter comes into contact with varied types of people in unique circumstances. From his experiences, the reporter later can harvest ample fictive details.

With rare exceptions, all reporting companies require that a professional report writer rewrite the freelancer's submission before the report is made final. This removes the pressure which causes some to try too hard to write impressively.

As the eighties began there was still a significant demand for commercial reports covering applicants for life insurance, fire insurance, and casualty insurance. Reports for automobile coverage have been restricted somewhat by the almost chaotic state of federal laws governing privacy and credit reporting.

Economic conditions are making reports on FHA and VA mortgagors more numerous and more profitable.

Research companies continue to be a good source of low-paying assignments.

Because of federal laws regarding privacy and credit reporting, it is usually best to get information from the subject of the report. Checks of courthouse records can be made quietly without causing any possible offense to anyone. In certain cases a reporting company will authorize and specify contact with others such as bankers, former employers, and medical personnel as appropriate.

Where the Jobs Are

Reports are submitted by freelancers to commercial reporting companies only in answer to specific inquiries. There is absolutely *no* market for unsolicited submissions. A freelancer starts receiving inquiries by letting the appropriate companies know of his availability.

How is this done? First, each prospective reporter must determine which companies are good bets in his own area. Then he must contact them.

Some commercial reporting companies have branches, with full-time employees, in practically every city or large town. These use freelancers only in rural and remote areas. Other reporting companies have only a few branches, and make use of independent reporters to a greater degree, including using independents in many large cities.

Thus, if a potential reporter lives in a sparsely populated area, his best prospect would be the larger reporting companies. In cities and large towns, the larger reporting companies would likely have full-time salaried employees, and in such places the smaller reporting companies would be the best prospects.

The following are several of the major commercial reporting firms in order of size.

Equifax is probably the world's largest commercial reporting company. It maintains an office or employee in practically every city of 15,000 or more.

REFERENCE INTERVIEW

RE: Applicant _____ Case # _____ Date: _____
(capitalize, last name first)

Name of Reference: _____ Occupation: _____

Address: _____ City: _____ State: _____

Known Applicant how long? _____ How well and in what way? (i.e. friend, former supervisor or business associate) _____

Is reference related to applicant? _____ Last time seen? _____

DESCRIBE HERE WHAT REFERENCE KNOWS ABOUT **APPLICANT'S** EMPLOYMENT:

Present Employer: _____ Address: _____

Date: _____ Position: _____
From   To

Previous Employers

Name & Address: _____ Dates: _____ Position: _____
From   To

_____ Dates: _____ Position: _____
From   To

_____ Dates: _____ Position: _____
From   To

If Reference is a business associate or supervisor, cover Applicant's employment, duties, capabilities, salary and reason for leaving: _____

_____

JOB ABILITY _____
Technical — Achievements — Performance — Skills

THE FOLLOWING SHOULD BE INFORMATION ABOUT APPLICANT AND HIS FAMILY

Present and Previous Residences and dates: _____

_____

Education _____
High School — College — Graduate School — Degrees Received

Organization Memberships _____
Professional — Social — Civic

Military Status: _____
Veteran — Active Reserve — Branch of Service — Rank

Civic Activities: _____

Hobbies: _____
Sports — Music — Arts — Scouting — etc.

Marital & Family Status _____
Names and ages of children

Name, educational background, etc. about spouse _____

Spouse employed? _____ Where and how employed? _____

Health of spouse and children? _____

Applicant or member of family have any chronic ailment or disability? (Describe) _____

_____

Applicant or spouse have any drinking problem? _____

What do you like most about Applicant? _____
Personality — honesty — integrity — etc.

What weakness can Applicant improve upon? _____

How does reference rate Applicant's REPUTATION? _____
General — Professional — Social

Loyalty to U.S. _____ Type of Associates _____

Applicant ever been in trouble? _____

Any member of family in trouble? _____

Recommend without reservation for job of trust and responsibility? _____

WHY? _____

Investigator: _____
Office: _____

FORM 34-1
11-69   USE REVERSE SIDE FOR PERSONAL COMMENTS OF REFERENCE.

Typical form used by commercial report writers in gathering information for clients.

It has regular part-time field representatives who gather information from which they make their reports. If a freelance writer would like to work as a field representative, all he has to do is contact the nearest local branch office manager and place an application. If there is no office in your city, contact the home office at Box 4081, Atlanta GA 30302 for the office nearest you.

Hooper-Holmes Bureau usually has offices only in cities of about 50,000 or more. If your city is smaller, consider this company as a prime potential source of good volume. At least one office is maintained in practically every state. Check the phone book for the largest city in your state for the probable controlling office. Home office mailing address is Box 428, Basking Ridge NJ 07920.

Dun & Bradstreet has branches in most cities of about 75,000 or more. If there is a branch in your city, prospects of revenue from this source are poor. If there is no branch, ask your banker for the address of the branch which handles your city; or check the largest city in your state. Home office is 99 Church St., New York NY 10007.

American Service Bureau has offices in over eighty-five metropolitan areas within the United States. Freelancers are used primarily in rural or sparsely populated locations. For further information about the need in your particular area, write to the American Service Bureau Home Office, 211 E. Chicago Ave., Chicago IL 60611.

To locate an appropriate office, take the following steps: check all company names through the white pages of your local telephone directory. For each company with no listing in your local phone book, call directory assistance for the nearest large city. Or write the respective home offices, asking for the address of their branch which handles your area.

If you decide to work in this line, you will want to know these things about the business: First, it is quite seasonal, with peaks in spring and fall, and the low point in December. Most of these companies require that you report for them exclusively and not for any other company at the same time. Most of these companies pay once a month, between the tenth and the twenty-fifth, for work done the previous month.

Convention Freelancing

by Dave Kaiser

Writing convention news and feature stories for business publications and producing daily convention publications are two lesser-known but lucrative markets for enterprising freelancers.

Many writers miss these opportunities because they feel this work is available only in resort and convention areas, when in fact it is to be found in any city where there is a trade or professional organization.

To discover which organizations are active in any community, first check the Yellow Pages under Associations. Also look for individual ads under various classifications that would indicate which associations particular businesses are involved in. (This type of ad will say "A member of the Association of . . . ")

Local, regional, city, and chamber of commerce publications are the second place to look for news about the activities of chapters of associations in any given geographic area. Most publications of this sort have an events calendar, which will provide fresh information on upcoming association activities.

One key method of ascertaining what activities are taking place in any particular industry related to your convention prospect is to consult the latest edition of *Writer's Market,* and contact the leading publications in that category. Ask to be placed on the publication's mailing list for sample copies so that you can know what is going on both on a national and local level.

Daily newspapers and weeklies serve as a last-resort source of information. Again, watch the newspaper ads as much as the stories to determine which associations area businesses belong to. Events in daily newspapers are usually too current to do anything about, but at least this information shows the writer what area associations are up to.

Small Can Be Profitable

Convention activities that are potential moneymakers for freelance writers vary from the small event with less than a hundred people expected to larger conventions attended by thousands.

The first step in arranging convention coverage is to check with industry publications for news of future gatherings. Often the annual convention routine is much the same from year to year, with a spring regional convention (or conventions) followed by a summer or fall convention for the whole organization. Some writers follow this routine each year, attending a half dozen regional meetings and then the large national one.

One reason for contacting leading industry trade magazines is to find out exactly what activities they have planned for a given event. In the case of regional conventions, it is doubtful that the publication has planned anything, and your awareness of the fact that the event is happening in your backyard is often enough to land a freelance job providing material about key topics and photos of speakers.

If, however, you find out the publication is planning to have a representative at the convention, offer your services as a local writer who knows the territory and who can fill in when the assigned reporter finds he has two meetings to cover at once. In many instances publications have planned to send two reporters to a convention, but after being contacted by a local writer decided to use the freelancer and save the airfare and other expenses involved.

Convention coverage is basically the same for a one-day affair and a two-week national event. You should get a copy of the convention schedule as far in advance as possible and keep up with the planners on a weekly basis to find out about speaker or schedule changes.

Preconvention Possibilities

A source of income often overlooked is preconvention coverage: providing basic information about the area, hotels, entertainment, and attractions. This type of service is invaluable to editors when they are faced with the extra-large issues leading up to the convention. Establish your credentials with convention officials from the beginning and produce news material on keynote speakers, schedule changes, and any other pertinent information. At the same time, you should try to get photos of prominent convention planners, association officials, and even tourist attractions to send in to interested publications.

This sort of advance material can amount to as much as 40 percent of what you'd make by covering just the convention itself. It can be prepared at leisure, from material provided by outside sources, such as the local chamber of commerce and the convention committee.

Setting Priorities

When mapping out your convention strategy you need to determine exactly what events are on the schedule and to decide their importance. A get-acquainted cocktail party, for instance, will rarely be worth covering, while a ribbon-cutting ceremony is a must.

Most conventions open officially with a ribbon-cutting, and a lot of writers figure that's the first event of any significance. This is a mistake. Many association officials hold directors' meetings, have special presentations, and do much of their important business in the several days before the convention starts. After the ribbon-cutting they are so busy conducting actual business they have no time for interviews.

The important news which will bring front-page coverage in the publication and extra pay usually occurs at the very beginning (or even before the beginning, as just noted) or during the last day of the convention. This is when decisions are made about important association activities, upcoming events, and next year's convention.

Most conventions, even the smaller ones, usually schedule seminars or guest speakers during the morning and exhibit hours during the afternoon.

It is important to cover the seminars and keynote speakers for news coverage, while the afternoon exhibit sessions give an opportunity to circulate on the exhibit floor, talk both to people attending the convention and to the exhibitors, and write a separate story on this topic.

Advance planning by the writer is also required to set up a schedule which will enable seminars to be covered, photos to be taken, film delivered to the lab, stories written, prints picked up, and the whole package assembled prior to deadline.

Most publications desiring convention coverage usually move their deadlines to coincide with the convention dates and want the photos and copy a few days after the final exhibition day. On the final day, it is essential to get onto the exhibit floor, talk to both the booth personnel and to people on the floor to determine exactly how successful the convention was, how it compares with previous conventions, how much business was done, and to obtain everyone's outlook on the upcoming season.

What we have discussed so far concerns coverage of a convention for a trade magazine editor at, usually, his regular word rate as given in *Writer's Market*.

Larger conventions, however, will need the services of a freelance writer-editor to produce a daily newspaper of convention coverage.

The Convention Daily

Based on the duration of the convention, the first thing to determine with your client is the size of the publication and the number of issues to be printed. Most conventions are scheduled around a weekend, usually beginning midweek and closing Saturday or Sunday. A frequent alternative is an opener Sunday night, concluding Tuesday or Wednesday at noon.

Therefore, three or four convention issues can be published, to reach most of the people at the convention, and to announce or report on most of the events. Advertisers are usually willing to buy ads in an issue having initial distribution during either the opening of seminars or classes, or the opening of an exhibit area, whichever comes first.

Daily convention papers vary from very simple affairs similar to a monthly newsletter, to more elaborate issues with dozens of pages of news, photos, and advertising. The time that must be spent in planning varies accordingly — as will the rates you charge for your time.

Basic procedures for printing and distributing the issues are about the same, no matter what the size of the issue.

Printing is arranged according to format. A newsletter-type daily, giving brief news items and the upcoming convention schedule, with no photographs involved, can be produced in any quantity at a fast-print shop. Such an edition can easily be paid for with a few ads run across the bottom of each page; some publishers use legal-size pages.

Big Dailies Need Big Printers

Producing a larger convention daily gets quite a bit more complex. For 32-to-64-page issues, it is necessary to line up a high-quality printer who can produce issues with photographs and quality ads on a fast turn-around.

One rather simple method of doing this involves preprinting the middle twenty-eight pages of a thirty-two-page issue, then printing only the four-page wraparound at the convention. If the convention-site printer is expensive, you can have the preprinted section done elsewhere.

Otherwise, you must find a printer who can handle the size paper you are using, produce such a wraparound in a few hours, fold it around the preprinted portion, and distribute it to the hotels.

Rates depend upon the job, with the writer charging the association on a job basis, which is determined by estimating how many hours a given task will take and then quoting accordingly.

For instance, in the preparation of a four-page wraparound, it is first necessary to determine exactly what steps will be required to accomplish that job from beginning to end.

The writer is going to spend several hours just in obtaining bids for the printing and photo lab costs, determining if the printer and/or photo lab has its own pickup and delivery service, and other miscellaneous time-consuming activities.

What to Put in a Daily

Writer-editors covering convention events prepare short 200- to 500-word stories, the length depending upon their importance. Usually, a 1 p.m. deadline must be set for gathering or receiving story material. This gives everyone time to write up his material and have it ready to go to the printer by 3 or 4 p.m.

Careful preplanning of editorial content can save the cost of one or more writer-reporters when action is heaviest at the convention. The most troublesome problem will sometimes be stretching actual convention news to fill space. It's best to have a reserve of prepared copy to use as filler material.

One such feature can be an outline history of memorable events from previous conventions (like the time they brought the elephant into the lobby of the Fontainebleu Hotel). Conventiongoers tend to be annual repeaters, so this kind of story has nostalgic appeal. Special attention should be given to the last convention held at the site of the current one, with references to changes in the industry or profession and its association, as well as in the location.

Predictions about the industry's future made at previous conventions — five years, ten years, twenty years ago — with some discussion of whether they proved to be true or not is another reliable feature idea. This could possibly be accompanied by current predictions from prominent convention spokesmen.

You should have a dozen human-interest fillers of varied length, preferably involving industry figures, on hand. In addition, you can highlight interesting facets of the convention city — things to see and do there.

As soon as you have a copy of the full convention schedule, go over it carefully for reportorial demands. What sessions must be covered in full? What can you drop in on for a couple of photos only? What can you handle by asking questions of those who were there? Which speeches will have press copies available, either in advance or at the site?

Then plot out your schedule, and those of your assistants, if you have them. Include copywriting time and trips to the photo lab and printer, if necessary.

If you must depend on nonwriters to report on sessions, try to line them up in advance, so they will pay more careful attention to what is said or done. Try to get more information than you need for your convention paper, since the same material will be useful in later issues of regular newsletters or to related publications.

Costs Plus Writer-Editor Profit

Production costs have to be checked out individually ahead of time. Printing this kind of newspaper is not cheap; it will cost a minimum of several thousand dollars. However, it usually is supported adequately by advertisers that appear in the preprinted sections of the issue. Advertising can also be solicited from all tourist facilities in or near the convention site, as well as from regular accounts. These rates are usually high enough to support the photo lab, typesetting, photography, and printing costs.

Based on a press run of 5,000 copies, the cost of such a project could easily be $6,000, with $2,700 going for printing, $750 for typesetting, $450 for photography, and $2,100 for the writer or writers. It is usually up to the association to pay about $3,000 up front and the additional $3,000 on completion. All advertising solicitation and ads for the publication are provided by the association. This can prove to be a bonus for the writer, because when preparing a four-page wraparound the association often will sell several half-page ads for $500 to $1,000 each to cover your expenses and, in the meantime, lessening the amount of editorial material needed in the publication.

Where a less elaborate publication would be necessary, without any photos and featuring a schedule of events, the cost per issue would be higher, but so would the profits. Such an endeavor might cost $1,000 to produce and leave a profit of about $1,000 for several days' work by one writer-editor.

After convention coverage is completed, it is time to begin again and determine where the next convention will be held nearby, or what regional events will be held as preparation for a distant convention for which you could provide similar services.

Business associations with 30 to 300 members exist in even the smallest communities and counties and usually hold several local or state conventions each year. This could add up to enough convention business to keep an enterprising writer occupied on an almost full-time basis!

Educational Grant Proposal Writing

by Leon Fletcher

Today a great many schools are recognizing their need for professional help in writing a wide variety of materials—study guides, programmed materials, filmstrips, course outlines, guides for parents, faculty handbooks. But most important of all financially, to you as a freelance writer as well as to the school as an institution, are the opportunities in writing applications for the thousands of federal and private grants now available each year to all levels of education.

According to one recent report there are now 57 federal agencies administering 1,093 grant programs. In 1979 federal grants to education totaled $22,081,846,000. In addition, there are some 28,000 private foundations giving grants to education and other fields. Writing the applications for these funds has grown to the extent that most major colleges and universities and many larger elementary and high school districts have established special administrative offices to prepare the applications. While many of these schools employ full-time project writers, there is nevertheless a great need for the part-time freelancer who is knowledgeable in education: In addition, there are 88,025 educational institutions in the United States and every one of them is eligible for various funding programs. The vast majority of these can get the professional writing assistance they need only by contracting with education writers on a project-by-project basis.

My full-time job was as a junior-college administrator. My salary was—well, "adequate" if my president reads this, "good" if my acquaintances who may need impressing are reading. But one month I earned more money on education-writing assignments, working a couple of nights a week and on Saturdays and Sundays, than I did at my full-time position.

Three Types of Jobs

To provide that assistance, the freelance writer—especially one well versed in today's innovations in education—may be called upon for three types of services: editing the proposal, writing the proposal, and creating the project itself.

An editorial or review service. This is usually but a brief assignment, typically for one or a few days. The manuscript to be reviewed has usually been written by a regular staff member of the educational agency; an experienced and qualified outsider is sought to go over the material and suggest changes to ensure that it is written clearly, organized logically, and provides all of the details needed.

Here are some of the operating procedures I've found useful in completing such an assignment. First, I ask that an advance copy of the material be sent to me so that I can review it before I meet with the writer or the staff involved. Sometimes it is suggested that I come to an advisory committee meeting, for example, "so we can all meet together and cooperatively review the manuscript and discuss what changes are needed," in the words of a typical request. Then, of course, I am reading the material cold, making evaluations on first impressions only. Usually the content of an education project is such that there should be time for deliberate, reflective review. Often it is valuable, I find, to read a manuscript and then do some digging in a library to see what related material may be available to broaden the basis of my evaluation.

I usually look through the last few years of *Education Index,* which lists by subject the articles that have been published in the major education magazines. It is the academic equivalent of the familiar *Reader's Guide to Periodical Literature.* Then I look through the latest yearbooks, research encyclopedias, and other references which cover the subject of the project.

If the project is concerned with the use of educational television to teach typing, for example, I look first for reports or studies of educational television, then studies of the teaching of typing, then branch out into such possible tie-ins as teaching typing through films, teaching piano by educational television, then teaching other hand skills—sculpting might be one—by television.

Next I make it a point to ask that a copy of *all* of the instructions for submitting the proposal be sent to me. I emphasize "all" because there are some funding agencies that publish one statement announcing such details as who is eligible to apply and when the applications should be submitted, a second publication which contains the actual regulations, and a third publication which presents the step-by-step instructions for preparing the applications.

This way, when I meet for the first time with a staff that has asked me to review a manuscript, I can start right out with detailed notes and specific recommendations. Sometimes I prepare my suggestions as a written summary, with enough copies for all who will be at the meeting. But frequently I find it more effective to present my recommendations through discussion.

(The freelance writer must be very aware of the tone of voice he uses in his discussions with educator and administrator clients. Although the freelance educational consultant-writer is brought in as an "expert" to help the school win funds, the creators of the project are naturally proud of their baby as it is, and suggestions by the writer for improving its appearance must be made diplomatically.)

To begin such meetings I've developed a technique that seems to be particularly helpful. After the usual small-talk exchanges of introductions and comments on the weather have been completed, the project director will generally bring the group to consideration of the manuscript, often by picking up his copy and starting to thumb through it. Right then I quickly ask him and the others present to lay aside their written materials for a few minutes and, in a statement which includes as much informal language as I feel is appropriate, I suggest, "Before we get into this discussion—for just a couple of moments would you pretend that I've never seen this written stuff, and would you just shoot the breeze with me, telling me what this project is you've got in mind?"

Then I listen hard and write fast, trying to take notes on virtually everything that is said. This oral presentation of the project idea is usually more specific, vivid, interesting than the manuscript itself. I then use this conversational version as a contrast to the frequently stilted, jargonistic, obscure statements that have become the written version, and set the tone for casting the proposal in a language that is somewhere in between.

Thus the staff and I have begun focusing on what are usually the major points of emphasis in any assignment to review a manuscript. Generally there is a need to clarify the goals or purposes of the project. Often there will be an attempt to sell the reader by referring to "educational research which shows . . ." But that research isn't cited because the facts may be so well-known to the project staff that they overlook the point that these details may be desired, perhaps demanded, by the reader before he is convinced. The tendency is often to use jargon for its own sake, to use semi- or even pseudo-scientific terms in an attempt to build authority, and to use a long string of references to simulate scholarship. By asking the staff time and again to "set aside the manuscript for a moment and tell me in your own words what this paragraph means," I seem to be successful in most reviewing assignments to pinpoint ideas, clarify expression, and develop logical structure.

The Second Type of Service

Writing the presentation means taking a collection of detailed, specific, usually lengthy materials which a college, for example, has been gathering over a period of time, and turning all of it into an organized, interesting, unified manuscript.

Often the collection of material is overwhelmingly long and detailed. I once wrote an application for funds for a college with a particularly creative innovation as the subject. Because of the outstandingly distinctive features of the proposal, a brief of the project had been requested by a high federal official. The eight college professors who wrote the first version had included a twenty-two-page, 381-item bibliography. One page of the text had nineteen research references; there were sixteen pages of "Overview of Related Research and Development." Fine documentation, perhaps, for review by a research team, but certainly not appropriate writing for the eyes of a busy Washington executive. My version got all this background information down to a page and a half with plenty of paragraphing, underlining of key words, and subheads to emphasize essential points.

A technique I have found effective in giving direction and structure to a large mass of educational material is to ask those who have been working on the project to dictate a summary that covers three points:

What information is available?
What does it mean?
How is it going to help what kinds of students learn what kinds of things in what kinds of situations?

One application I worked on was for a major grant to establish criteria to diagnose dyslexia, a reading disability. When I asked that first question—"What information is available?"—the project coordinator told me, "The doctor here has more than five years' work on the problem, all written up; we've also outlined the program we want to establish, listed the staff, facilities, and equipment needed." My job, then, was merely to simplify the writing and select from the abundant information only that which was absolutely needed in the application, then structure that information into the various parts of the application form.

My second question—"What does it (that information) mean?"—elicited an exceptionally pointed answer. "It means that both the medical and education professions really know very, very little about this problem."

When I asked my third question—"How is your proposal going to help what kinds of students learn what kinds of things in what kinds of situations?"—the coordinator showed once again this project had direction, purpose, value. "We'll be able to help all kinds of kids who have dyslexia learn how to read better in school and out."

But not all applicants are so clear-cut in their planning. I once met with a group of art teachers seeking funds for "some kind of art project."

"What information is available?" I asked. "Well, we have our personal experiences, and we can all tell you about that; but, well, we haven't done any research or study, if that's what you mean."

So I didn't need to ask my second question—"What does that information mean?" And how was that art project to help which children learn what? As you have probably guessed, the answer to that was vague indeed.

The dyslexia application brought in around $500,000. The art project was one of the few assignments I refused.

As I mentioned earlier, when you, as a writer, enter as a newcomer to a group which has been working over an idea for some time, gathering the detailed information, writing that material into at least some form of presentation, you often face individuals who are quite protective of what they have produced. (And understandably so.) I have found that, in the early staff meetings I attend as a writer, it helps to be complimentary, encouraging, enthusiastic about what has already been written by the staff—provided, of course, the material can justify at least some sincerity. (They *know* their writing is not all that "great"—that's why they called for you!)

Then, I never submit only a part of my written version. Rather, I want the staff to have in their hands the complete package of their material as I see it. When they have just a portion of it they often bombard me with "This is a key concept you haven't even mentioned," and "Here's a point which must be added early in the presentation."

Sometimes I ask the staff, in the planning sessions before I begin to write, to indicate by underlining in their material those "basic points" they consider absolutely essential to their proposal. Then I consider myself free to select from the remaining material only what I believe needs to be included. This, of course, turns out to be another way to help them establish clearly and specifically what it is they wish to communicate in the finished presentation; the lack of an exact idea is the one most frequent, most significant weakness. Once it is overcome you're more than halfway to the printer's.

The Third Job Type

Creating the project itself. An educational agency may seek help from a writer in the designing of a project as well as in the writing of the grant application. Usually some teachers or administrators have suddenly been dazzled by all the reports of federal and private funds which are now available to education, and so they want to get some of those dollars, too. The writer is asked to "meet with us some afternoon so we can kick around what kind of a project we might go for."

Such an introduction could well serve as a warning to the writer that he's in for a difficult time and might want to consider passing up this request for his services. Far too often such an introduction masks a blunt request to write a proposal to bring in dollars, as contrasted with a proposal to help some specific aspect of education.

If you are a writer qualified in education, and informed about CAI (Computer-Assisted Instruction), single-concept films, student-response systems, audio-tutorial instruction, multimedia presentations, team teaching, programmed instruction [see separate chapter on this specialty], and other recently developed techniques of teaching—then you can certainly be valuable to a school as a designer as well as a writer. But creating new ways of improving learning is a giant field in itself, and the educational writer whose qualifications are not strong in these areas would be best advised to restrict his services to that writing he can do effectively.

Finding Clients

How might the freelance writer make himself known to prospective clients? He should compose a one-page summary of his writing qualifications, experience, achievements; describe how this writing relates to the interests and needs of a school; and include references to the availability of funding programs appropriate for the needs of the particular school. (Among the standard sources of this information are the *Grants*

Register, detailing funds available to individuals; *Annual Register of Grant Support,* focusing on funds for groups; and *Grant Data Quarterly,* providing more current information. To search out grants available in specific fields, consult the *Catalog of HEW Assistance* or *Sources of Information on Funds for Education.*)

This latter part of the summary should show a knowledge of the needs of the specific school. Obtain this by reading the local news reports of what programs the school is studying, developing, having difficulties with; attend a few meetings of the school's board of trustees to get further information, particularly about programs being considered for establishment or expansion by adding faculty or constructing new buildings.

Send this summary to the chief administrator of the school, and also to the individual teacher at the school who is active in developing innovations in instruction.

Thus, contacts should be individualized for the particular school as well as for the particular program that may be developing at that school. With few exceptions, the freelance writer will be facing two distinct types of institutions, with no middle ground: (1) the school that's continually developing new programs and frequently needs a writer's assistance; and (2) the school which has not yet developed any new program requiring resources beyond its own staff and funds, and needs a writer to help launch its initial innovation.

How Do You Charge?

There are two methods of billing clients. Certain education writers, some of whom have organized into professional service groups to offer developmental assistance to schools, charge a percentage of whatever money may come from the applications for funds they write. This figure can be as low as 1 percent for a straight writing job on, say, a $250,000 application; perhaps 5 percent if the task includes considerable research and design of the project, along with writing; occasionally higher for an especially complex or extensive proposal.

This percentage is usually included in the funding application under expenses for a development or preparation stage of the project. Sometimes it's entered as a cost in the dissemination of the results of the project.

What happens when the applications are turned down? No pay at all to the writer—but percentage fee arrangements are typically entered into only when the project is truly extensive and significant. Then someone on the staff of the applying agency usually meets with the funding agency well before the deadline for the application and tries to get some encouragement that the project is likely to be approved. If there's no encouragement, the project is usually dropped.

I work on a fee basis. The amount of that fee might be set in some kind of relationship to your full-time salary, particularly if you are in the field of education or other area related to the writing you'll be doing. I know education writers who do contract assignments at daily rates of $200 and up. If you're a certified teacher, and especially if you are a specialist in a particular field, your fee can be much higher. According to a 1983 issue of *The Professional Consultant* (20121 Ventura Blvd., Woodland Hills CA 91364), a newsletter for consultants, the rates charged by educational consultants range from $265 to $686 per day for an average of $459 per day. These are all plus expenses for travel, typing, telephone calls, research assistance, etc.

Almost without exception the institution asks the writer what his charges will be for the specific assignment.

I state what my charge per day is and give an estimate of the number of days I will need to complete the assignment. The estimate I give is for a range of days—say six to eight. Obviously it is important to have a clear understanding of the extent of the services the writer will provide—the time to rewrite a specific document can be estimated quite accurately, but if research is part of the assignment, the sources may be very time-consuming to develop. The day after the initial meeting with a school I send a letter describing quite specifically my understanding of what I'm to do and what I'm to be paid.

While some schools have established fees they pay consultants, there is seldom the need for bargaining.

I started some ten years ago writing pieces for professional education journals, very few of which pay at all. I developed my writing technique and moved into popular magazines. Today, as a freelance education writer I'm earning a good income. You can set *your* own rates based on your background and get into a field that has a very great need for a great many truly qualified writers!

Writing the Proposal

Every effective proposal, whether for a contract or grant, a federal agency or private foundation, contains a concise explanation of what the applicant plans to accomplish. It must prove his competence. The format generally follows this order: title page, abstract, statement of problem and method, budget, and biographical information.

Title page. The title must be concise and specific. If it is the kind of title that William Proxmire could ridicule, the proposal will be turned down. Key words that will serve indexing and retrieval purposes must be written in a meaningful pattern.

Abstract. The abstract should in no more than 200 words state in simple terms the problem, the purpose, the method, the scope, and the results anticipated. Managers glance at abstracts; only if a message comes through do they turn to the proposal itself.

Statement and method. A common flaw in proposal descriptions is the failure to emphasize the central objective of the proposed project. You should put that first and make it stand out. You should then relate what you propose to do with what has been done in the past. It is important to anticipate what equipment, if any, will be needed to carry out the project. It is vital to make clear what facilities and other forms of support will come from the institution making the application. If the cooperation of other bodies or institutes is essential, it is necessary to secure it in advance of submitting the proposal. Any advance planning results in a better proposal description. A proposal reader should be able to say what new understanding will result from the project. If the writer does not clarify the significance of the project, a reader cannot explain or justify it to others.

Budget. Under individual headings, details should be given for: Salaries, Equipment, Material and Supplies, Travel, Publication Costs, Direct and Indirect Costs.

Frequently the budget must demonstrate that the parent institution supports the proposed work to the extent of making a concrete contribution to it in a percentage of salary or in overhead or facilities or all of these. A foundation-type granting body may be reluctant to support on a national level what is denied help on a local level. An institution's contribution should be described under the heading Cost Sharing. Contracting agencies do not require any participation; for that reason, university administrators tend to favor government contracts over grants.

Biographical information. It is entirely possible that an agency or foundation is satisfied with the worth of a proposal but uncertain whether the person or institution submitting it is the best one to do the job. It is the function of this section to persuade them that he, she, or it is.

— *Michael S. Porte*

...dentally, this campaign went over its goal by $200,000.)

...ut human beings at the center of your fund-raising writing. Be ab-
...tely honest and sincere. But keep emotion under control. Sentimen-
...y turns people off if you are approaching them for money. Your
...er handling of human distress will touch the heart and release that
...er urge to help others in trouble.

...ere's an example from my brochure for a psychiatric clinic for emo-
...nally disturbed children:

> A six-year-old boy is unable to sleep the night through. Often his
> distraught parents find him wandering through the dark rooms of
> his home, unable to tell where he is. Shy with other children, he
> keeps on the fringe of their groups, prefers to play alone. For long
> periods he will rock in a chair, silent. Neighbors call him the
> "strange one." Secretly his parents fear that he may be "crazy."
>   This child is *not* crazy; he's emotionally disturbed. The Guid-
> ance Center is bringing him back to normal through therapy.

Campaign Materials

You'll do the *campaign brochure* first because it contains all the data
and appeal themes. It's the sourcebook for the rest of the campaign
literature.

Use lots of photographs. Twenty is not too many for a sixteen-page
brochure. You must have pix that shout the story out loud. To show just
how one client agency helped children and adults handicapped by
cerebral palsy I spent a day snapping pictures of children turning
doorknobs, putting on their coats, playing drums, trying to hold a pen-
cil, walking in bright sunshine, smiling—workers in the background.
Out of sixty candid snaps, I got twenty that told it all.

You can hire a talented pro to do this work for you. But why not
become your own top-notch photographer? It's legitimate to charge your
client the going rate. If you are already a camera buff, the opportunities
are limitless. But it isn't all that hard to learn photography. Don't swea...
trying for texture—just get the focus, light, and composition right. C...
for close-ups—freckles and eyelashes. Invest in a quality camera. Bu...
how-to pamphlet (Eastman Kodak's are grade-A). In six months...
picture taking, my camera paid for itself.

Photos need captions—short word gems. Tell the readers what...
can't know. For example, "Jane stands proudly on her artificial...

You'll prepare *agendas*. Campaign directors love you when y...
this burden off their backs. Meetings must produce action; ot...

Fund Raising

by Alan R. Blackburn

I've written more than a million words—and every word was printed.
I've retired early with a comfortable income, and still keep my hand in.

Yet you have never heard of me—nor are you likely to in the popular
press. I write for a lucrative hidden market: fund raising.

Nonprofit organizations—charities, hospitals, museums, colleges,
community causes, and churches—constantly solicit money. These
groups rely on professional writers—freelancers like yourself—to reach
their prospective donors. Fund raising is a highly respectable pursuit approved by chambers of commerce and better business bureaus.

Here's how to find this market, write for it, and sell yourself to it.

First, make a list of philanthropic agencies and institutions in your
city. You'll find them in the Yellow Pages under their categories, such as
Social Service Organizations, Hospitals, Colleges and Schools, etc. Your
best prospects are the smaller ones. Big ones use their own staffs or hire
out-of-town fund-raising firms. But try them all.

Walk into the top person's office, be it the president of a college or the
director of an agency. *Don't telephone in advance.* What? you ask. Isn't it
better to make an appointment? Not when you're *selling* yourself. There
are good reasons for walking in on your prospect unannounced:

You're *there,* in person, right now—not waiting another month to suit
the prospect's convenience. Telephoning in advance telegraphs your
punch—your prospect ducks. Fortune favors the bold.

Tell the secretary you'd like to talk to the boss about fund raising and that you don't mind waiting. Chances are fifty-fifty you'll get in.

If you don't, *then* make an appointment. At least the secretary knows you. Secretaries are important people. They open doors. Make friends with them.

I've called on scores of top executives this way. Fund raising is a continuing concern for the nonprofit executive. The agency *always* needs more money. Executives will shoehorn you in between appointments long enough to hear what you have to offer.

Once I walked into a natural history museum on the hunch they might be interested in a color-slide presentation of their work. The director himself saw me, and I left with a contract to run their annual fund-raising drive!

Walking in cold works. Try it and keep score.

Getting Experience

But before making such calls, you must have some experience in fund-raising writing. Here's a choice of ways to take the plunge:

Apprentice yourself to a local professional fund raiser. Usually there's a need for a part-time writer, and you'll earn while you learn. Look in the Yellow Pages under Fund Raising Organizations.

Take a crack at working for a *nationwide fund-raising firm.* To obtain a list of the big firms write to American Association of Fund-Raising Counsel, Inc., 25 W. 43rd St., New York NY 10036. These are top-of-the-line, and you'll get their fair-practice code. It will pay you to observe it. For cities outside your own, your library has the phone books.

Don't neglect your United Fund. It's your best source for data about the local fund-raising scene. It may even need a writer.

Volunteer for fund raising at a local church. There's hardly a church that doesn't raise money every year by letter appeal or personal canvass. Many use tested routines. Offer your services free. They'll be grateful, and you'll be paid many times over in experience.

Once I was asked to do a citywide cerebral palsy campaign, but they didn't have any money to pay me. That year I put out my best for them and charged them nothing. The campaign was a success; they became my paying clients for the next eight years.

I got my start as an apprentice. I was packing my bags on graduation from college when my former headmaster offered me a job as development secretary raising money for my prep school. It turned out that one of the school's board members was a top executive of one of the leading fund-raising firms in the US. I learned the basics from scratch and liked

it. I stuck with fund raising and later set up my own firm, [...] cessfully for twenty-five years. I estimate that 80 percent [...] did was writing!

Fund raising is divided into two activities: organizing an[...] a professional campaign, the key staff members are the cam[...] tor (organization) and the publicity director (that's the wri[...]

The campaign director tangles with people and rarely h[...] writing. This is where you come in. You write the campaig[...] and publicity. But you don't *just* write, you research by readi[...] talking with staff, and saturating yourself with your client's [...]

Limits of Sentimentality

To get the hang of this kind of writing, visit institutions in y[...] Pick up their fund-raising publications. Study each piece—it wil[...] a lot about the way to write for a campaign. Ask yourself if you c[...] well or better.

Now, what's special about writing for this market? It is *appe[...] ing*—a mixture of facts and emotion. Your words must persuade [...] to volunteer their services or write out a check.

Make no mistake about it: Fund raising demands quality writi[...] will test all the skill you've acquired in nonfiction *and* fiction techni[...]

When I wrote a brochure for the Society for Crippled Childre[...] raise money for a new building, I burrowed through piles of techn[...] material and talked with staff. I was searching for an angle. Sudde[...] there it was! Building specifications called for an entrance door t[...] would open automatically as crippled children wheeled up to it (this w[...] back when such doors were not common). The architect referred to [...] casually as a "magic door." I had my lead.

Here's what I wrote for the first page under a picture of the door:

Help them open the magic door* to a brighter day

This is the magic door—entrance to the new Heman Rehabilitation Institute on Cleveland's East Side.

Across this threshold thousands of handicapped children will step into a world of hope.

We ask you to help us raise $500,000 to complete and equip this vitally needed rehabilitation center.

This is the first and only capital campaign for the Society for Crippled Children since its founding in 1940.

*There actually is a magic door. It swings open by itself when a child approaches.

they're just social gatherings. An agenda is a whip to get things done by deadline. With each agenda item provide space for the chair to write in who's agreed to do what, and when. Allot time to each item for discussion. Plan the meeting for one hour, no more, or you'll lose your people. At the end put the date for the *next* meeting to keep the action moving forward. Attach all data needed for discussion to the agenda.

Is all this necessary? Yes. It pays off. Just this year I helped a church chairperson with her agenda technique, and presto! a committee that had been dragging its feet went out and raised an unexpected $27,000 for world missions!

You'll write *speeches* for campaign leaders. [See separate chapter on this specialty.]

You'll write *publicity releases.* Make them one-pagers. Cram them with facts and names. Send along a couple of your best photographs.

You'll write *personal letters* by the score. A hospital campaign I was involved with lacked gusto. The chairman called me in. "I don't have time for what we need," he complained, "which is a lot of personal notes."

I got busy, shooting out short, friendly letters for him like this:

Jim —
    Saw you got Harry Blaine on your team. That's a ten-strike. He's a busy guy but he's got important contacts.
    See you Wednesday night at the captains' meeting.
    Again, thanks.

                         George

You'll write *form letters.* Put wallop in the first sentence. Here's the start of a letter to enlist church workers:

Dear Friend,
    Jesus called on people—He didn't write them letters.
    So we want you to help us do away with letters like this one, and *call* on other members Sunday, November 9.
    We'll give you details at the meeting on . . . .

Never write a letter longer than one page—half-page is better.

In short, you'll do *all* the writing: workers' manuals, pledge cards, posters, requests for foundation grants. The secret of this business is that most people can't write—or can but hate to. You do it for them and charge a fee.

What to Charge Your Clients?

Experience will be your best guide as you get the feel of the market in your city. I never work for an hourly rate but charge a flat fee for the campaign-writing package. The reason: When you work for a fixed fee, the client knows in advance what you will cost him. He likes that. You'll like it, too, because it doesn't tie you down to clockwatching. (Keeping track of time messes up my creativity.) Also, you may bang out an A-1 letter in five minutes or wrestle with it for hours. I think it's fairer to your client and to you to average out the charge.

But if your client prefers to pay by the hour because he's used to it with his advertising firm and law firm, by all means use an hourly rate.

Here's how I go about setting a flat fee. Paradox: You *do* estimate the hours all the writing will consume. From past work, I set down my guess as to the *average* time each piece may require, including research. For example, a brochure may take perhaps twenty hours for research, spread over two weeks, and thirty hours to write, get it approved (not easy from committees), lay it out, and see it through the printer's. That's worth at least $3,000. Add up *all* the pieces in the campaign, and that's your flat fee. Compare this to what you would expect from magazine articles.

How many pieces to a campaign? An effort that expects to raise several million from a few foundations and wealthy people may need only one first-class presentation of the case. But a citywide canvass with a goal of a few hundred thousand may take a lot of writing.

Only experience can give you the answers. That's why a period of apprenticeship is indispensable.

Some personal advice: Your greatest asset will be dependability. There's a lot of money at stake in a campaign. You can't let your client down. If you do, don't expect repeat business. Read widely in psychology, art, science, and finance (particularly the *Wall Street Journal*). These are topics your clients talk about. Groom well, dress well—you're dealing with the Establishment. You're not sitting in your study writing; you're out among 'em. Make them feel you're one of them.

This is a good, clean business that will give you a living. If along the way you become a full-time professional fund raiser (writing *and* organizing), the sky (almost) will be the limit of your income.

You'll also feel the glow of serving up something extra to your fellow human beings, especially those who need help.

Why not reach for the phone book and start looking up churches, hospitals, welfare agencies . . . ?

Genealogy and Local History

by J. Stouder Sweet

Alex Haley isn't the only writer to have benefited from the phenomenal popularity of *Roots*. The interest in genealogy that it aroused creates a market for freelance writers everywhere. People are more aware now of their ancestors in both a familial and societal sense, and will pay to have their past preserved in published form. The writer with a taste for history and a nose for research should consider the possibilities of writing family trees, family biographies, and local histories.

Genealogical Research

Family trees are a good place to start. You might want to try telling your local librarian or county clerk about your services, or placing an ad in the *Genealogical Helper* (see below).

Genealogical searching can be done anywhere there is a courthouse. And you might find you have a local monopoly on it. You'll look up wills; records of probate, deaths, marriages, births, divorces; land records; old telephone directory listings; cemetery records; pension information; tax lists; church records—anything that might carry personal information from long ago. And of course local and state libraries should be consulted for research material.

In a large city, vital records may be kept by the Board of Health; very early ones may be found in churches. Old census questionnaires are stored in the US National Archives in Washington, but many local libraries have microfilms (and you can also buy them yourself). Each census lists the head of the household and the various individuals in it. (You can't find yourself in them—only the very oldest are public.)

You can earn six to ten dollars an hour for this sort of research if you are a certified genealogist. Certifications are issued by the Board for Certification of Genealogists (P.O. Box 19165, Washington DC 20036) and the Genealogical Society of the Church of Jesus Christ of Latter-day Saints (50 East North Temple, Salt Lake City UT 84150). If you are not a certified genealogist, adjust your fee accordingly, to perhaps $3-$5 a hour, or ask your local librarian if he can tell you what you might reasonably expect.

If your family tree searches lead you outside your local community, you may want to know about these publications: the *Genealogical Helper* (Box 368, Logan UT 84321) is a monthly publication that covers the whole subject, with news, names of individuals looking for information or offering services, lists of libraries and archives, etc. See the *Helper* for many applications of small personal computers for indexing and name searching. The *D.A.R. Magazine* (1776 D St., NW, Washington DC 20006) features a genealogy column. People who want to join the D.A.R. and other ancestry-based organizations will hire genealogists to prove their lineage.

of their families. One freelance writer who specialized in family histories provided several versions of such a service. If the family had already assembled the basic information and only needed to have it edited and typed, he'd charge $100. A history that involved a lot of research might be billed at $1,000. Generally, fees averaged from $200 to $500. In each case his clients only wanted one bound copy in typewritten manuscript page format.

If the family had many members, all of whom wanted copies of the history or memorial biography of some family celebrity, then your best bet would be to work with a local "Insta-print" company, which has the ability to make masters for either photocopying or multilithing. Your price for the booklet to the family members, therefore, would include your costs and a markup for your handling of these details.

Local-Interest Pamphlets

What other opportunities exist in your area for historically based writing? Travelers on the Pennsylvania Toll Road, for instance, will find pamphlets on Pennsylvania Dutch art and customs in the Howard Johnson restaurants along the way. You can hardly go anywhere without encountering historic sites. Could you write locally based, illustrated pamphlets to be sold in racks in stores and at the sites themselves?

You might be surprised to learn how little it costs to print "short run" pamphlets by offset. Anyone with a multilith and facilities to make paper printing masters can do this. Assembling and stapling the pages yourself will save you some money. You can promote the booklet at lectures you give before local groups. Have a pile of copies for sale at the door.

If you don't want to speculate on your own investment in a locally based pamphlet, don't overlook the possibility of having it produced by the local historical society or chamber of commerce. Centennials and other historic occasions often create the desire for such a booklet [see separate chapter in this book on Business Writing: Anniversaries], and local groups or well-to-do private citizens often underwrite such projects.

Missing Links in History

Literally thousands of commercially distributed local histories were issued by hundreds of publishers in the US between about 1875 and 1930. The authors were characters right out of *The Music Man*—and also made real contributions to the communities they visited. These old volumes were about half local history and half biographies of leading local citizens, and are in many cases the only source for information on particular aspects of local history and personalities. On practically every page of *The Dictionary of American Biography* (edited by top scholars), the list of sources is heavily loaded with these old "mug" books. If it hadn't been for such vanity publications, a lot of historical material would never have been published at all.

Are there some missing links in local history you can provide, and earn freelance income at the same time? It's worth investigating!

Government Public Information

by Ted Oglesby

I live in a rather progressive Southern community of about 18,000 which is the hub of a ten-county region. After a three-year stint as news and public affairs director of a local radio station, I served ten years as editor-publisher of a weekly newspaper.

One conclusion I came to during this time is that the general public does not understand its local government.

And the workings of all levels of government are becoming more and more complex. The larger dailies and magazines do an adequate job of covering the state and national scene, but it is at the grass roots level that communication between government and citizens breaks down. It isn't intentional; it is caused by economic necessity.

I recognized this problem in my community and found what I believe to be a solution.

I offered to be the county's public information officer on a time-spent fee basis. I would attend the required meetings. I would research the many problems. I would leave the hard-news reporting to the media but would write in-depth, explanatory features, material the media might not ordinarily come up with themselves under normal circumstances. These features would be individually prepared for each of the local print and broadcast media, written in the particular style of each, aimed at their specific audiences.

In addition, I would be available to design and prepare information tracts and brochures explaining how taxes are spent to be mailed with annual tax notices. And I'd be available for other special public relations projects.

We agreed upon a monthly retainer for a maximum amount of work plus a fee for all work performed in excess of that maximum.

I visited the city government, then a public authority, with the same results. In my relatively small community I secured three monthly retainers totaling about one week's work per month, leaving me three weeks monthly for extra work (at a fee) for these clients and for my *other* freelance writing.

Perhaps equally important to me as a writer is the access to unlimited material for magazine articles. In the brief time I have been engaged in this pursuit, I have found at least a half dozen ideas which I believe can be marketed to a dozen magazines.

I will admit that I may have had a slight advantage in light of my recent tenure as a crusading editor in the community, but I stoutly maintain that any freelance writer with the ability to research and write toward specific audiences can do the same.

How does one charge for this type of work?

It's a compromise between what you think your time is worth, your expenses, and what the client is willing and/or able to pay. If, for example, you arrive at $20 an hour for your figure, then establish how many hours a month it will take you to provide the services you want to offer the local government. You can then suggest a monthly retainer of that amount.

This offers you a guaranteed payment each month for freelance work and offers the local governing body services at a lower rate than it would have to pay in salary and fringe benefits for a full-time employee.

Editor's Note: If you live in a city large enough to have regional offices of some federal government agencies, you will find opportunities there, too, for occasional freelance work. Make some phone calls to the Contracts Management Office of the agencies, who will be listed under United States Government in the white pages of the telephone book (or, in some larger cities, in a separate section of blue pages). If they use freelancers they'll ask for your credentials and put your name on their "bidder's list" to contact when a writing project that their staff can't handle comes along. (Any projects whose fees are expected to exceed a certain amount are required to go up for competitive bids.) How do you know what price to quote for the job? The agency will provide a summary of the job's requirements so you can see the scope of the work involved, and your bid will be determined by how much you think your time is worth and how much you want the job. Keep in mind, also, that freelance writers can get help in wending their way through the bureaucratic maze (and in learning which projects might have been set aside from competitive bidding in the interests of opportunity for minorities) from the Small Business Administration, which has offices in most large metropolitan areas.

Newspaper Stringing— Long Distance

by James McLendon

Wire services are worldwide, multi-million-dollar news networks with huge staffs of reporters, editors, and photographers who deal with an almost limitless fund of news sources and outlets. True, but not always. You can start your own wire service for a quarter. The price of a daily newspaper can start you on your way as a one-man wire service.

To illustrate: You read in your local daily newspaper that a New Jersey tourist has been beaten and robbed in your small town in Florida. Digest the facts in the newspaper story before you, and then call the local law enforcement agency that handled the case for further in-depth details and possible later developments. You will be asking for information that is public record, and free to you.

After you have gathered your own facts, write your news story, and then get on the telephone to the appropriate New Jersey newspaper for your sale.

You've got localized human interest material, it's immediate news for the paper you are calling, and if the regular wire services have not carried the story, it's profitable for you.

A tightly worded 250-word news story is usually worth between $15 and $25 if you are that rare bird who can beat the local wire service to the punch!

When you call the out-of-town newspaper, call collect to the city desk. You are in the role of a correspondent, and in most instances the newspaper will gladly accept your call.

Once you get the city desk or the city editor on the telephone, outline your news story to him. If he accepts it, phone it in word for word, and punctuation mark for punctuation mark, as you have it written.

And make sure the editor takes your name and address so he can send you your check!

The sales possibilities do not end with your initial news story. If the incident is of a serious enough nature, there may be follow-up assignments; or, if there is a potential feature-length story in your news item, ask for an assignment for the paper's Sunday magazine section.

Sunday supplement feature stories vary in price from about $25 to about $200 with most large daily newspapers, and generally run about 1,000 to 3,000 words in length, with pictures.

Pictures are an important part of your one-man wire service, so be sure to mention their availability to the editor you call. In some instances, the editor will request that you put your photographs on a jet flight immediately to his office.

Your one-man wire service can also feed information to radio and television stations in out-of-town areas.

Opinion Research Interviewing

by Michael H. Ketcher

If you have a healthy curiosity about how people live and what they think, and would enjoy going into strangers' homes and asking probing, personal questions about their thoughts, lifestyles, and financial circumstances, then opinion research interviewing may be the job for you. The skills and experience you'll gain are bound to enhance your writing.

Hundreds of opinion research companies—from the huge syndicated polls, like Gallup and Harris, to tiny market research firms based in somebody's kitchen—conduct thousands of surveys yearly. These companies have a constant need for freelance interviewers. Over the last few years I've worked as an interviewer for several such companies, to help tide me over between full-time jobs and support my freelance writing habit as well.

A steady income is not the only benefit that freelancers can gain from working in opinion research. The interviewing techniques and "people skills" I've learned have been invaluable in my development as a writer. Writing is solitary work, and regular contact with others can be stimulating.

Nevertheless, writers should usually resist the temptation to use their survey respondents as subjects for articles. Contrary to what many people believe, most of the individuals who respond to surveys are so flattered that someone actually wants their opinion that they will gladly tell you almost anything you want to know. Sometimes they'll even give you information—regarding their income, for example—that they wouldn't tell their best friends. Therefore, interviewers should always respect their respondents' confidentiality. For a long time, in fact, the Gallup Organization had a policy of not hiring writers—especially newspaper and television reporters—because it didn't want the respondents' confidentiality abused. Such indiscretion is grounds for dismissal at most opinion research companies. But it could be worse. Census Bureau interviewers who abuse a subject's confidentiality can be fined $5,000! For their own protection, writers should be careful about using their subjects too literally as material.

Market Research

When most people think of opinion research, they usually think of political polls. Yet few of the surveys I've worked on have actually been concerned with such lofty topics as the President's popularity or the state of the national economy. Most deal with such mundane subjects as what company makes the best olive oil, which brand of margarine tastes the most like butter, or which brewery's advertising is most effective. Nevertheless, I've worked on a variety of interesting projects, including a CBS Election News Poll, readership studies for national publications like the *Wall Street Journal,* and viewer studies of current films. One company even offered me thirty-five dollars per day, plus expenses and a gas allowance, to travel to each county seat in Oregon, Idaho, and northern California and interview election officials. I turned the job down because I didn't want to be on the road for five months.

While I've interviewed people in such diverse places as bars, subways, and theater lobbies, most surveys are conducted either door-to-door, at a shopping mall or street corner, or by phone from either the research company's office or the interviewer's home. Companies hire people by the survey, which can run anywhere from two or three days to two or three months. The average is about a week.

Market researchers generally work on evenings and weekends; hours are flexible and companies will allow you to refuse assignments if you have other obligations. Most interviewers get themselves listed with at least two or three companies so that they can be sure of having work whenever they want it.

Pay ranges from the minumum wage ($3.35 per hour) to over $5 per hour, depending on the company, your skill at interviewing, and your ability to negotiate for top dollar. A few companies pay by the interview, and again, rates vary. Most companies will also reimburse you 18.5 cents per mile if you use your car, and for parking, bridge tolls, and any other expenses incurred. The only tools that you may have to supply are pencils, a legal-size clipboard, and sometimes a phone. (You will be reimbursed for long-distance or toll charges.)

Requirements for interviewers are: fearlessness in approaching strangers, the ability to accept rejection gracefully, and a modicum of common sense, intelligence, and patience. Legible handwriting also helps. Some companies will pay extra if you're fluent in a foreign language.

There are two things to find out when applying for a job as an interviewer: will you be an employee or an independent contractor, and how soon will you be paid. Because of some vague Internal Revenue Service rulings, a few companies—especially those that provide work space, telephones, and other tools—insist that their interviewers become employees and fill out a W-4 form so that income tax and Social Security can be withheld. If you're an independent contractor, however, you're really self-employed and are responsible for self-employment tax (if you make more than $400 in one year) and your income tax, since there's no withholding. Unfortunately, some market research companies, like some publishing companies, take as long as two or three months to pay. Others pay within a week. Employees are generally paid faster than independent contractors.

Where to Find Jobs

There are plenty of freelance market research jobs available, especially in large metropolitan areas. The best way to find these jobs is to look under Market Research in the Yellow Pages of the telephone directory, call the companies listed, and ask them if they hire interviewers. Those companies that do will probably ask you to come in, fill out an application, and perhaps attend a short training session. If you live in a non-metropolitan area, contact national market research firms to see whether there's a need for an interviewer in your part of the world (see list of addresses at the end of this chapter). To get additional addresses consult the *International Directory of Marketing Research Houses and Services* (better known as the Green Book), published by the New York chapter of the American Marketing Association (420 Lexington Ave., Suite 1733, New York NY 10070) and available in most larger libraries. While some of these companies deal directly with the interviewer, most hire through local supervisors, so when writing, ask for the name, address, and phone number of the supervisor in your area.

Public Opinion Polls

Some of the more interesting surveys are conducted by the larger nationwide polling organizations (see list of addresses at the end of this chapter). For example, the Gallup Organization regularly surveys the public on important national and international issues from their 362 sampling areas in the United States. Each assignment takes five to six hours, and the interviewer has a week to complete the job and mail it back to the home office. Pay starts at the minimum wage ($3.35 an hour) plus 19 cents a mile for travel.

The Louis Harris Poll also hires freelance interviewers; if you write to the national office your letter will be forwarded to the appropriate regional supervisor. The pay varies with the job.

Another possibility is the National Opinion Research Center (NORC), a nonprofit corporation which gets contracts from government agencies to do opinion research on a variety of topics, including health care, the labor force, and education. NORC has a hundred sampling points across the country and advertises for interviewers in the help-wanted section of newspapers. Or, if you write to NORC's main office in Chicago, your letter will be forwarded to the appropriate regional field manager.

The US Bureau of the Census, which conducts regular monthly surveys on a wide range of social issues, pays their researchers better than any of the private companies do. However, interviewers meet strict deadlines, and may be asked to work in high-crime areas. Attendance at a paid training session is also required. Pay is $5.28 per hour ($6.63 in inner city) plus 20.5 cents a mile. Some government benefits—such as sick days, leave, and pension—are also given.
Some government benefits—such as sick days, leave, and pension—are also given.

In addition to its regular monthly samples, the Census Bureau hires interviewers (called enumerators) for the Decennial Census. Enumerators track down and interview people who don't return their census forms by mail. The enumerator must meet a daily quota and is paid by the piece rather than by the hour.

After applying to opinion research companies, if you don't hear from any of them within a week, call them and ask if they have any upcoming projects. If you let the field supervisors know periodically that you're out there and ready to work, they'll think of you first when a job comes up.

Research Companies

Audits and Surveys, Inc.
1 Park Ave.
New York NY 10016

Burke International Research Corp.
1529 Madison Rd.
Cincinnati OH 45206

Chilton Research Services
201 King of Prussia Rd.
Radnor PA 19089

Dale System, Inc.
250 W. 57th St.
New York NY 10019

Field Research Corp.
234 Front St.
San Francisco CA 94111
(Hires mainly in California)

George Fine Research, Inc.
55 W. 42nd St.
New York NY 10036

Gallup Poll
Princeton Survey Research Center
53 Bank St.
Princeton NJ 08540

Louis Harris & Associates
630 Fifth Ave.
New York NY 10020

M/A/R/C
4230 LBJ Freeway
Dallas TX 75234

National Analysts
400 Market St.
Philadelphia PA 19106

National Family Opinion
Box 315
Toledo OH 43654

Opinion Research Corporation
Opinion Park
Princeton NJ 08540

Quality Control Services
11042 Manchester Rd.
St. Louis MO 63122

Simmons Marketing Research
  Bureau
219 E. 42nd St.
New York NY 10017

Starch, Inra, Hooper
566 Boston Post Rd.
Mamaroneck NY 10543

Walker Research Co.
8000 Knue Rd.
Indianapolis IN 46250

The Census Bureau also hires freelance interviewers.
For information write:

United States Department of Commerce
Social and Economic Statistics Administration
Bureau of the Census
Washington DC 20233

Printers' Writing Jobs

by C. G. Welton

If you get just as much pleasure out of seeing your name on a check as you do on a magazine article, take a good look at the printers in your town. This often overlooked source of income is not only a ready market, but can pay extremely well. Equally important, few freelancers seem to go after this business, so you have little competition.

Some years ago, when I gave up the "security" of a job with an insurance company to freelance full time, I sold a printer on the idea of writing a series of advertising pieces . . . at $25 a week. A few years later I was netting nearly $10,000 a year from this source alone.

Every town has at least one printer. Printing Industries of America, the printers' trade association, has 10,000 members, but the Census Bureau says there are over 26,000 commercial printers in the US. Most printers are so busy managing the business and selling that they have no time to listen to their own advice about the value of the printed word. But ask one if he shouldn't be producing printed advertising for himself and he'll tell you, "Sure, but I don't have time."

You couldn't ask for a better opening. Whip out a couple of ideas you've armed yourself with and show him what you can do for him. Tell him you're prepared to write a series of monthly mailings that will cover more territory than he or his salesmen could working twenty-four hours a day . . . and at a fraction of the cost.

All right, you're not a printer, so where do you get your ideas? Go to the public library and study the trade magazines. If your library doesn't have any, borrow copies from several printers before you make your pitch.

One of the best sources is *Graphic Arts Monthly,* where George Griffin's column "How's Your Advertising?" is a gold mine of ideas, good and bad. He reviews specimens of printers' advertising from all over the country, offering penetrating comments that constitute a course on the subject. Don't swipe them, of course. Use your imagination.

After you've sold the printer on doing his advertising, don't stop there. Tell him you'll write copy for his customers, thereby enabling him to offer still another service. You might subtly point out that this can also mean more printing orders from his existing customers.

Rarely is there a buyer of printing who wouldn't be buying more if he had someone on tap who could write copy. Ask the printer if you could work up some ideas for his best customers that will help them sell more fuel oil, or insurance, or whatever.

Or ask him for a list of prospects he'd like to have as customers. Use the same approach here; help them to sell more. Point out to the printer that even if he doesn't get an order, at least he's offering *ideas* while his competitors are just selling printing. The novelty of this sales approach is practically guaranteed to result in some additional printing orders.

Some of the freelance jobs I secured through association with a local printer included: a folder prepared as an announcement of the merger of two graphic arts companies—fee: $350; a folder written to emphasize a Howard Johnson Lodge's convenience to Civil War points of interest—fee: $110; a folder written for an auctioneer who came into the printer's plant and asked if someone could "fix up a folder" for him—fee: $25; a yearbook written annually for a philanthropic foundation—fee: $750.

Editor's Note: Writers who have letter quality word processing printers or typewriters which use a carbon ribbon to produce the sharp, black characters necessary to photo-offset reproduction can also work with printers whose smaller customers need only camera-ready typewritten copy rather than more expensive typeset pages. If you have the kind of proportional-spacing typewriter that approximates the justified (even) margins seen in magazines and newspapers, that's even better. How much you should charge per page depends on the going rate where you live and should be a rate that you think is fair to you and still allows the printer to add a markup before charging his customer. Also, don't forget letter shops, churches, banks, and other businesses which often have small printing equipment but no means of typesetting.

Programmed Instruction Materials

by Bill Williams

What comes to mind when you hear the term "programmed instruction"? Well, unless you draw a blank—and lots of people do—you probably envision a student sitting in front of something like a TV monitor, trying to pick the transistors of some gigantic computer. And you *could* be right; quite a bit of PI is now presented in a computer-assisted format.

But the truth is this: Much of the really practical programmed instruction in use today is presented in the simplest way possible—the old reliable pencil-and-paper format. Now, I'm not going to invite IBM out into the alley in this article. All I want to do is explain briefly what PI is, how it can be developed in simple forms, and how you, as a freelance writer, can cash in on the move toward self-instruction both in schools and industrial training situations.

What PI Is

As you probably know, several years ago a group of scientists known as behavioral psychologists began proving some theories they'd thought were true for a long time. Among other things, they showed the world that most animals—pooches and pigeons, rabbits and rats—could be induced to perform in a desired manner ... *if* they were rewarded when they did the right thing. In fact, the behaviorists determined that they could change the behavior of animals by rewarding correct responses to stimuli and withholding rewards from (or even punishing) their "students" when undesirable behavior was exhibited.

It wasn't long before our heroes (who were smarter than the average pigeon) figured out that this knowledge could be applied to the everyday learning processes of just plain folks. With this thought in mind, some of these hardy pioneers set out to develop methods of doing just that: applying the basics of behavioral psychology to down-to-earth teaching methods.

What PI Does

The methods used to change human behavior along the lines of behavioral psychology have developed rapidly over the years, although in the eyes of most PI writers the state of the art is still quite primitive. Basically, however, here's what programmed instruction does.

PI presents the material to be learned in relatively small pieces called *frames*. A frame consists of a certain amount of information, to which the student is asked to make a response of some kind—fill in a blank, complete a sentence, discriminate between two or more possible answers, or complete some small portion (or perhaps all) of some task, etc. This frame contains, or *is*, if you prefer, the stimulus, in behaviorist terms. In other words, within a frame of a programmed instructional text, the student is led toward making the response his instructor wants him to make.

Once the student makes his response he is rewarded. How? By being told that he has performed as the instructor wanted him to. As you can see, it's pretty important here that the student not respond incorrectly too often; unless the program tells him he's *right* much of the time, the student will become just as discouraged as if he were sitting in a classroom, unable to answer his teacher's questions because he couldn't understand the thirty-page chapter of a text he didn't get around to reading the night before.

The problem, then, is this: How does the programmer lead the average or below-average student to the correct response the majority of the time without boring him or his brighter colleague? As you can see, this takes more than a little writing skill. The programmer must hit a delicate balance between boring a bright student and losing a dull one. And the biggest problem in the field of PI today is that too few programmers can attain that balance!

PI Types and Techniques

If you've ever worked on a factory assembly line, one of those jobs that require you to do the same thing time after time, day in and day out, then you know how dull this routine performance can become.

By the same token, a student who is working his way through a regular textbook will soon begin to yawn and rub his eyes. Tired? Maybe. Bored? You bet! And programmed instructional texts are equally boring if the student is asked to perform the same kind of action throughout. For this reason, a variety of programming techniques have been developed over the years.

Before we discuss a few of these techniques, let me point out here that there are two basic types of programming. One is called *linear,* because the student begins with the first frame in the program and works his way through the book in a straight line to the end. The other major type is *branching* programming, in which the student skips around in the program, based on the answer he chooses in each frame. If he chooses a right answer, he is given new material and another set of answers to choose from in the frame he branches to; if he selects an incorrect response, he goes to the frame indicated by that response, receives remedial instruction, then is sent back to the original frame for another try.

As you can see, the branching technique can save a sharp student a lot of time. There is some evidence, however, that the linear method is more effective, at least when a student is expected to repeat answers verbatim, or perform an exacting task. If you decide to study PI in detail, you'll find that there are some very effective and efficient ways to combine both linear and branching elements in a single program.

There are three common linear program techniques: *constructed response* frames; *discrimination* frames; and *BABOON* frames. The most commonly used of these is the constructed response frame, which looks like a sentence with one or more blanks in it. Actually, there's a lot more to it than that. The student must be asked to supply, or construct, a relevant response—something that pertains directly to what the program is trying to teach. Special care must be exercised to avoid making this type of frame too simple for the student. Here's an example of a constructed response frame:

1. In certain types of programmed instruction frames, the student is asked to build, or construct, his response. For this reason, these are known as ＿＿＿＿＿＿＿ response frames.

Looks simple, doesn't it? And that's one problem with this programming technique. It looks so simple that it's overworked, and in many cases too little thought is given to proper construction of the frame.

Discrimination frames are another effective and popular technique.

(In fact, one programming expert I know claims that the entire *world* consists of one huge discrimination—a constant choice between two or more possible answers.) They ask the student to select the correct response or responses from among the choices presented. Here's an example:

2. When a loan is executed, the person borrowing the money is expected to pay it back. Write "loan" beside any appropriate descriptions below.

_____A. John's uncle dies, leaving John $1,000 in cash.

_____B. Fred painted his friend's house and received $100 for the job.

_____C. Ralph bought a car and agreed to pay the bank $125 a month for three years.

This is just one type of discrimination frame. The student might be asked simply to check the correct answers, or he might be asked to look at some artwork, or an actual object, and make his decisions based upon what he sees.

Finally, we come to what's known as a BABOON frame. In this type of frame, the student is given a choice between answer A or answer B. In addition, *both* A and B can be correct, or *neither* A nor B might be correct. Take *A, B, BO*th A and B, *Or N*either A nor B; shake them all up; and you *could* come up with the term BABOON—as someone, at some point, obviously did! At any rate, a BABOON frame looks like this:

3. In loading a hole for blasting, then, those items of major concern are (check only *one* answer):

_____A. The amount of explosives and resulting powder factor.

_____B. The burden and spacing involved in the blasting pattern.

_____C. Both A and B are correct.

_____D. Neither A nor B is correct.

This type of frame enables you to test (or make the trainee discriminate using) several items, without working through an entire series of frames.

Developing Programmed Instruction

Developing a PI text involves a combination of several types of writing. It resembles a research paper or technical article in that you must research your subject thoroughly before you write that first word. It's like journalism in that you'll probably end up interviewing one or more experts on the subject at hand. And it resembles article and short fiction writing in the sense that you will write in a style designed specifically for the audience you're trying to reach—whether you're teaching a high school dropout an assembly-line task, or a group of physicists how to conduct a new type of laboratory experiment.

If you're writing for industry or schools, you will probably be assigned a given subject or area of study, rather than proposing the program yourself. For instance, if you're working as a specialist in, or a consultant to, the training department of a manufacturing firm, you may be asked to write a PI text that teaches a given assembly job to production workers. Or in a school situation, you may be assigned the task of writing a PI text on the basics of Modern Math. At any rate, assignments are common in the field of PI.

On the other hand, suppose you are an expert at some particular task, or in some special field of study. Let's say you have developed a new system of self-instruction in playing the guitar. Or perhaps you have a friend who is a whiz at chess and whose knowledge of basic moves might lend itself to a programmed format. In this instance, you would prepare a portion of the text, outline the rest of the idea, and send it to a publisher who puts out PI materials (or even standard textbooks—they just might be looking for general-knowledge PI materials to publish), just as you might submit a sample chapter and outline of any other book-length idea.

In either event, once you have the go-ahead you can begin your research in earnest. It would take a lot more space than we have here to detail the entire process of research and study that goes into a PI text. However, it should be pointed out that you must apply the "systems approach" to the subject, if you're to come up with the most efficient (least possible frames) and effective (best teaching) method of programming your subject.

In the systems approach, you start with the end product—let's say the ability to make certain chess moves and know when to use them—and work backward to see what knowledge is necessary to attain these skills. You talk with your experts, make notes, outline everything that's pertinent to the development of the required skills. Keep in mind that the first step is to set the objectives of your program: where you're going. The objectives are of the utmost importance. They must be *behavioral* objectives, items that can be measured in terms of *performance*. Remember, the objectives you set for your program are just as important as, if not more important than, your programming approach itself.

Next, you must determine, with the help of your experts once again, how much material must be taught and to what depth, or level of understanding, in order to accomplish the objectives you've established. In this step, you should end up with a list of teaching steps (facts or skills your student must grasp, in one way or another) known as a *teaching points outline.* You'll save yourself a lot of grief, at this stage, if you double-check every point to make certain it's accurate and that you intend to teach it to the level of mastery your experts think desirable.

To determine whether you are teaching each point to the desired degree of mastery, you can develop a terminal frame—the final frame of the section of the program dealing with that point—on each item on the teaching points outline. A further check with your experts will tell you whether you are asking too much or too little of your students on each point. Now you are ready to write the frames which will fill the gap between "ground zero" and mastery.

A basic PI sequence will consist of three frames to teach a given point. Now, some points are so difficult that you'll need more than three frames to teach them adequately; and some are so easily grasped that only two frames will be required. The number of frames necessary to teach any given point will become apparent only after you have written the basic program and begun validating (testing) it on students. And that's where the fun begins. Every PI text, if it's going to do the job it should, must result in a 90/90 ratio. To most programmers, this means that 90 percent of the students who take the program must learn 90 percent of what the program is intended to teach. There's no such thing as a student who "just can't hack the material"; if a PI text doesn't work to the 90/90 ratio, it's the program's (and the programmer's) fault, not the student's.

What this means is that you must write your basic program, usually relying on a three-frame sequence throughout to give yourself some starting point, test it, rewrite based on the test results, test again, rewrite, and so on, *ad infinitum* (or *nauseam,* if it takes longer than you'd at first hoped). Sound like a lot of work? Well, it is. On the other hand, it pays well. And besides, if you've never seen a two-week training job cut down to a day and a half, or if you've never heard the thanks and praise of a trainer or teacher who has suddenly had the drudgery of the hard-to-teach, boring parts of his job lifted from his shoulders, or if you've never seen an individual who's been considered nearly "untrainable" suddenly begin learning ... then you're in for some rewarding new experiences when you begin writing PI.

PI can be learned by anyone who has a logical mind and a basic knowledge of writing in the first place [see bibliography of this book for titles of PI-writing texts]. At this point, there are a lot of programmers who are doing fine work but whose biggest problem is the English language itself. If you decide to get into the field, you'll probably be a couple of steps ahead of the game; at least you'll know how to put things down on paper in an interesting and correct manner. And once you've mastered paper-and-pencil programming techniques, you'll be able to expand the applications of these basic techniques into even broader, more sophisticated media.

Format for PI Submissions

Most publishers have their own special final printing formats for programmed instruction, so the important thing for the writer to remember is that the frame and its answer should be typed closely enough together to show their relationship, yet with adequate separation to allow use of the draft for validation testing.

I usually use $8^{1}/2$ x 11 paper, double-spacing the bodies of all frames, with about four spaces between a frame and its answer. The answer appears below the frame itself, each frame being numbered, and I usually draw a solid line across the page between the frame and the answer so I can use the draft in validation. The students can use a blank piece of paper, or cardboard, as a simple mask. They simply read the frame, make a response, then move the mask down far enough to expose the answer I've given them beneath the line drawn across the page. To go to the next frame, all the student has to do is move the mask down to the next line, read the frame above the line, make his response, then move the mask down again to expose the answer, etc.

The writer can get a lot fancier than this, of course, with such variations as the frame on one side of the page, the answer on the back, or at the top of the next page, with only one frame per page.

The PI Market

As I said, there are several major textbook publishers who are interested in publishing PI materials on subjects broad enough to sell widely. Among these publishers are McGraw-Hill, Prentice-Hall, and Pitman Learning, Inc., to name a few. And, as mentioned earlier, you could come up with your own freelance programming ideas, do just enough of the research and frame writing to submit a sample and an outline to these people, then sit back and wait for a go-ahead.

Another method of marketing PI material is to approach major businesses in your local area and show them what you can do for them. To do this, of course, you will probably have to show them some samples of your work. By approaching several companies with an offer of your talents, chances are good that one of them is going to say yes.

And a yes from a company that has training problems you can handle can come in many forms. The company might pay you on a consultant basis, keeping you on the staff in a consulting capacity until you have completed the work they feel you can do for them. (And you're not likely to finish overnight.) Or perhaps you will find yourself in a full-time position doing what you like best—writing. Just as possibly, you might end up with an assignment on a freelance basis to prepare one or more PI texts to teach a variety of tasks the company needs help with. If any one of these comes to pass—well, you're on your way.

Payment for PI Materials

Some commercial publishers pay a flat fee, while others pay a royalty. Relatively short texts (32 to 64 pages, for example, with 60 to 200 frames) on simple subjects might be assigned for a fee of $1,000 to $2,500—more, if the publisher wants a particular piece badly enough. More complicated materials, perhaps involving multimedia programming, can pay several thousand dollars, and a royalty arrangement can frequently be worked out with the publisher. Obviously, prices vary greatly, depending upon such factors as: length of the published work; amount of research required; how technical the material is; how much knowledge the writer brings to the task, as opposed to the amount of input the publisher/client is required to provide; and, perhaps most critical of all, the writer's reputation for meeting deadlines with materials that work.

In my efforts to get writing assignments from companies today, the fees I ask are based on all of the factors listed above—plus my experience and my estimates of how long it will take to produce the material. Then, based on my overhead, a profit figure I've worked out with my accountant, and my feelings as to how smoothly the task will flow (through reviews, rewrites, etc.), I usually quote on the basis of $100 per hour of my time for in-house writing and editing, $1,000 a day (plus expenses) if I have to go somewhere to research and/or write.

Another approach to pricing is to charge by the hour of instruction provided by the materials. For example, if the intent is to use two to three hours of trainee time in the program, then multiply the maximum estimated trainee time by a pre-established figure. For the "usual" type of material, this per-training-hour rate should start somewhere around $3,000-$3,500; and for, very technical training, fees on this basis can range from $3,500 to $5,000 per training hour . . . or higher. A lot depends on the intuition you'll soon develop as to what the training is likely to be worth to the prospective client.

What About Staff Jobs?

PI consultant fees vary, depending mostly upon the programmer's reputation (often more on reputation than on ability, in fact). The lowest fee I've heard of is $500 a day, and the high is about $1,000 a day. Needless to say, at $1,000 a day, most projects are of very short duration. Salaries of full-time programmers vary according to the programmer's experience, the industry in which he's working, and the type of material he's writing. A programming trainee might start at $12,500. Usual salaries for experienced programmers seem to range from $20,000 to $40,000 a year, with most programmers averaging $22,000-$23,000. Again, reputation in the business has a lot to do with the salary commanded. And if a programmer works his way into a supervisory situation over a group of programmers, $45,000 (supervisor) isn't at all out of line, in many industries.

Rights Retained by Author

This varies by publisher, but most commercial publishers producing general-interest programs work out rights arrangements very similar to those on any other book to be sold to the general public. Best thing to do is check the individual book publisher's contract regarding these terms.

In most cases of program assignments for specific projects, and programs written for certain companies to alleviate their training problems, the author retains no rights. He receives his flat fee for the job, and that's all. This is not a particular problem, however, since most of this material has no real market outside the specific area for which it's prepared.

Getting Started

Don't get the idea that you'll be able to set up a company of your own overnight to prepare PI materials for publishers, school systems, or industry in general. This could happen, of course; it has happened, in fact, but not overnight, to a few friends of mine. Your most likely chance of immediate success is one of the two routes I've mentioned above—freelance an idea to a publisher, or show local companies what you can do for them in the way of relieving some of their training burden. Then perhaps some day you'll be in a position to begin building a staff of programming experts of your own.

There's an old saw in the field of programmed instruction that goes like this: "Programmed instruction is fun, fun, _____." Well, for the freelance writer who wants to expand his capabilities, or who wants to find a permanent home in a writing position with some company, here's one that fits even better: "Programmed instruction can mean money, money, _____!"

Public Broadcasting

by Nancy Abbott Young

You are a serious writer with a quality script and a desire to see it develop into a television or radio production of special artistic integrity. You have put something of your education, hard-won experience, and soulful self into this effort, and you want to reach an audience that has a "serious, qualitative" predisposition. You may want to avoid Hollywood-style commercial programming on principle. Or you may have tried those channels, and been discouraged by the lessons of rejection, or even the lessons of success! At any rate, you are ready for an entirely new approach to TV or radio production. Naturally, you turn to public broadcasting.

You fire off a letter to the Public Broadcasting Service, National Public Radio, the Corporation for Public Broadcasting, or your local station. And that is where the adventure begins. Writing the script was nothing compared to the Herculean effort of moving it through the public broadcasting system—or "non-system," as insiders jokingly refer to this labyrinth of stations and networks we cherish as our primary alternative to commercially sponsored TV and radio.

But take heart. The effort of marshalling your script through this bewildering, amorphous maze is not without its possible rewards. Public television's 302 stations and NPR's 286 stations offer a unique opportunity to the freelance writer and independent producer.

Alphabet Soup: CPB/PBS/NPR

The Corporation for Public Broadcasting (CPB), the major source of federal funds for program production, has recently reorganized its operations through the creation of a Television Program Fund. The Fund is charged with the development and implementation of a five-year plan, one of the major goals of which is the encouragement of independent producers. The reorganization affects submission and acquisition guidelines throughout public broadcasting. It will also have a decisive long range effect on whether public television will actually develop its promised showcase of homegrown talent—including the development of "American Masterpiece Theater," radio dramas, scripted adaptations of short stories and novels, poetry performances, documentary nonfiction, and innovative public affairs programming.

Priority areas under the new Program Fund include: children's programming, minority programming, popular cultural affairs, public affairs, and science and information, with a focus on individual health.

The Television Program Fund is the main path of access to CPB funding. CPB is usually approached by the production entity itself, and writers are best advised to contact either a local public broadcasting station or independent producer first with their proposals or scripts. The funding process includes request, negotiation, and monitoring. Proposals are evaluated by peer panels and advisory panels rather than by staff assessment.

The Program Fund will provide producers and writers with detailed guidelines for proposals so that they may have all the material necessary to compete for funds. Contact the CPB Program Fund, Corporation for Public Broadcasting, 1111 Sixteenth St., NW, Washington DC 20036.

The Public Broadcasting Service is the national broadcast and distribution arm of public television. New technology resulting in transmission by satellite (something the commercial networks haven't picked up on yet) makes possible a whole new range of national program distribution. PBS will soon divide its programming into three networks: PTV-1, for prime-time cultural and public affairs selections; PTV-2, for special audience and innovative shows; and PTV-3, for instructional and children's programming.

PBS is also reorganizing its programming priorities. The desire to nurture American productions—as opposed to supporting another decade of Edwardian drawing room imports from Great Britain—is fierce among the increasingly organized groups of independent producers in this country who are clamoring for airtime on public television as never before.

PBS is *not* a producer, however, so script reading is a negligible part of its activities. PBS deals in fully developed scripts of broadcast quality—with funded operations only.

Despite the lack of production and script-reading facilities and staff, PBS is nonetheless interested in pursuing new frontiers in creative production. The best place to send your proposal within PBS is, depending on your subject matter, either the Department of Arts and Humanities or the Department of Current Affairs (PBS, 475 L'Enfant Plaza West, SW, Washington DC 20004). Enclose a résumé that lists your previous production credits and establishes the fact that you are a professional writer experienced in TV or radio.

If you have written a script, note that PBS does not use waiver forms (see below) as a policy, and it is entirely possible that your script will be returned unread. However, your name and résumé will be forwarded to the newly formed Drama Project, and you are promised equal consideration there for production review, and possible referral if you haven't been able to line up a local producer on your own.

National Public Radio (NPR) is the third organization in Washington's alphabet soup. Three of NPR's most popular shows—"All Things Considered," "Morning Edition," and "Earplay"—accept freelance submissions on speculation. The first two, which use public affairs analysis and commentary, news and human affairs, and arts profiles and interviews, are interested in ready-for-air taped submissions only. Write for complete guidelines: Acquisitions Producer, NPR, 2025 M St., NW, Washington DC 20036. [See Radio Interviewing chapter in this book for information on NPR interview submissions.]

"Earplay" is the contemporary radio drama series produced by NPR in conjunction with station WHA in Madison, Wisconsin. This immensely popular series seeks to establish a market for radio writers equivalent to that of the British Broadcasting Corporation, where as many as seventy-five new dramatists are introduced to the public each year! "Earplay" producer and originator Karl Schmidt sees a great potential audience in this country for original radio drama during the next decade.

"Earplay" pays its writers $2,000 for first rights and $1,000 for previously produced works. Script length is sixty minutes. Noncommercial radio rights in the US are acquired for three years' unlimited broadcast from date of distribution. Script submissions and inquiries should be sent to: Script Editor, "Earplay," Vilas Communication Hall, 821 University Ave., Madison WI 53706.

Regional Networks, Workshops, and Consortia

Public broadcasting is organized into five major regional networks, all of which have member stations that produce new programming. If you're interested in contacting them concerning scripts or proposals, first query the Director of Programming within each region:

Central Educational Network (CEN)
4300 W. Peterson
Chicago IL 60646

Eastern Educational Television Network (EEN)
120 Boylston St., 5th Floor
Boston MA 02116

Eastern Public Radio Network
1 Center St.
New York NY 10007

Pacific Mountain Network (PMN)
Suite 170-B, Diamond Hill
2480 W. 26th Ave.
Denver CO 80211

Southern Educational Communications Association (SECA)
Box 5966
Columbia SC 29250

There are also *instructional* television organizations within the regional networks. Educational programs are their first priority, with the emphasis on audiovisual materials. Again, a query to the Director of Programming is always appropriate. The cover letter, resume, and list of previously produced materials are important with this market as elsewhere. Negotiations are usually up front, with all fees negotiable and frequently subject to state funding guidelines. The producer usually buys all rights. Fees may vary from $100 for a wraparound (the introduction, continuity, and summary which tie together an interview, and which may range from thirty seconds to five minutes) to $2,000 for a full (thirty-minute) script. For a list of stations in your area offering instructional programs, write to your regional network.

One especially encouraging recent development is special-audience programming. The following organizations are not necessarily production houses, nor are they always open to unsolicited submissions. But—if your script or project idea relates to their interest area, it's probably to your mutual advantage to query the Director of Programming:

Children's Television Workshop
1 Lincoln Plaza
New York NY 10023

Black Programming Consortia
WOSU-TV
Ohio State University
2400 Olentangy River Rd.
Columbus OH 43210

Native American Public Broadcasting Consortium
Box 83111
Lincoln NE 68501

Latino Consortium
c/o Rick Tejada-Flores
KCET-TV
4401 Sunset Blvd.
Los Angeles CA 90027

Your Local Station

PBS, NPR, and the regional networks are composed of hundreds of local stations, and you should be sure to research the production possibilities in your own backyard.

The Corporation for Public Broadcasting has two station handbooks available, gratis, to the public: "Handbook of Information Sources for United States Public Television" and "CPB-Qualified Public Radio Stations." Write to the Office of Public Information, CPB, 1111 Sixteenth St., NW, Washington DC 20036.

Further information on community-licensed radio stations may be obtained from the National Federation of Community Broadcasters (NFCB), 1314 14th St., NW, Washington DC 20005. This list is also available free of charge; it includes the smaller, non-CPB-qualified stations.

Working with Independent Producers

As stated earlier, the freelance writer may seek to collaborate with an independent producer, i.e. one who works for himself and is in complete control of the content and budget of the project.

Independent producers are fast becoming a vocal and effective force within public broadcasting. Many local, regional, and national organizations of producers are open to contact by writers with scripts and project ideas. (See your Yellow Pages under Television Program Producers and Radio Broadcasting Program Producers.) Funds are always a pressing consideration, and again, there is no coherent access plan to production. However, freelance writers and independent producers are natural allies, and contacts should be explored and developed.

The Association of Independent Video and Filmmakers (AIVF, 625 Broadway, New York NY 10012) is a national trade association of independent producers that seeks to strengthen ties with the organizations independents need, and is developing a comprehensive list of independent producers working in the US. Individual membership is available at twenty-five dollars per year to freelance writers, who can announce script services in the membership's newsletter, *The Independent.* AIVF considers a good script an absolutely essential part of any production, no matter how glorious the camerawork. Another association that publishes a newsletter for independents and public broadcasters is Global Village (454 Broome St., New York NY 10013).

Independents abound in radio. Pacifica Network, which pioneered the concept of listener sponsorship, seeks public affairs and arts programming designed to heighten social consciousness. Contact the director, Pacifica Program Service, 5316 Venice Blvd., Los Angeles CA 90019.

The award-winning Children's Radio Theatre (1609 Connecticut Ave., NW, Washington DC 20009) specializes in original plays and stories for children and their families. Any format or suitable subject is welcome in thirty-minute scripts. Fees are negotiated individually.

The North American Poetry Network is a distributor of poetry cassettes and is in the process of developing a poetry directory for public broadcasting. Poetry cassettes or reel-to-reel demos, maximum thirty minutes, should be sent to: Black Box, Box 50145, Washington DC 20004. A cover letter listing the poems on the tape is welcome. The editors will read radio theater scripts, but prefer a query first for that genre.

Audio Independents, Inc., a group that has obtained foundation funding for three years, is devoted to the development and dissemination of works produced by independent radio producers and audio artists. It welcomes inquiries at 1 Lincoln Plaza, New York NY 10023.

Packaging Your Wares: Cover Letter and Presentation

Once your script, scenario, outline, or treatment is written, and once you determine the production sources you will approach, the next consideration is the presentation, or "packaging," of your work. This will involve a query or cover letter, a synopsis, and perhaps a production proposal. Make sure your work has copyright or Writers Guild registration before you present it (see below).

The query or cover letter is crucial. Do not assume that your work will speak for itself. Furthermore, in your cover letter you will have to speak not only for your work, but for yourself ! The producer is looking for a "sense of the person" he is going to negotiate and work with. Establish your professional identity and emphasize your proven self-discipline. Demonstrate your knowledge of public broadcasting, mention any interest on the part of any other producers or agencies, and any possible support from sponsors or underwriters. Show that you have done your homework, researched the field, and are willing to work within the bottom-line limitations of your proposal. If you demonstrate your research abilities, experience, and discipline, along with an ability to follow through on production leads and contacts—if you show that you are willing to help move the ball yourself (possibly with underwriting help from a corporation or community organization)—the prospective producer is more likely to take you seriously. Remember that in public broadcasting budgetary constraints are a constant, and staffs are generally small, but enthusiasm for a "natural" can run fanatically high!

You may want to include with your cover letter a short synopsis (one or two pages) or a production proposal. The latter should mention topic, approach, format, production team, and budget. A project timetable and example of previous work may also be attached. Samples of previous work should be treatments, synopses, or critical reviews rather than bulky scripts or videotapes, which might or might not be returned. You could add a note saying "Full script/videotape available on request."

The important point to remember about presentation is that your writing doesn't stop with the script. Extend your best abilities into the cover letter, prospectus, and proposal.

Protecting Yourself: US Copyright and Writers Guild Registration

Since the pursuit of production is a public process, involves circulating your work often to several sources simultaneously, and is highly competitive, proper protection of your writing is absolutely necessary. Just as producers have their waiver forms for unsolicited manuscripts, authors must have registrations to protect their rights and establish an original claim to the expression of an idea, script, treatment, or synopsis in a legal and binding fashion. Whether you use US Copyright protection or Writers Guild registration, the nominal fee and formal procedures are well worth the effort.

Standard copyright protection is available for all submissions where the idea has been developed into an actual script. Work must be substantially complete, though it may be as yet unproduced or unpublished. Since your copyright in a work exists from the moment of creation, be sure to type Copyright, the year, and your name on the cover page of any script. If you wish to register it, however, the US Copyright Office (Library of Congress, Washington DC 20559) will send applications and copyright information on request. Registering your script for copyright involves sending the completed application, a check for ten dollars, and one copy of the script to the Copyright Office.

The Writers Guild of America has established a second form of registration protection. Their Manuscript Registration Service, set up for members and nonmembers alike, establishes the completion date and the identity of the work. While it does not confer statutory protection, the service does provide evidence of the writer's prior claim to the authorship of the work involved.

Writers Guild East (555 W. 57th St., New York NY 10019) accepts not only full scripts but also "synopses, outlines, ideas, treatments, scenarios." Each work must be registered separately. A registration is valid for ten years and is renewable. WGE will send you an application guideline along with a registration envelope upon request. The registered work is placed in the envelope, sealed, and vital information (name, address, title, form of material, signature) is recorded on the outside of the specially designed envelope. A $15 fee ($20 if the manuscript is more than 125 pages) must be remitted with the envelope. This material will then remain in the Guild's charge with the seal unbroken. Unless the author terminates registration or there is a court order to release the work, the manuscript, receipt, and envelope are not allowed to leave the Guild office for the duration of the ten-year service.

Writers Guild West (8955 Beverly Blvd., Los Angeles CA 90048) operates a similar manuscript registration service.

Their Protection: Waivers

It now appears that what was once a fairly random non-system within public broadcasting is giving way to a mandated, more regulated method of program selection and funding. Theoretically, this reorganized system is more open to independents (including freelance writers), but there *may* be a parallel trend developing, whereby submission procedures will become more rigidly defined and bureaucratically complicated. Stringent guidelines for submissions could be developing in the area of unsolicited manuscripts.

Stations and production houses increasingly will try to protect themselves from future lawsuits by issuing "waiver forms" or "evaluation agreements" before unsolicited manuscripts are even glanced at. Such waivers are based on the premise that producers are under no obligation to writers—whether their ideas or material are subsequently used or not. In essence, writers are forced to waive certain rights as the price of having their ideas or work even considered in the first place!

Here is an example of a producer's waiver form for submission of program ideas and materials, to be signed and returned by the writer:

WAIVER

I understand that it is your established policy not to read or consider program material except in compliance with the expressed policy that I, as the contributor, am willing to rely entirely upon your discretion in determining whether my idea is novel and original; whether it is used by you as a result of my having submitted it; and, what compensation, if any, should be paid in connection with such use.

In order to have you read or consider my ideas and material, I agree that they are submitted to you upon the above conditions.

NAME: _____

ADDRESS: _____

PHONE: _____

SIGNATURE: _____ DATE: _____

TITLE & DESCRIPTION OF MATERIAL SUBMITTED

_____

_____

_____

PROPOSAL ATTACHED: _____ _____
                              YES   NO

Conducting Business: Billing Procedures and Contracts

It is difficult to ascertain a standard schedule for royalties, flat fees, and residuals in public television or radio. Fees vary with program, station, region, and institutional funding guidelines; each situation must be queried individually. Fees paid by public TV stations in the past have varied from $35-$100 per minute down to flat fees of $100-$500 for thirty- to sixty-minute scripts.

In 1981, the Writers Guild of America negotiated a contract covering Public Television minimum compensation rates for freelance writers for national and regional programs. A copy of the contract, which is in force until 1985, and its accompanying Rate A schedule can be obtained for $7. A copy of the basic minimum rates for commercial television is available for $1 from Writers Guild of America, 8955 Beverly Blvd., Los Angeles CA 90048.

Fees will also vary with the degree of the writer's participation in the production itself. A writer working with an independent producer, for instance, may become an associate producer or director in the course of actual production.

As always, the major consideration is to get fees and other contractual agreements, including ultimate copyright privilege, *in writing* as soon as possible. Whether you are dealing with a small independent producer or an established station production house, your attitude should be the same: maximum protection for the created work and for yourself as author. You are not doing the producer a *favor;* you are rendering a service. Moreover, anyone connected with a worthwhile business venture understands, respects, and anticipates this attitude on your part. You're better off avoiding transactions with anyone who doesn't likewise desire to put-it-in-writing as soon as possible.

The 1980s are a time of challenge and change within the entire public broadcasting industry. You are in the first wave of writers learning to deal with a new "network" operating under the aegis of the public trust, in a relatively new industry.

You are going to have to pound the pavement. You are going to have to follow all the usual rules of clean copy, simple, effective writing, and courteous approach. And a good script may not be enough—presentation is important, as are persistence and discipline. You will have to learn new skills: simultaneous submissions to stations and independent producers; more effective proposal writing so that you can present a complete package to a production house upon request; and, perhaps the harshest lesson of all, how to navigate financial constrictions at all levels but see your dream emerge unscathed. But if you succeed, an eager public awaits you!

Public Relations for Libraries and Other Nonprofit Organizations

by Virginia Blankenship

As a newcomer to the community of Hazard, a mountain town in southeastern Kentucky, I became a regular visitor to the Perry County Public Library. On several occasions the librarian and I discussed current books. After a few such chats, the zealous woman inquired of me one day: "Would you by any chance consider doing some book reviews for the local newspaper, the *Hazard Herald?*"

"Why not," I replied. It was, after all, an opportunity to write for publication. No pay, of course, just a byline, but—a new writing experience.

Until then my writing had been without pay and consisted of little more than letter writing, journal keeping, taking minutes at community meetings, serving as press secretary to women's organizations, constructing lesson assignments, submitting stories and articles to freelance markets (and watching them return). Yet this apprenticeship served its purpose! Within six months the book review column was popular reading. I was offered the unexpected opportunity of joining the regular staff of the public library as a "library journalist." This time, I'd be paid for writing.

I soon discovered that today's social-minded libraries are constantly thinking up new ways to bring the public in. As a recent White House Conference on Library and Information Services pointed out, libraries are in a unique position to help communities become aware of and meet individual and social needs. The Conference passed a resolution that the funds allocated to each state be increased by a fixed percentage, and that this extra income be used for professional public information programs.

What is the objective of a library in a community? What are the many services offered? How can the citizenry benefit? As a library journalist I wrote promotion pieces expounding the answers to these very questions. Book reviewing expanded into compiling reading lists, announcing new books received, dashing off current library news items, composing feature articles, writing radio public service announcements; any-and-everything I could to bring the Perry County Public Library and its services to the attention of its reading public.

Within a few months, I was corresponding with the leading publishing houses, acquiring news releases of new books coming into the market. With this material, I developed a specialized newspaper column, "A Library Journalist Looks At Authors, Books & Publishers," which the library sent out through the Pine Mountain Regional Library System of Kentucky for use by other libraries in our district.

As a library journalist, I soon found myself helping with other public relations jobs. Library exhibits were planned. Colorful bulletin board ideas conceived. Catchy window displays invented. Local artwork highlighted. All of this was a daily team effort among the enthusiastic, public-minded library staff.

I also conducted tours for student groups from around the county who visited the public library regularly on special educational field trips. Kindergarten classes were shown children's films on a weekly schedule. Every month or so I'd take a collection of picture books to the retarded children's school, an especially satisfying assignment; and on two occasions, I appeared on local television as a representative spokeswoman for our community-spirited library.

Writing for the public library, I've found, offers an opportunity well suited to the aspiring journalist. In its day-to-day service it covers the complete range of nonfiction writing, from terse headlines to full-length feature articles.

The public relations aspect of it furnishes the writer with interesting outside contacts who can keep him amply supplied with ideas for freelance writing projects.

Publishing outlets, such as local newspapers, have need for what a library writer turns out. These items are service features to a community, and since the writer is paid by the library, the budget-wise editor welcomes this voluntary source of copy.

Consequently, a polished, productive library writer may draw a regular salary, become a welcome public relations personality in and around the community, and earn extra freelance writing fees after regular working hours.

If you're looking for a writing opportunity, why not try the public library? But don't ask if a PR job is available. Design a job around your individual talents and then sell yourself and your ideas as a package. Contact the head librarian or members of the library board.

Other PR Clients in the Community

From the library job I moved into another PR project.

I was a volunteer member of Hazard Community Ministries, a Christian-oriented organization whose goals were to discover unmet human needs in our small community and to attempt to meet them. It sponsored an emergency food pantry and a teen center.

For several years the group struggled to develop its outreach programs as well as its local funding. Our efforts seemed hopeless—the organization was not winning the needed financial support to keep it going. We were on the verge of shutting down.

My library experience had taught me the necessity of maintaining a highly visible image within the community in order to gain widespread support. I knew a PR program was vital. So I began to think creatively, to plan and design on paper a PR approach to our problems.

I went to the next regular "gloom and doom" meeting prepared. Waiting for the proper moment, I made the group a business proposition. If they would take me on as a part-time employee for a trial period, I would try, with their cooperation, to develop a PR program that would draw attention to our purposes and goals and, ideally, gain more community support.

My first project was to put together a Community Contact Directory for local distribution. Next I detailed plans for approaching the media through newspaper articles and radio/TV public service announcements. I proposed contacting government agencies our group could be of service to and asking for speakers to attend our monthly meetings. And I suggested that I should attend fiscal court and city commissioner meetings as the group's organizational representative.

That's how it began. With the helpful participation of the members, my PR work resulted in an impressive turnaround. Our standing in the community today is respectfully recognized. We have grown to be Hazard-Perry County Community Ministries, Inc. The necessary financial support is being provided. In fact, we are actively involved in raising a large sum of money for a county recreation center, something we would not have dared to dream of a few years ago.

My monthly retainer fee from Hazard-Perry County Community Ministries varies from $100 to $300, depending on my output for that month. As a PR person I have a marvelous opportunity to make use of all my communication skills, and I'm learning the ropes of fund raising. [See separate chapter on this specialty.]

If public relations writing on the local level interests you, you will be pleased to know that there are ready aids to help you develop your expertise. To add to your basic skills in nonfiction writing, you will find extensive reading in the subject areas of Public Relations, Advertising [see separate chapter], and Business Management/Organization most helpful. Community college courses are also a possibility. And to find out the nearest location of a professional chapter of the Public Relations Society of America, write PRSA, 845 Third Ave., New York NY 10022. You'll learn a lot from these professional contacts. The more involved you are, the more adept you become.

Editor's Note: In small library systems, the job of PR specialist may be a part-time or full-time position paying $50-$10 an hour. In larger cities, public relations specialists would charge $35 an hour and up for freelance part-time work.

In large metropolitan library systems, the public relations director and his staff do everything described in this article, and in addition *initiate* a great many programs, designed either to bring potential patrons into the library and its branches or to take library services out to the community.

The public relations director may be involved in setting policy in some library systems; in others, he may have additional responsibilities, such as book selection or reference services.

PR staff salaries are keyed to the library's overall operating budget. The range is currently $12,000 to $28,000 for a PR director, $10,000 to $15,000 for an assistant. To get an idea of library budgets and pay scales, consult *The Bowker Annual* (of library and book trade information) at—where else?—your local library. It gives figures for specific library systems in the US and Canada.

Writing for a University Publication

Since I live only two blocks from a university (Penn State), it was a natural place for me to look for a part-time writing job. I found the ideal position on *Feedback,* a four-page newspaper type of brochure published six times a school year for the counselors in more than six hundred high schools in Pennsylvania. The brochure describes new developments at the university and elaborates on existing programs listed in the university catalog. The articles, which contain both factual information and human interest, involve interviewing members of the faculty and staff at Penn State.

When I interviewed for the job, I was pleased to find that the staff was quite impressed by my list of freelance publications. I got the job the following day.

I am expected to turn in three one- to two-page articles for each issue. After an initial coordinating conference, I am on my own. I interview on my own time and write the articles at home. I turn in three articles every six weeks. Most of them don't take more than a single interview. The part I enjoy the most is meeting the people I interview and finding out about new research and developments, which often lead to other articles for me as a freelancer.

—*Margaret B. Duda*

Public Relations for Schools

by Wanda Voncannon

If you are looking for a part-time writing job, you might want to consider the possibilities in your local city or suburban school districts. I work part time as a public relations person for our city's public school system.

Not only has this job afforded me the opportunity to exercise my writing skills, it has favored me with a certain amount of recognition in our community as a journalist.

The work schedule usually requires fifteen to twenty hours a week. Part of this time is spent in front of my typewriter at home, so I have been able to devote ample time to my family.

Whenever I explain my position to anyone, they invariably ask: "How did you luck into a job like that?" I like to believe that it was about 50 percent luck and 50 percent guts. By "guts" I mean being able to convince the school superintendent that I was the best news writer he could get when I was actually quaking in my shoes, afraid that I couldn't deliver what I promised.

I have learned that if a writer shows a good deal of confidence in what he is selling, even if he is not really so confident as he seems, he will inspire confidence, not only in a superior but, surprisingly, within himself.

Every school administrator knows the value of good school-community relations. He also knows that one of the best means of presenting activities and accomplishments of his school is through newspaper coverage. What he may not know is that there is a freelancer in his community who is skilled in putting his ideas and his school's achievements into public light.

I had no college degree, but I had two years of journalism experience in high school. This experience was a help, but if a writer knows how to stack a story (the inverted pyramid style, giving the bare details of who, what, when, and where in the first paragraph and then enlarging the scope), then he has a good start on any news story.

One of the most important steps toward convincing school officials that they need a press representative is to go right to the top. Start with the superintendent. He usually has the most influence with the school board, and if you sell him, you've practically got it made. Of course, if you happen to know someone in the system who can speak highly of your writing abilities, there's no harm in name-dropping.

If you have worked on a paper, even if it was only in high school or college, a few of your best clippings could make a good impression.

Get to Know Your Editor

There is one person who can make or break the efforts of a press representative: the editor of the paper to which the writer expects to submit his articles. (In large metropolitan and suburban school districts, of course, you may have to work with half a dozen editors or reporters.)

The first rule of thumb is to get to know him and instill in him confidence and respect for your ability to produce. Learn his personality and his moods, and play by his rules. The editors I have worked with have been most helpful in discussing with me the methods and style they like best in presenting copy. But don't be surprised when the lead paragraphs of your first articles come out differently in print from the way you have written them. Study the difference. This is the best way to learn the style the editor uses and requires of his reporters.

The second rule is to work closely with the editor. Don't be afraid to discuss your story ideas with him before you write the article. He may have a particular slant from which he wants the story written. And by all means check with him first if you have any doubts about the timeliness of an article.

Don't be surprised if you are expected to double as a photographer, too, if you're in a small city. Newspaper photographers are overworked as it is without having to make the scene of every PTA meeting or school assembly program. This came as quite a surprise to me. But with the patient help of the newspaper's photographers and the aid of the proprietor of a local camera shop, I began to turn out decent pictures. It's just about as gratifying to see your pictures in print as the copy.

I have an arrangement with the newspaper wherein I take the pictures and write the cutlines and they develop the film and make the photos in the size they need.

In larger cities, of course, papers will send a photographer if you have a really unusual story, or you may occasionally hire a photographer.

For work in a small town, the rate may be only $5 an hour plus travel expenses, but in larger cities the rates are much higher (as are the demands of the job). In larger school districts, for example, school press relations may—in addition to working with a half-dozen different newspapers and broadcast media—also involve editing newsletters, writing teacher recruitment and adult education brochures, working up referendum campaigns, and many other diverse duties. In smaller cities like mine, getting news and features in the local paper is the main work.

Once you get started, you can keep abreast of developments in the field by joining the National School Public Relations Association, 1801 N. Moore St., Arlington VA 22209. They sponsor national seminars and writing contests.

Radio Ads

by Bob Jacobs

The electronic media have become so pervasive in American life that many fear George Orwell's "Big Brother" is already here. We all know about the billions spent by mysterious Madison Avenue on market research to sell us everything from hideous sprays that make us stop sweating to futuristic appliances. And thanks to Marshall McLuhan, we all know how effective the media are in conveying these messages.

Consider how much you personally have been affected by the media thought controllers. Do you use an underarm deodorant? Who told you about it and what convinced you that you needed it? And I don't even mean the *brand name*. You were sold the *idea* that it is *wrong* to sweat under the arms and to smell like a human being.

That selling was done by other writers, most of whom are no better than you. Radio and television *eat* writers like Mrs. O'Leary's cow ate hay. For you, that spells opportunity.

I was an operations and program director for a radio station in a small market on the West Coast. My problem was not programming the music—it was finding writers capable of turning out that endless stream of commercials. Good commercial copywriters are in continuous demand. There are 4,733 commercial AM radio stations on the air in the United States, and another 3,527 commercial FM stations: 8,260 potential markets you probably hadn't thought of before. Think about them now, and I'll tell you how to break in.

You to the Rescue

Whether you live in a big city or a rural village, there are radio stations near you. For once, you're at a big advantage if you live in a small town. Metropolitan markets are saturated with professional ad agency copy and campaigns.

For now, let's deal with WHIK (KHIK if you're west of the Mississippi). Small-market radio stations sorely need folks who can write like the big time. "Creative copy in the small market just doesn't exist," says John Dombek, vice-president and station manager of WQUA in Moline, Illinois. "The salesman writes it or the announcer writes it while he's producing it and the situation is pretty desperate."

The problem with small markets is one of economics. A small market is one where the population is under 50,000 and the three radio stations are competing desperately for every advertising dollar. Frequently the station owner is also the manager, head salesman, and primary producer of commercials. His disc jockeys are high school or college kids with an FCC third-class permit and a third-grade ability to write. And he has to convince Dorothy's Beauty Shop that his station can sell its services more effectively than the town newspaper.

Mr. Manager has a lot of statistical evidence proving that radio sells *better* than newspapers in general. In the first place, more people listen to the radio than read newspapers. Radio slips in the commercial almost subliminally. Record ends, commercial begins; the listener can't turn off a pair of ears the way a set of eyes can skip over printed ads while looking for the news. Those ears can, however, detect the amateur, poorly written, small-time commercials, because they have been exposed to the Real Thing on network radio and TV. So our manager is in a tough spot, indeed.

He spends his time and budget trying to hire salesmen for his station who can also write catchy copy and produce spots. Even if he is successful, these people will very soon burn out and begin to repeat themselves until all the sponsors sound the same. He has a small audience, so he must change copy frequently to keep their attention; he may need five new spots every two or three weeks. Believe me when I say that this guy is desperate to have *you* come to his rescue.

Commitment

You can make $100 to $250 a week doing commercials part time. And if you're really good—and hardworking—you can follow John Dombek and others right to the top.

John started nineteen years ago with WHOU in Houlton, Maine (population: 6,500).

"I worked an airshift from 5:30 in the morning until noon, wrote copy for a couple of hours, did the station logs for the next day, went home to eat, and came back at night for two hours to get ready for the next day. And I did it for eighty-five bucks a week!"

Then John moved on to WFDF, the NBC affiliate station in Flint, Michigan, where he began full-time copywriting after losing his voice. His concentration has paid off with twenty-three awards for his creative commercials, including a national American Advertising Federation award for the best sixty-second commercial.

John Dombek typed his way to top management. He attributes his success to one thing: "You have to make a commitment to the station. And you have to be versatile. You have to be able to write a spot for Joe's Dragstrip, a supermarket, and a funeral home, one right after the other. Then you have to be willing to sit down and type the logs or whatever else needs doing around the station. People like that can find work in this business, I guarantee you.

"Copywriting really taught me to write everything," he adds. "It is the real art of condensation: getting everything into that thirty or sixty seconds. Every novelist should write copy to learn how you get the most out of every word, every phrase."

So Open the Door

To begin with, select the radio station that you want to work for. Listen to it critically and a *lot*. Determine its format; this will dictate what audience you'll be writing for.

Every radio station programs itself to appeal to a certain segment of the population. The top-rated ones appeal to the 25- to 55-year-olds—the folks most likely to spend their money on the sponsor's products. Under very competitive circumstances (and which ones *aren't?*), the stations will fragment that audience into ages 18 to 39, over 40, etc. Radio does not generally serve the very young or the very old, simply because these people do not represent a sizable buying bloc. You may think that's unfair, but it remains a fact of the business.

Listen to your station. If it is primarily up-tempo, rock-oriented, you probably have a Top 40 format. Listen all day and note how often the songs and ads are repeated; this station is programmed for an audience that tunes in and out all day. During the school hours, you'll notice a subtle programming change: The station will play songs appealing to women in their twenties and thirties. You'll find the ads in this time slot will particularly appeal to young moms, if the program director has his act together.

Prime times on this station are the early morning hours, when people are driving to work or school, and four to six p.m., when they're driving home. These slots are called "a.m. drive time" and "p.m. drive time." Say "morning drive" and "afternoon drive" if you want to sound like an Old Hand. Most of the heavy advertising occurs during these slots, and the sponsors pay premium prices for the spots.

Listen Up

Top 40 is your most likely market, since these stations have proved to be the most financially successful. Here are the four other major formats:

Country and Western (C&W) is just that.

MOR (middle-of-the-road) is characterized by lots of Andy Williams, Tony Bennett, Dionne Warwick, and the Ray Conniff Singers.

Beautiful music or *easy listening* is very lush, mostly instrumental, with tons of violins: Mantovani, the 1,001 Strings; sometimes called background music, or Hits from the J.C. Penney Elevator.

Progressive or *album-oriented rock (AOR)* is always on FM and features a more strident and less conventional brand of rock than that heard on Top 40. (Commercials on these stations often deal in borderline sick humor and presume a passion for *Saturday Night Live* and *National Lampoon*.)

Listen carefully to the air personalities. Top 40 DJs frequently sound as if they've overdosed on Benzedrine: much shouting and screaming. C&W jocks usually try to make you think they were born in Tennessee and grew up whistling "Dixie." (They usually hail from L.A. or New York.) MOR folks are mild, mellow, personable, and give the impression that they know you very well. AOR announcers make a conscious effort to sound ever so cool.

Check out the amount of patter your station allows. MOR jocks, for example, talk a *lot* and like to do their own copyreading, since they are such good friends of their listeners.

Finally, listen for format consistency. You should hear essentially the same thing coming out of your radio speaker whether you turn it on at nine a.m. or ten p.m. If you encounter Frank Sinatra back-to-back with Led Zeppelin, then you're in tune with another kind of AOR: *all-over-the-road!* Avoid these people, because they do *not* know what they're doing, and they'll make you sound the same!

Appeal to the Senses

Now that you recognize the format you want, you're ready to think about the commercials you'll be writing.

First, remember this: Radio is a very personal medium. It is subjective, intimate, and emotional; it's almost always listened to by one person at a time. So avoid the Pronouncement. Direct your appeal to *one* person, as if he were sitting next to you.

Also treat the listener as if he were blind. Use descriptive, visual words; use texture and color. For example:

WRONG: Luigi's Pizza Parlor has very good pizzas. They also have sandwiches and beverages that will make your mouth water. Next time you want pizza, try Luigi's Pizza, 904 Main, Fleaburg.
RIGHT: Luigi's pizzas are delectable: thick, rich tomato sauce with the tang of old Italy in every bite. (Fade up mandolin music.) Mozzarella cheese so pungent and hearty you can taste it before it gets to your table. Complement the zesty pepperoni with hearty Chianti or a dark, malt-rich beer, and you've got a meal fit for the brush of Michelangelo. Come to Italy tonight at Luigi's, 904 Main, Fleaburg.

Remember that the listening habits of your audience vary only slightly from Key West to Portland. Your listeners have become used to national network campaigns, and they want to feel that their little station in Black Earth, Nebraska, is just as hot and with-it as WABC in New York. So avoid the down-home approach, unless you're using it for a specific business at a specific time of the year (like Christmas, when you might want to appeal to nostalgia).

Radio time is strictly measured. Your spot commercials must be either *exactly* twenty, thirty, or sixty seconds long. The most common small-market spot is a thirty. So believe John Dombek—*get concise!*

Smirks and Sentiment

Now you're ready to zero in on the manager of your choice. Do *not* go in and tell him so! Radio people rightly resent outsiders who tell them how to do things. You have to be humble, inquisitive, and *prepared*. A manager will only look at results. He won't believe you if you say you're a writer. But he will have to if you go in loaded to the gunnels with material. Prepare no fewer than five spec (on speculation) spots for him, researched and perfected, and you might just have him begging for more.

Listen to the commercials the station is running to find out what businesses in your town are already on the air. Then look at the newspaper and pick a sponsor who is *not*. This is a hot target for your manager, and if you give him a complete campaign that he can sell to that sponsor, you are in!

Plan your five spots around a campaign theme. For example, if you've chosen a camera store, think up a campaign slogan, such as "Picture Your Whole Family at the Photo Boutique."

Write your spots with some musical selection in mind. Read your copy aloud with the music in the background. The station, through arrangements with ASCAP or BMI, can use almost any commercial recording as background music for its spots. Pick out an instrumental arrangement of some piece that is familiar but not overused. This piece will become the signature tune for your sponsor throughout the campaign. Go through Arthur Fiedler and the Boston Pops recordings at your local library. For your Photo Boutique spot, you might try something lyrical, like "Simple Gifts" from Aaron Copland's "Appalachian Spring." Remember that the music—like the words—must have some emotional punch. Sentimentality *sells:* Just recall those telephone company commercials on TV that make us feel terrible because we haven't called Mom and Dad this week!

Ads Must Fit the Format

Key your delivery to the station format. If it's a "rocker," then upbeat and cute is what you want. Most rockers like humorous spots; not knee-slappers, but smirk-bringers. Use a couple of characters, if you like. Get them in some silly trouble that a trip to your sponsor will surely get them out of. (And don't be afraid to end with a preposition like that. Radio speaks the way people *do,* not necessarily as they *should!)* Here's a spot that I did for a motorcycle shop:

(Fade up harpsichord music: Igor Kipnis, The Best Of, Angel ST-5172) VOICE OVER: (It is the voice of a sweet little old lady) THIS IS THE LITTLE OLD LADY FROM PASADENA WITH A WORD ABOUT RICHARD MILLER MOTORCYCLES. RICHARD'S SIDEKICK, JOHN THE SALES MANAGER, IS GETTING TIRED OF BEING KICKED IN THE SIDE BY RICHARD FOR NOT SELLING ENOUGH MOTORCYCLES. SO HE HAS A DEAL FOR YOU, HONEY. 20 PERCENT OFF EVERY NEW MOTORCYCLE IN STOCK FOR KXGO LISTENERS ONLY. I LIKE JOHN AS MUCH AS NEEDLE-

POINT, SO DO GO DOWN AND BUY SOME *HOT WHEELS*
(*hot wheels* done in tough, Hell's Angel voice) FROM RICHARD
MILLER MOTORCYCLES. BEHIND RICO'S ON SOUTH
BROADWAY.

I based a whole campaign on this theme, which didn't win any awards,
but got the motorcycle shop away from the newspapers!

MOR stations like down-to-earth, heart-tugging appeals to friendship, generosity, nostalgia, and so on. An MOR sponsor wants his clients
to think of him as good old dependable, courteous, friendly Fred, the
camera store owner who's been there since Eastman invented the box
Brownie. Here's an example:

(Fade in music: Scott Joplin, "Maple Leaf Rag")
VOICE 1: (friendly, mellow) THE PHOTO SPECIALTY SHOP
HAS THE FINEST LISTENING ROOM IN HUMBOLDT
COUNTY.
VOICE 2: (W.C. Fields character) WHADDAYA LISTEN TO AT A
PHOTO SHOP?
VOICE 1: TO THE BEST STEREO EQUIPMENT FROM J.V.C.,
PIONEER AND ALTEC.
VOICE 2: AT THE PHOTO SPECIALTY SHOP?
VOICE 1: WAIT A MINUTE. DID YOU KNOW THE PHOTO
SPECIALTY SHOP WAS THE *FIRST* WITH TAPE RECORDERS
IN EUREKA BACK IN THE FIFTIES AND THEN WITH
STEREO TOO?
VOICE 2: IS THAT A FACT?
VOICE 1: YEP.
VOICE 2: AND THEY ALSO HAVE CAMERAS AND STUFF?
VOICE 1: YEP.
VOICE 2: THE FIFTIES, HUH?
VOICE 1: YEP.
VOICE 2: DO THEY GIVE FLATTOPS, TOO?
VOICE 1: NO. JUST FRIENDLY PERSONAL SERVICE. SEE
STAN AT THE PHOTO SPECIALTY SHOP: 511 F, EUREKA.

C&W sponsors like more of the same, with cowpies thrown in.

Emotion, Action, Change of Pace

Emotion is the key word. Do your spots in an absolute flood of empa-
thy for Modern Man—or Persons, if you're so inclined—ensnared in a

web of insecurities, fears, and fantasies. We all want to be accepted and well thought of, right? So use your own insights into the feelings you want to get across. Are you uncomfortable walking in for dinner at a restaurant *alone?* Do you settle for hash and eggs or a TV dinner when you really want to go out for a steak, but you're embarrassed to be single? Well then, tell all the lonely people that Dale's Steak House makes single people feel right at home. Think of other situations where you can turn natural fears into motivations for action!

And prey on the greed inherent in most of us, too. The "big guys" on Mad Ave. do it all the time! Fear, greed, and fantasy are the big three words to keep in mind when you're working on inspiration for commercials.

Use action words—lots of verbs and colorful adjectives. Radio advertising is like posthypnotic suggestion, so give positive directions: SEE AL AT THE PHOTO BOUTIQUE TODAY!; GO TO 904 MAIN STREET NOW!; HURRY TO THE SALE OF A LIFETIME; LET THE PHOTO BOUTIQUE PUT *YOU* IN THE PICTURE.

Use a catchy opener: a clever phrase, a snatch of music, hysterical laughter, some sound effect like a car crash. To illustrate:

(Pop on sound effect: BOMB EXPLODING)
ANNOUNCER: THE PHOTO BOUTIQUE EXPLODES WITH
A SPRING SALE!

Another simple way to get attention is to change pace. If your "rocker" shouts and screams all of its spots, then one that comes on very soft, with the announcer even whispering, will stand out of the pack and get attention for itself, as well as for you.

You Can Say That Again

Now the most important part of all: Radio relies on repetition. In any single announcement you have only thirty or sixty seconds to do your thing. That "thing," as far as the sponsor is concerned, is getting *his name* imbedded in the listener's mind. You cannot give a laundry list of all the wonderful items for sale at the Photo Boutique. Keep it simple. Open with the sponsor's name, use it at least once in the body, and close with it, along with his address. When your listener has heard the spot two or three times, you will have done the primary job of radio advertising: airing the trade name.

Finally, to look like a real pro, type your spots in ALL CAPS. Double-space it and put instructions about sound effects and music (in parentheses). Eight lines of double-spaced, all-cap words with your margins set at 30 and 75 will equal thirty seconds of spoken dialogue. You can squeeze in sixteen lines for a sixty-second spot if you keep the words *short* . . . and do! Leave all of your four-bit words in Roget. Write in crisp, short sentences. Write the way people *speak*.

And be imaginative! Radio is unique in its ability to delight the mind's eye. To prove the point, in a radio commercial for the Radio Advertising Bureau (RAB), Stan Freberg turned Lake Erie into a hot fudge sundae just by saying he was going to do it, then using sound effects: airplane engines humming, the cherry "bomb" whistling, and the giant *ploosh* as it drops into place. Don't be so clever, though, that your sponsor gets lost in the whipped cream!

Getting Prepared

Pay the most attention to your own preparation. Remember, any writer's most constant friend is research. Go into the target store without telling them why you're there. Try to feel out what sort of people are in charge. Their point-of-purchase advertising and personal approach to customers will tell you almost all you need to know about them. Research their kind of business, too. Remember that many stores get cooperative advertising from manufacturers of products that they sell. This means that the camera maker may pick up 50 percent or so of the cost of airing your spot for the Photo Boutique. The co-op book published by the Radio Advertising Bureau has a complete list of all cooperative manufacturers, along with exactly how much they will spend in terms of percentages. Most stations subscribe to the RAB service and this information will be available to you once you land your job. To get co-op money, however, at least 70 percent of the spot must be about the manufacturer's product; the rest can tell where to buy it: THE PHOTO BOUTIQUE IS LEICA HEADQUARTERS THIS CHRIST-MAS . . . and so on.

You're armed now with all you need to break into small-market radio copywriting. Just listen to those spots on your local station. Of *course* you can do better! But don't come on too strong with Mr. Manager or you'll threaten yourself right out the door.

How you sell depends on a lot of things: your manager's mood, your own dedication and perseverance, and the way the moon and stars align. In some markets, you could freelance if the manager likes your work. Pay might be $5-$10 per spot, depending on how much the sponsor spends. The manager might make a commission deal with you—15 percent of everything you sell, for example. Most likely, though, he will offer you a full-

or part-time job if he likes your work. As John Dombek pointed out, you'll
be expected to do some other things around the station, too. For four to six
hours a day, you should expect to make no less than $100 a week. It can
range on up to $300 if the station is prosperous enough and you continue to
work well. So don't just sit there reading—*do it!*

SPEC SPOT: THE PHOTO BOUTIQUE   RADIO STATION WHIK

Writer: Jane Doe
        405 Slick Street
        Fleaburg, Ohio
        555-1234

MUSIC BED: 1812 OVERTURE; LONDON PHASE 4 RECORD:
           ROBERT SHARPLES CONDUCTING THE LONDON
           SYMPHONY ORCHESTRA WITH ROYAL WELSH
           GRENADIER BAND: FINAL CANNON AND BELL
           MOVEMENT

(SOUND FX: LARGE EXPLOSION)

                    <u>ANNOUNCER</u>

           THE PHOTO BOUTIQUE EXPLODES INTO SPRING
           WITH (Music fades up under voice)
           A VALUE FESTIVAL! PICTURE THAT SPECIAL
           PERSON OF YOURS THIS YEAR IN THE EASTER
           PARADE WITH A PHOTO BOUTIQUE CAMERA.
           TIME SLIPS AWAY TOO SOON TO LET
           ANOTHER MEMORY GO BY WITHOUT CATCHING IT
           FOREVER. THE PHOTO BOUTIQUE WILL SHOW
           YOU HOW WITH A CAMERA PRICED JUST FOR
           YOU. PUT YOUR FAMILY IN THE PICTURE AT
           THE PHOTO BOUTIQUE. 904 MAIN STREET.
           DO IT NOW!

(Music fades up and out)

Radio spots are presented to the station in this format.

Radio Continuity

by Ted Schwarz

Radio stations need an enormous amount of continuity material—the interesting (?) and witty (?) things staff members are supposed to say between records, interviews, or whatever else comprises their particular format. Though disc jockeys are hired for their gift of gab, few are capable of producing interesting or humorous *original* material for their audiences. Most rely on canned services which supply jokes and other information on a syndicated basis to stations around the country. These seldom have strong local appeal, but they enable DJs to get by. Occasionally you encounter stations that let their people "wing it"—talk off the top of their head—which, in numerous instances, has reinforced my belief that many of those heads are empty.

For several years I supplemented my income by writing for radio stations, primarily in major-market areas. I was never turned down by a station to which I offered my services, though I did find the pay range varied significantly from area to area. When I finally settled in the scenic Southwest (known for beautiful climate and ridiculously low salaries), I found local stations paying less money for *full-time* staffers than I earned *part-time* back East. However, interest in my work was just as strong. Your freelance writing, too, can get an equally warm reception.

Almost *any* type of material is desirable for continuity, within the customary bounds of AM/FM taste. But there *are* some staple crops. One is the calendar of historic events—short historic items for each day of the year:

July 2, 1937: Amelia Earhart, pioneer aviatrix, and her copilot, Frederick Noonan, were lost in the Pacific Ocean somewhere between New Guinea and Howland Island while attempting to fly around the world. The disappearance is still a mystery.

Sometimes an item can be extremely short, such as one I found for July 12, 1933: "A new industrial code set the minimum wage at an unprecedented forty cents an hour."

Other items go on for page after page when the disc jockey plans a special presentation on some public figure whose birth or death occurred on that date. However, the medium is such that long material must be broken up with commercials and music on most stations. Therefore, long pieces must be written so that the disc jockey can read segments in no more than one minute's time (from 120 to 160 words, depending on the individual DJ's delivery). These must be complete in themselves, providing information on a limited aspect of the person's life.

I did this with the Beatles, for example. For a February 7 program I gathered material from 1964. On that date the Beatles left England to make their first appearance before an American audience. Their trip to New York City was described in detail, with facts about their fans and excerpts from their press conference:

"Will you sing something for us?"
"We need money first."
"How do you account for your success?"
"We have a press agent."
"What is your ambition?"
"To come to America."
"Do you hope to get haircuts?"
"We had one yesterday."
"Do you hope to take anything home with you?"
"Rockefeller Center."
"Are you part of a social rebellion against the older generation?"
"It's a dirty lie."
"What about the movement in Detroit to stamp out the Beatles?"
"We have a campaign to stamp out Detroit."

And so it went, providing a bit of nostalgia for the disc jockey to read between old Beatles songs. Some stations might have recordings of such interviews, but it's not your job to worry about that. As a writer you must provide a range of material that can either be read or used as a guide when the staff is researching their own files for early tapes.

Inspiration and Information

Where do you get calendar information? I always start with specialized resources such as *Chases' Calendar of Annual Events,* books such as *What Happened When . . .?,* and various almanacs. I have also called upon the dozen or so volumes that comprise *Time* magazine's old *Time Capsules,* which can be found in the remainder piles of bookstores, in used-book shops, and in many libraries. For local material I go to newspaper files, looking back five, ten, twenty, and twenty-five years for each date. (Obviously you must be several days ahead of the station's needs at all times or you may have trouble meeting airtime deadlines.)

The various guidebooks have to be supplemented, however. I have used history books and biographies, after starting with calendar-type reference books, to do supplemental research quickly.

Radio stations also need special features that can boost ratings, be sponsored by local businesses, or meet a special public interest. One steady demand is for information about the achievements of various minority groups.

One of my series ideas was "Women of Greatness," capsule summaries of the achievements of women in numerous fields. Each was written so it could be read in one minute, or slightly more. (I take a watch with a second hand and glance at it as I read the material aloud. After a few such readings, you will begin writing the proper length. When starting out, however, I seldom wrote less than a five-minute piece for my first draft, three minutes for my second draft, then tighter and tighter until I had everything in a minute's time.)

Items could be used as needed throughout the day or at special times. They could be sold to a sponsor, or used as station continuity material. In short, they had *versatility*—which stations love. A couple of examples:

Women of greatness—women whose efforts have altered the face of society. She was an Austrian-trained physicist working in the unexplored field of atomic energy shortly after the turn of the century. Lack of knowledge of proper safeguards resulted in burns and illness from the radioactive materials she handled. In 1910 she heard Albert Einstein lecture on the enormous power he believed would be found at the center of the atom. She began searching for this center, discovering element 91, protactinium, with her co-worker Dr. Otto Hahn, in 1918. In 1938 she fled Hitler, going to

Sweden to work. The next year she made Einstein's theory a reality. She became the first person to split an atom and reveal the tremendous energy stored inside. Her co-worker, Hahn, received the Nobel Prize for his efforts, but she was denied the award because of her sex. She spent her later years trying to find peaceful uses for atomic energy. She was Lise Meitner—physicist—discoverer of protactinium—first person to split the atom—woman.

Yucks and Bucks

How do you get radio jobs? Not in any conventional manner. If you go to the personnel director of a large station and say that you're a writer looking for continuity work, you will probably be told the station doesn't use anyone like that. There will be no job openings. Why? Because few radio stations are aware of the writing talent available in their areas. Only in the biggest broadcast centers, such as New York, will there be anything resembling an open market for your work. Other stations realize the availability of talent only when it is forced upon them. They never ask personnel to hire such people.

So what is the answer? Go to the station and make an appointment to see either the program director or the general manager. Always go in person. Though you probably won't be given an appointment on the spot, there's always the chance that you'll catch the program director at a free moment. Few will refuse to see you if you are in the lobby waiting.

Be selective in the stations you go after. Never bother with a station that has disc jockeys who give time, weather, and little else. Stay with those that either have men and women who do a fair amount of talking between records, or those that have talk shows, special guests, and other programming which indicates they could use original material.

Explain to whomever you see that you are a professional writer interested in providing the station with original material for the disc jockeys to use. Stress only straight continuity material, unless you can show samples of humor you have published in the past. Stations are bombarded with individuals who think they "write funny." All their friends laugh at their jokes and think they are another Bob Hope or Phyllis Diller. Of course, the jokes are often either old, crude, or just plain dumb, and the stations' top brass are likely to be skeptical of so-called humor writers.

If you haven't sold humor in the past, do not bother to mention this talent until after you have the job of writing "straight" continuity material. Then bring in some samples and see if they are interested. Once you're on board, they'll be more willing to look at what you've got.

What kind of pay can you expect for your efforts? It will vary with the market. The lowest offer I ever received was minimum wage for full-time work. The highest was $200 a week for part-time. Ideally you should agree to work either a minimum number of hours a week or, better, provide a minimum number of pages of copy. The latter is preferable, because it is hard to judge time for research and creating material. Stations either stand in awe of your production or wonder why you don't turn out far more when they are paying you by the hour. A specific number of pages, though, they can understand. Thus, my first job required a minimum of fifteen pages of humor a week for $75—$5 a page. What is the potential from such work? On a full-time basis, anything from $150 a week to $600 a week and more for staff jobs in the major cities.

In some cases you may want to retain all secondary marketing rights. Humor used locally can often be sold nationally either through syndication or, with slight changes, as cartoon captions. This is something you should discuss *after* you have begun working, though. Never bring up something like this in advance, because it may discourage the station from hiring you.

Meantime, be certain to write for the station's audience as defined by the program director, not by your personal beliefs. Demographic studies are done by the station for their advertisers. These offer the best clues as to income, sex, education, and general background of at least the majority of the listeners.

Multiple Sales

When your writing is good enough to sell to one radio station, you can be certain that there are other stations that will be equally interested in buying your work. Fortunately, it is possible to sell your humor, general continuity material, and/or special features to noncompeting radio stations throughout the United States. The writing must be general enough to appeal to people throughout the country—but much of what you write for your local station is apt to fall into this category.

The first step toward multiple sales is to send a query letter to program directors at stations throughout the country. Try to learn the broadcast range so you do not contact competing stations. Generally stations are not heard much farther than a hundred miles from their transmitters. I play it safe and contact stations in cities at least two hundred miles apart. For names of the stations and their addresses, use either *Broadcasting Yearbook,* available in most libraries, or the annual *World Radio-TV Handbook,* published by Billboard Publications. (The latter will provide you with addresses for radio stations around the world, if you want to expand your contacts to other English-speaking countries.)

Tell the program director that you are a professional writer currently supplying continuity material, humor, or whatever to station ZZZZ, and that you are interested in the possibility of selling to his station as well. Enclose a sample of your work. Offer to provide additional material on speculation if desired. Explain that the station will have exclusive use in its broadcast area. Enclose a self-addressed stamped envelope with adequate postage for the return of the sample.

There are two ways to price your work if a station is interested. I prefer to offer it "at your usual rates," since I am never certain what to ask. Others set a price based on the number of pages. Often this is a minimum of five dollars per page; some services go higher. You will be paid a set amount each week, the number of pages to be negotiated.

Special feature material is handled similarly. I would supply a week's scripts, or a minimum of five—whichever is greater. If you are selling a series, tell how many episodes will be offered. Generally you will have to supply material three weeks in advance so there is time for recording it and selling it to sponsors.

One last point. Radio station personnel constantly play the game of musical stations. Never address a program director by name if the information comes from an annual guide. Chances are he or she has moved on. A Dear Program Director is nonpersonal, nonsexist, and will reach the person in charge.

Radio Editorials

by Bob Jacobs

The National Association of Broadcasters and the FCC have both strongly encouraged the broadcasting of editorial opinions by station management. The philosophy is that the airwaves are there to serve the public interest first, and to entertain the public second. Expressing opinions about issues of interest to the audience is followed with the requirement, dictated in the FCC Fairness Doctrine, that equal time must be given for response. Not only must it be given, but public response to editorial opinion must be *actively sought* by the station.

Most stations can't afford the luxury of turning over the job of editorializing to the general manager or to a staff writer. Both of these people are too busy with commercial work to do the research and come up with a considered opinion every day. For example, the general manager of stations WOSH-FM and WYTL-AM in Oshkosh, Wisconsin, recently solicited students at the local branch of the University of Wisconsin to take over the job for him. Out of a student population of nearly ten thousand, only one person applied for the job!

As an inveterate radio buff and hungry freelancer, I recognized a new market. Management is starving for editorial opinion and, if you're a normal freelancer, you have *plenty* of that commodity to sell.

My opinion was heard by just over a hundred thousand listeners to station WAPL-FM in Appleton, Wisconsin, five days a week. And I got the job simply by writing a sample packet of five opinions and taking them in person to the station operations manager. His first and only question was whether I could keep up the flow. After a year of my steady stream, he's stopped asking. Now he just signs the checks with gratitude.

How Much?

The amount of money you can make depends on several factors. Here are the major ones. How large is your radio market? Obviously a station in Dismal Seepage, Arizona (population: 2,500), doesn't make as much money as a station in Los Angeles, California.

How desperate is the manager? If he is in a tight spot, you can dicker on price somewhat.

How good and consistent are you? If your spots start getting lots of attention, if the cards and letters and phone calls pour into the station—in short, if you generate response—then you become increasingly valuable.

As a guideline, I'll fess up to what I make, if you *promise* not to tell the IRS! When I started, WAPL made me the princely offer of five dollars a spot. A year later I was up to $15. Now at WOSH I make $20. That may not sound like a lot, but look at it in terms of an hourly wage. As a freelancer I read and research all the time, anyway. *Time, Newsweek, Omni, Science Digest, American Cinematographer, Cycle World,* and my two newspapers, plus the nightly news on television, are all regular sources for my opinion. I'm also very fast at the IBM Selectric. So, in an average week, in amongst the other articles and books and scripts I'm working on, I figure that I spend maybe two hours on "That's My Opinion." That means that WOSH is paying me $60 an *hour*. And by golly, that's better than even my doctor makes! If I got serious about it, I suppose I could go to as many stations in noncompeting markets as I wanted and make a fairly full-time thing of it. As a casual supplement to my income, while Ballantine Books ponders my latest novel, I'm quite happy with the wages as they stand.

What Do You Say?

First of all, check with your manager to find out how long you have to say it. Most editorials run between ninety seconds and two minutes. I made up a form for myself with a 1 1/2-inch margin on each side of the page. With double-spacing, twenty-eight lines comes out to ninety seconds exactly.

What to say depends on the target audience. Your manager can and will tell you what the station's demographics are. If the station you're writing for is aimed at teenagers, then you will try to talk about topics of concern to them: the drinking age in your state, teenage "cruising" in a time of energy shortages, morals, drugs, and so forth.

If your station, like many, tries to pick up an audience between the ages of 18 and 34, then your own feelings are the limit. My station is one of those. Topics I've covered recently include violence on television (pro), abortion (pro), telephone company profits (con), the 55-mph speed limit (con), and Ralph Nader (con). Note from my pro/con bias that I *try* to be controversial, not safe. Remember that it's your function as editorialist to elicit *response* from the listener, not necessarily passive agreement. This doesn't mean that you can be flip and irresponsible. It does mean that if you *try*, you can find valid arguments on both sides of *any* contemporary issue.

WOSH, as do most radio stations, runs a disclaimer at the end of the show, to wit: I always finish with, "I'm Bob Jacobs and That's My Opinion"; then the announcer says, "It certainly is. And it doesn't necessarily reflect the opinions of WOSH's staff, management, nor any of our sponsors. If *you* have an opinion on any subject, write to WOSH, P.O. Box 1490, Oshkosh, Wisconsin 54901." In this way they both disclaim any responsibility in possible slander suits *and* fulfill the FCC requirement to actively solicit rebuttal.

Some radio station managements run editorial opinion as their own and no disclaimer is tagged on. They do have to solicit rebuttal, however.

Check Your Facts

Even though the word "opinion" implies that what you say is not set in concrete, you have an obligation to be accurate and to be able to produce verifiable data if challenged. I keep a file of all my sources for such occasions and twice have had to dredge them up for the station: once to show where I got my data on telephone company profits *(Time)* and once to show figures I had used for oil company profits *(Newsweek)*.

A Good Laugh

Many people feel that editorials have to be bleak or at least pontifical. Not me! As Molière and others have taught us, we can often teach best with a good satirical poke in the ribs. At least once a week I try to leave 'em laughing. I also try to present information not found in your typical hometown news rag. An example, "Fuel of the Future," is included in this chapter.

Go To It!

Follow my format, write up a handful of your opinions after listening

```
        FUEL OF THE FUTURE
        THAT'S MY OPINION #27          by BOB JACOBS
1    Hydrogen is clearly the fuel of the future.  It's a
2    simple combustible element which makes up 90% of all
3    the matter in the universe.  The supply is endless.
4    The by-product of burning it in your car or your
5    heater or your stove is water; from which MORE hydro-
6    gen can be obtained! The Germans have a bus running
7    on hydrogen now.  In Utah, a Dodge Omni has been run-
8    ning on hydrogen for three years.  You fill its tank
9    with water, an electrolyzer produces hydrogen and
10   off you go.  A scientist at Columbia University has
11   a project to satisfy all the Earth's energy needs
12   with a 200 square mile body of water filled with
13   plants and bacteria.  IF we start NOW, hydrogen could
14   be meeting almost ALL of our energy needs by the year
15   2000; simply, cleanly and cheaply.  Here's the ques-
16   tion.  Why is our ten BILLION dollar a year depart-
17   ment of energy only giving 18 million dollars to
18   hydrogen fuel research, while it comes up with rid-
19   iculous schemes to deprive us of gasoline?  The ans-
20   wer as I see it is that the oil companies, the lob-
21   bies which REALLY control the DOE, are afraid of
22   hydrogen.  Why do YOU have to hear about it from ME?
23   Why do I have to get it from an obscure science jour-
24   nal? It's time that the DOE answers to we the people!
25   Let's all drive as much as possible.  Use up the gas.
26   Then the oil barons and bureaucrats in Washington
27   will HAVE to give us what we're going to have anyway.
28   All the cheap, clean fuel we need with hydrogen.
29   I'm Bob Jacobs and That's My Opinion.
30
```

Format the author uses for his radio editorials. Twenty-eight lines equals ninety seconds of airtime.

to a couple of radio stations in your area, and take them in. Make your appointment with either the general manager, the operations manager, or the program director. In small markets, this will no doubt be the same person! I tape my own show at the station, which has had the side benefit of making me a local celebrity: It's good for at least one free beer a week and several rousing arguments. If you don't have a radio voice, your station will provide one. What you *do* have is the gift of writing. Keep it succinct, lucid, and lively, and a station should leap at it.

Radio Interviews

by Michael S. Bucki

Only one radio reporter has ever interviewed Lester Maddox at the controls of a Goodyear blimp, cruising and dipping and swaying and diving a scant 1,500 feet above Atlanta's *growing* skyline. . . .

Obviously, I lived in order to pass on the Good Word: You can recycle your interviews for print to nearly *nine thousand* new markets—radio stations.

How? Whom do you approach? What equipment do you need? How much should you charge? Read on.

All broadcast stations, to renew their licenses every three years, must determine community needs and plan their "community affairs" or "public affairs" programs accordingly. In the past, most commercial stations put little money and less effort into these programs—often a telephone talk show aired at 6 a.m. Sunday was par for the course.

Recently, however, some stations have faced serious challenges to their license renewals from community groups. And the Federal Communications Commission is listening to these complaints.

The FCC's attentive ear is your foot in the door, if you'll pardon my anatomy. The program director, news director, or community affairs director (all the same person at small stations) is more likely now to listen to an intelligent proposal from a talented individual (like you) who knows the community, has the contacts, and is equipped to do some reporting.

Equipped? Yes, I *do* mean literally. Sorry, but most radio stations aren't going to lend recording equipment to just anyone who walks through the door. Does that mean you must invest hundreds of dollars in expensive gear? No. Standard cassette recorders range in price from $75-$200.

You and Mike

Know your equipment and what it will do. Run tests—especially for background noise interference—before you interview. Always carry extra batteries and cassettes. Test and tote both microphones.

Two mikes? Yes. When you purchase your moderately priced cassette recorder, plan also to spend that much for a good omnidirectional microphone.

It will allow you to record professionally from the start of your career. To record with a directional microphone, you must aim it toward what you're recording. This can be difficult during an interview. If you pay close attention to aiming the mike, you'll find you're not listening carefully. You'll miss opportunities for good follow-up questions. If you listen carefully, and if your subject jumps in with his answer rather quickly, you'll find that while you're moving the microphone back in his direction, his first words aren't recorded at the same clear intensity as most of his answer. And radio listeners want to hear *everything* clearly.

So buy yourself a good omnidirectional microphone. Use name-brand cassettes—Sony, TDK, Ampex, or Memorex, for example. Spend from three to eight dollars per cassette. (Watch for sales, of course, and check into the possibility of buying them in bulk, wholesale.) Cheap tapes have a tendency to crawl inside the motor of your machine, leaving you with a tangled mess that ends the interview and costs money for repairs.

The Interview Itself

When you're firing questions, be honest and be yourself. In the north Georgia mountains where I was recording a documentary, I was often asked for *my* answers to the questions I was asking. "Is America a land of equal opportunity?" I asked the octogenarian owner of a country store. He gave a racially inflammatory answer and retorted, "What do you think?" I said I disagreed, but respected his right to an opinion. He nodded, and the interview continued. Had I lied, or tried to pretend that I was as "folksy" as he, the interview could have ended right there. Instead, I was able to ask, "How are you going to celebrate the Bicentennial?" and record his tobacco-chawin', molasses-slow reply: "Well, when's it comin' up?"

Be honest when you're doing on-the-street surveys, too: Introduce yourself and explain your project before you stick a mike in someone's face. Recorderphobia has reached epidemic proportions since Watergate. You can best offset it by squaring away at the start.

When interviewing politicians, or experts, be tough. Be the devil's polite advocate, even if you agree with the interviewee's ideas. While she was interviewing Henry Kissinger, Barbara Walters used a method that requires nerves of steel but is worth the risk. She repeated her question, between his answers, three times. She never said, "You didn't answer my question, Mr. Secretary." She simply repeated her question—word for word. Get tough.

Listen carefully—not only to the interviewee's answers, but for background sounds that can make your spot more authentic. Let's say you're interviewing the local pinball champion. Interview him in a quiet room away from the machines, or—if he needs the visual impetus of the machines—in the pinball war room, while the machines are quiet. Afterward, tape as many of the ping-pangs and flip-flaps as you'll need to fit under the entire interview. Later, in the studios, you'll mix the two sound tracks so that the whiz kid's every word is heard clearly over the background of the pinball machines.

At Large in the Studio

Now for some production hints:

Know your market. After the station has indicated interest in your interviews, you'll have to call the public affairs director for permission to use the studio facilities. But before you do, know his preferred length, format, and slant for spots. Before your *initial* contact with the station, of course, you will have found out when the station's public affairs programs are aired, and you will have listened to them and *studied* them.

Learn to be your own best editor. Would you send a magazine editor a word-for-word transcript of an interview, with a note attached saying, "Here's the profile I promised"? Hardly. Well, the news or public affairs director wants a little respect, too. You must edit your material before it gets to him.

But editing cold, in the studio, is like trying to write an article over the phone. So I'd suggest that you buy a tape recorder with a footage counter for your interviewing. *Before* you go in to edit, make a log of the tape interview, corresponding the counter numbers to the highlights of the conversation. You needn't transcribe *everything*. But you should write down the last few words of the quotes you intend to use. You might want to follow them with the designations CUT POINT, PICKUP

POINT (PUP) and CUT TO. (For example, one of my interview subjects, a clinical psychologist, put together a film for divorce counselors to use in divorce adjustment groups. I used dramatic vignettes from the film's sound track to augment and illustrate our conversation.)

Then, when you go to the studio and begin working with the engineer, you'll copy from the cassette onto a reel *only* those quotes needed to make up your piece. Knowing where everything is on the cassette will save both you and the engineer much time and grief. It will also keep that door open for you.

Here's an editing tip: Pay close attention to the "ands" in your subject's conversation. Often what follows an "and" is an interesting but unnecessary embellishment of what preceded it. If your follow-up question elicits a more succinct answer, edit from that "and" in the first answer to the start of the next answer. Does this mean you have to drop your question? Yes, if the answer is well understood without it. I know that's a blow to your ego, but the listener wants to hear the subject, not you. (When National Public Radio airs my pieces, only my mother asks "Why didn't I hear more of you?") So stifle your ego and pay attention to the "ands." Mother doesn't write the checks.

Writing for the Air

All right—*now* you can write up the spot. You'll have to write to fill your time requirements. If you want to use 2:40 of your subject's conversation in a three-minute piece, for instance, you'll have to write twenty seconds of material. In any case, your story must have a beginning, a middle, and an end. The middle is usually the interview itself, so that needs no belaboring.

How about the beginning? Depending on your station's preferences, you or the announcer might read the intro. Either way, it must be scripted. The intro should:

Hook the listener: with a catchy first sentence; an excerpt of ten seconds or less from the interview; or sound effects (*if* they're appropriate).

Establish the subject's credentials, or the event's importance.

Identify the interviewer.

Hint, in the last line of the introduction, at what is to come in the spot.

If the piece is ten minutes or less, your introduction must be under thirty seconds (40 to 60 words). For ten- to twenty-minute pieces, keep the introduction under one minute (100 to 120 words). For twenty- to sixty-minute documentaries, try to keep the intro under ninety seconds, but use two minutes of airtime, if you must. Transitions in the piece should be under fifteen seconds—or thirty, at most.

What about the end? That too should be scripted, and here's an example:

> OUTCUE: . . . and that's why changes in the law are so important to changes in societal attitudes toward divorce.
> ANNOUNCER: Dr. Sheila Kessler, author of the book *The American Way of Divorce: Prescriptions for Change,* and creator of a film which is used by counselors throughout the United States in divorce adjustment groups.
> BUCKI: This is Mike Bucki for WABE, radio.
> OR: In Atlanta, this is Mike Bucki, for National Public Radio.

The Ropes and the Rates

I hope you took careful note of the last line. It should tell you that you might be able to sell your piece twice—once to your local NPR affiliate or local commercial station, and again to National Public Radio.

National Public Radio pays:

Actuality clip	00:01-01:59*	$ 25
Report	02:00-02:59	$ 40
	03:00-04:59	$ 55
	05:00-09:59	$ 75
Mini-documentary	10:00-14:59	$125
	15:00-29:59	$200

Complete programs

30:00-58:59		59:00 and up
$ 75	Speech	$100
$100	Panel program	$125
$100	Interview	$125
$150	Magazine	$200
$175	Performance	$250
$275	Documentary	$500

*one second to one minute fifty-nine seconds, etc.

I'd suggest that you also use that pay scale as a guideline for commercial stations. In smaller towns—those with a population of under 50,000—you may have to accept up to 50 percent less than the above. In cities of more than a million, you should be able to match the above prices, at least for pieces over ten minutes long. Now, $200 for an hour—

long documentary may sound all right to you if you know nothing about radio. But hear this: With fourteen years of interviewing and tape editing experience behind me, I still needed four weeks to produce my first hour-long documentary.

If you're new to this game, you might approach your local noncommercial station first. It may not pay much. (It may not pay at all.) But it is probably willing to teach enthusiastic volunteers, because it usually programs more public affairs material than the commercial stations do. And, if it is a National Public Radio affiliate, it will help you submit pieces to NPR for money.

Have you a good tape recorder and a quality omni microphone? Extra cassettes and batteries? Is your earjack or earphone plugged in? Did you run a test with each microphone before leaving the house? Then what are you waiting for?

This transcript of the author's taped interview with poet Gwendolyn Brooks shows the format used for the National Public Radio Modular Arts Series interviews.

For: National Public Radio's Modular Arts series.
From: Mike Bucki, WABE, Atlanta
TITLE: SHOULD BLACKS WRITE POINTEDLY TO BLACKS? (Interview, with sound illustrations, of Pulitzer Prize winning poet Gwendolyn Brooks)
SUGGESTED INTRODUCTION:
BROOKS: (auditorium ambience): . . . in Negro History Month you're supposed to remember the Negroes. You're supposed to rummage up the Negroes from their dull little corner and say "Hi!"
(FADE UNDER QUICKLY AND HOLD, BUT VERY FAINTLY UNDER):
ANNOUNCER: The time—Black History Week, 1976. The place—Spellman College, an all-women, mostly black, liberal arts college in Atlanta.
BROOKS: . . . and what a pleasure it is to be here with all these home folks and friends. And I've been invited to involve you with poetry. Poetry is life distilled, and I shall distill for you.
(AGAIN HOLD FAINTLY UNDER):
ANNOUNCER: The distiller of life is Gwendolyn Brooks, winner of the Pulitzer Prize in 1950 for her volume entitled "Annie Allen." Wrote the Library Journal, quote, "The composition and vividness of her poetry goes beyond any one group to reach out to

all humanity.", end quote. In more recent years, however, Miss Brooks's works have reflected a mounting commitment and involvement in being black. Her poetry, more and more, is charged with power and urgency.

BROOKS: Blackness stretches over the land. Blackness—the black of it, the rust red of it, the milk and cream of it, the tan and yellow tan of it, the deep brown middle brown high brown of it, the olive and ochre of it; Blackness marches on.

(FADE UNDER AND OUT DURING FOLLOWING):

ANNOUNCER: The change in her work is a result of a conscious effort, as she explains:

BROOKS: (background ambience has changed): Since 1967 my address has been specifically to blacks. I'm often asked Well, why do you do this? Isn't poetry—poetry?

(Thereafter the interview continues with Miss Brooks illustrating certain points with her poetry.)

Résumé Writing

by Jan A. Noble, Sr.

Writing employment résumés may not sound exciting, but don't sell it short. It can easily furnish a writer with an almost immediate source of income of $150-$200 a week, and enable him to meet new, interesting, intelligent people.

Initially, writing a résumé will take about two and a half hours (including one hour for interviewing your client). But you can eventually trim that to an hour and a half, and charge $60-$120 per résumé, depending on your location.

Like some dances, résumé writing can be learned in four steps: advertising your services; selling your services to a prospect; interviewing; and writing the résumé.

Advertising Your Services

Place a classified ad in your local newspaper. If possible, run it under the Help Wanted Administrative-Professional section. In some cases, you'll have to run it under Business Personals, but fight for a help wanted—you'll double the response.

This will do the job:

RÉSUMÉS
Professional — Confidential
Call 000-0000.

You can embellish upon this if you want to spend money. Be sure your ad runs often enough to show that you are really in business.

Call or visit nearby employment agencies. Offer them a 5 to 10 percent commission on all résumés that you write as a result of referrals from them. Then follow up with a letter to confirm your agreement with a particular agency. Later, you might leave a supply of business cards with the agency for prospective clients.

Don't hesitate to contact even an agency that advertises that it prepares résumés; maybe they want someone to take the chore off their hands.

Client referrals are the best source of new clients. Do a good job for each client, and he will pass along the word to his friends.

Selling Your Services to a Prospect

Okay, your ad ran in the paper yesterday afternoon, and already a prospective client is on the phone, with high hopes and guarded questions. His overriding concern is the cost of the résumé. Your best strategy is to quote a fixed fee, then to tick off your services. Tell your caller that he will get one original and one carbon (or more); that you need only one hour of his time for a personal, in-depth interview; and that you work by appointment only. Tell him when he can expect delivery of the completed résumé.

Early in the conversation, ask your prospective client what type of work he is in. This helps establish rapport, takes him off the offensive in the conversation, and gives you insight into the caller. Emphasize the necessity of a good résumé: Without it, he may never get into an employer's office even though he may be eminently qualified for a job; with a good résumé, he could command a salary that would pay more than the cost of the résumé in the first few days. Tell him that if he is dissatisfied with the résumé, you will refund his money in full. But don't promise anything but a professional résumé prepared confidentially. You can't guarantee that it will get him a job or that it will get him an interview with a particular employer.

Now ask him when he would like to be interviewed. Schedule the interview for the earliest possible date. The longer the time lag, the greater the possibility that he will change his mind. Get your client's name and telephone number. This will minimize the likelihood of a no-show.

Interviewing

When your client arrives for the interview, make him comfortable. Offer him a cup of coffee.

Begin by asking him what type of work he is in and what he is looking for. Next, ask him for a brief rundown of his employment history, beginning with his most recent job. This will give you a broad idea of how far back to go and how much material to cover.

Now get into the details of personal background, military service, educational background, and employment history.

Encourage your client to talk about his achievements. Some people are shy about their accomplishments, or they fail to recognize the importance of them. Be alert for clues to significant accomplishments, and changes he's suggested or made. Seek out numbers and facts, and present them in the best light available. For example, if a sales manager increased sales from $1,000 to $2,000 at his old job, say that he doubled sales. But if he increased sales from $900,000 to $1,000,000, don't say he increased sales 10 percent — say that he increased sales by $100,000.

Don't let your client go off on tangents. Budget your time and pace the interview. Getting your client settled in and getting all of the statistics as well as a rundown of his jobs should take no more than twenty minutes. The rest of the hour should be devoted to discussing the jobs your client has held, focusing on the elements pertinent to the job he wants.

What were his responsibilities? What projects did he initiate? What ideas did he contribute? Did he supervise or guide the activities of others? Answers to these questions will help make the résumé professional rather than perfunctory.

Writing the Résumé

Use short phrases, but be concerned with proper punctuation. Underline and capitalize words if it adds to the effect—but don't overdo it. Use the language of your client's profession, drawing from your interview notes. (Watch your spelling.) Here's what your résumé might include:

Résumé of. Name, address, city, state, and zip. Telephone number with area code.

Summary. This is a sales pitch. It should entice the prospective employer to read the rest of the résumé, saying to himself, "This is the kind of applicant we're looking for. I'd better talk to him." It should cover: what the client is (energetic, versatile); what he is seeking (challenge, greater responsibility); what his achievements are (increased profits, provided leadership); what he will do for the employer (reduce costs, increase sales). If the client is willing to travel or relocate, say so in this paragraph.

Personal background. Marital status, number of children, age, height, weight, health, and leisure activities.

Military service. Include this information if it fills a blank in his

RESUME OF

ERNEST WORKMAN
1234 Fifth Street
Halcyon, Pennsylvania 18500
Phone (555) 555-1212

SUMMARY: Energetic self-starter seeking opportunity in television news. Experienced in dealing with people, both inside and outside the media. Strong educational background. Have displayed initiative in setting up and conducting interviews under a variety of circumstances. Hardworking and results-oriented.

PERSONAL
BACKGROUND: Single--Height 6'0"--Weight 165 lbs. - Health --excellent. Age 23 years. Hobbies and personal interests include aviation, politics and photography, especially 35mm.

EDUCATIONAL
BACKGROUND: Halcyon State University, Halcyon, Pennsylvania - received Bachelor of Arts Degree with major in radio-television, minor journalism. Earned 3.8 GPA. Courses at Halcyon State University included radio and television, continuity writing of commercials, audio, video, history of broadcasting, journalism law, broadcast law, radio and TV production courses and radio and TV broadcasting techniques, among others. Extracurricular activities at HSU included serving as vice-president of Alpha Epsilon Rho, national honor broadcasting society-HSU chapter; Gamma Beta Phi, national honor society; HSU academic honors program; member of administrative advisory council, Halcyon State; student government senior and graduate class representative and Phi Kappa Phi National Honor Society, administrative health advisory committee.

University of Pennsylvania, Philadelphia, Pennsylvania. Currently working on Master of Arts Degree in Political Science. Graduated from Halcyon County High School, Halcyon, Pennsylvania.

OTHER: Hold Third-Class License-Endorsed. Belong to Radio-Television News Directors Association, National Pilots Association, Washington, DC, Pennsylvania Pilots Association, professional member of Alpha Epsilon Rho (national chapter) and Sigma Delta Chi--national society of professional journalists.

EMPLOYMENT BACKGROUND

Aug. 1978
thru present: Currently employed as press aide for Democratic candidate for governor, John Doe. Address: 213 St. Clair St., Philadelphia, Pennsylvania 19154. Phone: (555) 555-1213. General responsibilities include handling the media and assisting in campaign. Answer

Employment Background Continued:

questions and sometimes assist in answering letters. Set up
and make arrangements for up to two press conferences per week.
Responsible for developing and maintaining good media relations.
Write press releases. Responsible for rewriting some speeches.
Have done numerous actualities and sent them to stations for use.
Function as advance man, which requires traveling, calling the
media and setting up appearances for the candidate. Have
visited from 20 to 25 cities and towns in Pennsylvania.

1/79 thru
present: University of Pennsylvania, Philadelphia, Pennsylvania 19157.
Presently employed as a college instructor teaching a broadcast
class. Was instrumental in setting up this broadcasting class,
which is the only one offered at UP. Teach general production
techniques and newsroom operations. Class is undergraduate,
junior level.

6/78 to
8/78:   Pennsylvania State Government - Capitol Annex - Harrisburg,
Pennsylvania 17120. Phone: (555) 555-1214. Employed as summer
intern for State Auditor John Doe, who is now gubernatorial
candidate. Was first employee to work with the media. Handled
the press for the auditor. Made writing contributions to newsletter. Performed some photography for newsletter. Participated
in writing and rewriting speeches. Set up press conferences.

12/76
thru 5/78:   TV2, Halcyon State University cable TV and WHAL-FM, 50,000-watt
stereo, Halcyon State University radio, Halcyon, Pennsylvania.
Employed in numerous positions for this university-operated TV
and radio station. Worked as announcer on radio station including
co-hosting three-hour, live program, "New Day." For TV station,
produced and anchored evening news, produced and directed program,
"News Conference" which invited state office holder guests, along
with three representatives from the media on a once per week basis.
Was responsible for camera, audio, photography, switching and
reporting. Interviewed and conducted numerous activities in
conjunction with the broadcast facilities. This included attending
White House Press Conferences, interviewing James Fallows, Chief
Speech Writer to President Carter, interviewing Morley Safer of
"60 Minutes," interviewing Seals and Crofts, and interviewing
Miss America 1977. Initiated getting Morley Safer to attend
university, including raising funds to pay his fee while chairman
of entertainment committee of student government. Was invited to
editor's conference at the White House, along with half-hour Q&A
with President Carter. Attended New York Field Study seminars
with network executives and news people.

*Professionally written résumés like this one provide the author with a steady
income from job-seeking clients.*

employment sequence or if it supports his career objectives. List dates, his branch of service, his rank when discharged. What special training did he have? Was he responsible for the activities of others? If so, how many doing what? Interview him thoroughly on this subject. Often a client mistakenly feels that he didn't do anything constructive.

Educational background. Start with the latest education and work backward. Do not go back further than high school.

For college and technical training, list the name of the school, city and state; degree obtained or credit hours; major and minors; class ranking and grade average (if available and favorable); awards, positions, and accomplishments. Detail briefly courses and projects related to career goals.

The more work experience your client has, the less important this section is. Conversely, if your client does not have much experience, this section becomes very important.

For high school, list the name, city and state; major and minor; class ranking and grade average (if favorable to the client); awards and accomplishments. If he graduated, say so.

Other. Optional section. List social organizations, related activities, and miscellaneous awards and accomplishments.

Employment history. State when each job began and ended. Begin with the client's most recent job and work backward. List the company name, address, city, state, and zip, and telephone. List the client's job title, and his immediate supervisor. State the nature of the company's business and its sales volume or number of employees. Example: "Employed as sales manager, reporting to John Jones, vice-president of marketing, for this $50-million manufacturer of widgets." List the client's responsibilities and accomplishments.

This is the heart of the résumé. Be brief, factual, and specific.

Now give the client's reason for leaving his job or desiring a change. Be terse, factual, and pleasant. If the reason for leaving is unpleasant, simply state, "Will explain personally."

Of course, you should state your client's earnings (and perhaps his *desired* salary).

Writing résumés for the long or unwillingly unemployed is more difficult than it is for those who choose to change jobs. What can be done for clients who have suspiciously long gaps in their job histories or tales of sudden ejections from their place of work?

All résumés have to come from a positive outlook. Clients who have had job difficulties may not think well of themselves. Then it becomes your job as a résumé writer to dig up all the positive things they've forgotten about or aren't aware of. Details about supervisory or organizing experiences are valuable, even if these experiences are not related to a regular job.

When it comes to wording résumés of difficult cases you can (1) explain sticky circumstances in a way that puts your client in the best light, or (2) say that certain circumstances will be explained by the client during the interview, or (3) resort to euphemisms—like "left job for personal reasons."

Personal references. These rarely enhance a résumé. When listed, however, they should include the subject's name, address, telephone number, and a brief description of his relationship with your client.

Close, meticulous work? Yes, résumé writing is that. It is also an instructive way to make a little money and to meet intriguing people—and it will tide you over until your novel is finished.

Another Market: Job Application Letters

Writing job application letters is another quick and easy moneymaker for the busy freelance writer who wants to turn spare time to profit. You can sell these simple one-page queries to a variety of nearby clients.

I advertise with a simple 3x5 card tacked up in local laundromats, shops, and family restaurants which allow free postings. You'll be surprised at the number of customers who will flock to your door in response to an ad such as this:

Looking For A Job?

I can help you apply for work with a personalized job application letter designed to showcase your talents in a friendly and courteous way. My fee is reasonable and I will even save you gas money by interviewing you over the phone and completing our transaction by mail.

If you would like to "break the ice" with a prospective employer, give me a call. I've had twenty years' experience in job research and résumé writing services. I'm sure I can help you.

D. R. Patterson
my address
city/state/zip
phone
(Hours — 6 to 11 PM daily)

Most people hate to look for a job. It's a tedious, worrisome operation that makes many applicants feel insecure and unqualified. You can counteract this inadequacy and earn an easy fee by writing dynamic sales letters for these people who falter at putting their best foot forward.

After all, who's more qualified to write a job application letter than the typical freelance writer? He's always begging for work anyway, so why *shouldn't* he be extra good at it?

The mechanics are simple: Tell the prospective employer who your client is, what he wants, and why he wants it. Write it from your client's point of view and play up his qualifications. Use an informal, direct approach, like the following sample:

Dear Mr. Smith:
I'd like to join your firm in Dallas as a quality control engineer. I'm looking for a more challenging position that will better use my skills.

I'm also interested in relocating to the Dallas-Ft. Worth metro-plex for the educational and social advantages which will benefit my family.

I hope the enclosed résumé of my 15 years' experience in quality control will interest you.

I'd appreciate the opportunity for an interview and will look forward to hearing from you.

Cordially yours,
John Doe

What fee should you charge? That's adjustable. I charge $25 for a dozen mailed copies of a job application letter. I keep it inexpensive because I know my client can use the letter many times and will appreciate the bargain. Besides, if I play my cards right, many customers will give me the spin-off business of preparing their résumé or doing job research, both of which can be more lucrative.

There's another bonus: You will continually sharpen your writing and interviewing skills by preparing such letters. You will also keep yourself more active in the constant effort of marketing your writing talents. Finally, you will be helping your clients with the important business of selling themselves.

— *Donald Ray Patterson*

Shopping Mall Promotion

by Connie Howard

There are now approximately 20,600 shopping centers and enclosed malls operating in the United States, with several hundred more on the planning boards.

Malls are *the* way of shopping in America, and they're also a whole world of job opportunities for writers!

I'm a case in point. When my husband's job meant a move for us from a large city to a small college town, I felt that my writing would be limited to whatever freelance magazine articles I could sell, not realizing there might be other, local freelance possibilities.

Happily, I fell into a job that allowed me to draw upon my fifteen years' experience in various fields of writing: shopping mall promotion.

Who Is Your Client?

You'll probably work for the Merchants Association, a group composed of a representative from each store within the mall complex. This group usually meets at least once a month to discuss general mall business and is then broken down into smaller groups to handle individual areas of business. You would work directly with the sales promotion group.

As advertising director, sales promotion director, publicity director— or whatever title you'd happen to have—you'd meet on a regular basis with the sales promotion group to set up the promotions that take place in the center mall or the parking lot to create traffic (shoppers) to benefit the entire mall. (Obviously, with enclosed malls this is a year-round proceeding, while ordinary shopping centers would have to consider the weather when arranging outdoor promotions.)

Where does the money come from? Each store within the association pays monthly dues based on their square footage. At the beginning of each year a budget should be worked out as to how much goes into each type of advertising, your salary, and promotions for certain times of the year (Easter, Back-to-School, etc.). Of course, you'll want to have financial leeway to take care of any sensational, not-to-be-missed promotions that may come along halfway through the year—as they always will!

What Is Your Job?

Now, to the crux of the matter: What will you do? For the sake of information, we'll discuss the freelance situation, where there's just one person handling the promotions and advertising, as opposed to the running of the giant malls where a complete staff is involved, or large city malls handled by advertising agencies.

First and foremost, you think up promotions. I like to keep something—large or small—going on all the time, with some promotions running a full week and others lasting a day or so. (Display-type promotions can easily be stretched out, while promotions involving people are best run for only a few days.) Plan your big promotions as far ahead as possible. These will fall into place naturally, as you'll discover when you're booking traveling acts or demonstrations who usually set up their own schedule before starting out on tour. You'll find that you won't have to pull your promotions out of your head exclusively. There are many resources available to you for ideas. The best and undoubtedly the most helpful is the *Shopping Center Newsletter,* published monthly by the National Research Bureau, 424 N. Third St., Burlington IA 52601. It offers a wealth of ideas.

For example, the average issue carries a four-page section with brief descriptions of dozens of promotions carried on in malls during the past few months. It always describes several promotions in complete detail, and includes sheets with reproductions of ads run by malls throughout the country. These ideas can run exactly as other malls ran them or you can borrow from them, changing them around to meet your purposes.

By having a center mall area available for promotions year round as well as a parking lot for large carnivals or other outdoor events, you'll find you have a definite advantage over downtown stores in the type of promotions you can plan. You'll also quickly find that nearly all the local clubs, schools, and charitable fund-raising groups will be coming to you with ideas they'd like to carry out to raise funds for themselves.

I personally try to aim for pretty much of a fifty-fifty basis. About half our promotions tie in with local charitable groups or organizations, and the other half are out-and-out sales promotions.

Fund-Raising Promotions

A good example of a charitable promotion is one I ran called "The World's Largest Backyard Muscular Dystrophy Carnival." MD's chief nationwide income producers, apart from Jerry Lewis's annual telethon, are the small backyard carnivals put on by neighborhood children for MD. We turned the entire center area of the mall into a carnival, using the fountain for a coin toss game, a turtle race, and a variety of other small games. Balloons were sold; the local Lions Club came in and ran a popcorn, cotton candy, and ice ball stand; the women of the Moose Lodge ran a bingo game; and many other local groups took part, with all funds raised going to MD. A highlight of the day was a personal appearance by Pittsburgh TV personality Paul Shannon, who also happened to be national backyard carnival chairman. Naturally, throughout the planning of the carnival and after arrangements for Paul's appearance were made, I flooded the newspaper with stories. To further promote the carnival I arranged an elementary-school poster contest: More than a thousand children turned in posters advertising the carnival. These were displayed throughout the mall before and during the event. All in all, the carnival left the mall center a shambles, but the stores reported unbelievably brisk business, we made over $1,100 for a worthwhile cause, gained thousands of dollars' worth of free publicity out of it, and I even received a personal thank-you letter from Jerry Lewis afterward.

Strictly Sales Promotion

An example of a straight promotion was our "Roaring Twenties Days." For this, we filled the center of the mall with thirteen antique cars. (We paid a flat fee to the club all the owners belonged to in exchange for their putting the cars on display.) To tie in with the era of the cars—most of them were from the twenties and early thirties— we had Roaring Twenties sales in all the stores, and ran a special tabloid section in the paper (for part of this I pulled old stories from the twenties and ran sections of them). In cooperation with the local newspaper I did a feature story on the antique cars and their owners, which appeared prominently the Saturday before the show opened at our mall.

You're a One-Man Band

Having a writing background while doing promotion work is a definite advantage. First off, nearly all newspapers are understaffed and simply don't have the personnel to send out to cover store promotions and such. But if you can keep a steady stream of newsworthy events going on—and then have the ability to write a professional news story or feature story—you'll find you'll have no trouble getting it into the paper. I've done feature stories on such happenings as a husband-and-wife art team, as well as dozens and dozens of straight news release stories. One word of advice—don't mail your stories, articles, or ideas to the paper. Take them in personally to the editor. Being on friendly personal terms with the newspaper staff you're working with is unquestionably a great advantage.

You can also do your own newspaper ads, even if you've never done one before. I do all my own, mainly because I feel that no matter how good an advertising department person is, he can't possibly work on dozens of ads in a day and put the same interest into every one of those accounts that I can working on just my own. In large cities you generally must come in with a finished layout sheet, but in smaller cities and towns the newspaper's advertising staff will usually lay out your ads for you, if you wish. I had done a great deal of ad *copy* work but had never actually laid out an entire ad before. My "schooling" consisted of a fifteen-minute explanation from one of the people in the ad department at our local newspaper, and then I was on my own. I confess that once I realized the cost of that ad I had some nervous moments till I actually saw it in print, but after that I was off and running and now do ads regularly without a second thought. There are, of course, books on this subject in the library to study for background information. [See this book's bibliography under Advertising and Public Relations.]

Writing your own radio commercials is a little harder—only because people don't always *listen* to what they're hearing but block it out unless there's a reason to give their attention to it. Again, it is something that can be learned. [See separate chapter on this specialty.]

That, basically, is what you will do as the advertising director or promotion director of a mall or shopping center. Obviously, the more you put into your job the more you'll find to write about. Some larger malls put out newspapers—which you could write—for the shoppers; some send features to both newspapers and radio stations. You might also do as I did and initiate a newsletter. I send this two- or three-page letter out to all the merchants about once a month, telling them what's planned for the next few weeks ahead, mentioning special stories about us that ran in the newspaper, etc. Most of the writing you do will be aimed at the local newspaper, so study it and see how they like their news and feature stories—strictly news or folksy?

Finding the Job

How do you get a job as a promotion director at a mall? If the mall is completed, with a number of stores already open for business, design your presentation and go to see the president of the association. If the mall is still in the building stages you can talk to the owner/developer.

The individual stores within any mall have advertising managers of their own, so they'll all be familiar with the benefits of advertising and promotion, and all malls have become increasingly knowledgeable about the effects of promotion in the past few years.

Your first job will be to sell yourself. Suggest a promotion or two, sketch out how you'd set them up in the mall, do a news release on them, and present what other publicity ideas you have. Offer to come to an association meeting and discuss your ideas with the group. Your salary usually should be approximately 15 percent of the total budget. However, once you've proved yourself, your salary can then be based on what the budget will allow.

A small mall, for example, might have an annual budget of only $30,000, which must cover newspaper ads, radio spots, the freelance advertising/sales promotion/publicity director's salary, and the cost of any promotions brought in. A large mall may spend $50,000 just for Christmas lighting alone. In small malls, the publicity director may only have to put in two or three hours' work for his $400 monthly retainer some weeks, and many times that other weeks, but there is usually complete freedom to schedule appointments at the writer's convenience. Some promotion directors work out of their homes; some have an office in the mall. In the latter case the director would work a more regular schedule for a regular salary rather than a percent of the promotion budget.

You'll find that if you're successful the world *will* beat a path to your door, because there just aren't many people around doing promotion work in small towns. And, because of the large acreage needed to build a mall or shopping center, most are located in the suburbs or in small towns. A large area around our mall has now become promotion-conscious, and I've had literally dozens of offers to do similar work for other shopping centers in the area, as well as for businesses.

If you like to write, love the advertising world, want to work at your own pace and schedule—then check into these great freelance opportunities in your community.

Speechwriting

by Mike McCarville

I've spent years writing for magazine editors and picking up checks for $50 to $500, but it wasn't until I discovered the rewards of ghostwriting speeches for politicians and business executives that my freelance career really took off.

The innocent request that opened the speechwriting cashbox for me came from the owner of a very small company. He was to be installed as president of a suburban city's chamber of commerce and, knowing I was a writer, asked me to compose a short speech for him. I did so, and pocketed a hundred dollars for the effort, a six-minute text that required little research.

Then a congressional candidate asked for a speech, which I wrote. He requested another, and another, then a fourth.

Suddenly it occurred to me that political speeches might be the surefire story-on-assignment-with-kill-fee, the pay-on-acceptance piece most writers find far too seldom.

While I've found this to be true in general, let me quickly add a whoa-up note: Simply writing what you might describe as a "speech" and then selling it to someone is no gilt-edged guarantee of megabucks.

Speechwriting, particularly for politicians, can be the most thankless, ego-shattering trip around. And while we're at the cold water tap, heed this Sad Speech Story: I recently spent ten days researching, writing, and rewriting an eight-page speech for a political candidate "on faith."

(Read that "on speculation.") He had requested it, I wrote it and delivered it to him. It is the finest speech I have ever written. He loved it. He gave it at least twenty-five times during his campaign, to appreciative audiences. I've still not been paid the $1,500 we agreed upon. (More about pay from politicians later.)

The Ghostwriting Market

Despite that story, there is a tremendous market in ghostwriting speeches, and it can be a lucrative one. The reason the market exists is simple: Most minor politicians and small businessmen can't afford full-time speechwriters. Most political candidates certainly can't, even though campaign budgets these days top the million-dollar mark with regularity, and "public relations" is often 10 percent or more of those budgets.

Yet every candidate, every officeholder, and most business people must, sooner or later, stand up and deliver a speech. That's where we come in.

We face two problems in writing speeches. The first is most obvious: How do we land the speechwriting assignment in the first place? Let's answer that question with a question: How do we sell our articles and photographs, our books, our radio scripts, our TV plays? We familiarize ourselves with the market. We write query letters. *We ask for the job.* If you want to write political speeches, the best place to start might be your home state's Democratic or Republican State Committee headquarters. Find out from your local party headquarters (they're in the phone book's white pages) who the executive director is and write a short letter, asking if anyone needs a freelance speechwriter. Follow up with a phone call or personal visit. You might also seek out local elected officials and ask if they need speeches written for them.

As for potential clients in the business world, how about chamber of commerce officials? Bankers? The executive director of the local Homebuilders' Association? Corporation executives? The list is as varied as the Yellow Pages. The owner of a small company making a new safety device, for example, might need help constructing a speech to introduce it. The president of a company embroiled in a controversy might welcome a professional writer's help in preparing his views, his side of the argument.

Now's the Time to Act

Let's say you've made contact with a local candidate for Congress (and remember, most campaigns gear up as much as a year in advance) and you have an appointment to discuss the possibility of speechwriting with him.

Write these questions on your notepad:

1. Is he a Democrat? A Republican? Independent? Liberal? Conservative?

2. Has he given speeches he himself has written?

3. Does he want a specific topic covered, or a general campaign speech?

4. Does his campaign have a professional pollster?

5. Does he joke easily? Can he deliver a one-liner without falling over the podium?

6. What's his demeanor? Is he low-key? Hyper? Professorial? Dogmatic? Rough? Glib?

When you meet, ask him Questions 1 through 4. Answer the last two for yourself. As you talk with him, listen for any peculiar speech patterns or key words you can use to write *his* speech. Try to imagine the language he would use if writing the speech himself. Make notes. If he's written speeches himself, ask for copies and study them later for style.

While you're with him, come to an agreement on a price for the speech he wants. If it's a fifteen-minute speech on national defense requiring research, a fee of $600 would be honest and you'll earn it, but that may be more than the market will bear. A range of $150 to $800 isn't uncommon for local or regional speeches, and some top national political ghosts pocket the higher figure just to write the first draft—*and they collect it in advance.*

In politics, this is known as "C.I.A."—cash in advance. If a candidate asks you to undertake a major speechwriting job, you should ask at least 25 percent of the fee on the spot, another 25 percent upon delivery of the first draft and the balance upon completion. Otherwise, you're working on spec and politics is a fickle enough endeavor without risking wasted time and effort.

So you've landed the assignment. What now?

Write, you say? Wrong! We face another step.

First, you must, in most cases, research. If you're lucky, the research will be done. But in most campaigns it won't be, and you'll be expected to do it.

If your man's a Democrat hewing to the party line, write the Democratic Congressional Campaign Committee and ask for all the party position papers. If he's a Republican, write the Republican Congressional Campaign Committee. If he's a conservative or liberal, of either party, you can obtain (often conflicting) viewpoints from the National

Association of Manufacturers, the League of Women Voters, and the Library of Congress. Soon, you'll have all the facts and viewpoints you need to write a fact-filled, well-balanced speech. [See list of research sources at end of chapter.]

If your candidate uses a professional pollster, ask to study the information on issues that his poll will provide. This will give you the mood of the electorate and possibly some other issues to develop into other speeches.

The Quiet Ghost

A basic rule that governs all speechwriters was well stated by business writer Robert Heinemann: "What you write for a client belongs to him. Cash your checks, and keep your mouth shut."

I learned this lesson the hard way. After completing one of my early speechwriting assignments, I told several local businessmen that I was the author of the speech that one of their colleagues had just given. The following day my client called and asked, politely, that I perform an erotic act with my typewriter. I learned a lesson, one that has been an ally since. That's why you won't see the names of any of my speechwriting clients here.

You wouldn't recognize most of their names anyway, since they were candidates for mayor, the city council, the county board of supervisors, the school board, or the presidency of the local chamber of commerce.

That's where the real dollars are in this business, right on your own Main Street.

You don't need national contacts or reams of research to write speeches for your local officeholders or candidates. Most times, you'll know enough about local issues and the "mood" of your neighbors to write a tailor-made speech your client should love. If you're short on research data, your local library is close at hand and the county courthouse probably isn't far away, if you need access to county records. Your city hall can be a rich source of information as well.

Know Thy Audience

A good speech has to be tailored to the audience and to the speaking situation. Is it a formal speech, the speaker at a podium with microphone before 250 persons? Or is it an informal speech, the speaker on his feet in the front of the room before 35 people? It also helps if the speaker has a sense of the situation himself, and most will.

If, for example, it is a larger group and the speaker's behind a podium, a fully written text is probably the best. (As for form: Set the margins at

20 and 80, use all caps, and double-space. Don't break a word at the end of a line, and don't go over the right margin to finish it, either: drop down to the next line. Underline all words and phrases that require emphasis.) If it's a small group, notes on 3x5 index cards and an air of informality is probably preferable.

Most situations will fall somewhere between these two examples, and it is those in-between speeches you'll probably be writing.

There are a couple of factors you'll need to determine in writing your client's speech:

What type of group will hear the speech? I know it's the senior citizens' group, but what are their interests? Social Security, for certain. Low-cost housing, equally for certain. Easy access to public transportation, undoubtedly. Presto! You have three subjects to cover in your rough draft for the client, providing the client agrees. If your client is a candidate for mayor of your city, he can speak on low-cost housing and public transportation with ease. If he's a candidate for Congress, add Social Security. If he's running for the school board, he can cover these three general areas rapidly, then move on to his plans for the schools. It's important that the speech convey a sense of rapport, a *kinship* the speaker feels for the audience. If this kinship is achieved, the precise words themselves become less important. If this kinship isn't achieved, however, the words had better be precise or some sharp septuagenarian is likely to cut your client off at the pass.

What's the speaking situation? Two hundred fifty persons at a banquet? Or 35 sipping coffee in metal folding chairs? If it's the 250-at-a-banquet speech, will those present have had a cocktail or two? If so, several minutes of humorous stories or rapid-fire one-liners can have them in the palm of the speaker's hand in short order. If it's the smaller group, a humorous opening is still fine, but it should *seem* spontaneous and self-deprecating to the speaker. This kind of humor should get your client's audience laughing, or at least smiling. And a happy audience is "with" the speaker.

Clarity Above All

Clarity is a cherished quality in speeches. It's the result of simple writing that contains all the elements of a good magazine article. Speeches must have a theme, a beginning, a middle, an end.

Often the selection of a theme is nothing more than the working title for the speech. It makes no difference if the speech is actually titled. That working title should grasp the essence of the speech, much as a headline written for an article grasps its essence. Particularly for politicians seeking news coverage of their remarks, speech titles should entice and arouse curiosity.

A while ago I was asked to write a speech for an oil company executive to deliver to a group of political leaders in Washington. Topic: America's energy industry. Instantly, the title came to me: "The Energy Industry: Is a Four-Letter Word the Only Answer?" (The four-letter word, incidentally, was "pray.") Since then, that speech has been given to dozens of local chambers of commerce and civic clubs in small towns all over America.

A local city council candidate wanted a speech pointing out how much money the city wasted each year. The title that sprang to mind: "Would You Lend Money to This Outfit?"

We wrote the speech as a profit-and-loss statement on the city, and the candidate used that speech sixty-one times in the campaign. He won by a wide margin.

Seven Tips for the Professional

For the ghost, performing speechwriting duties at established prices means turning out a professional piece of writing even if the speech is for a local candidate for tax collector or dogcatcher.

The biggest failing most beginning speechwriters are guilty of is that they lack professionalism. Being a pro doesn't mean you must have written fifty speeches already. It does mean you must approach the project in a businesslike, journeyman manner.

Here's a quick formula to help you achieve professionalism:

1. Ask the (potential) client for the job.

2. Establish a price for the job up front. (Remember C.I.A.)

3. Set a deadline for the first draft. Meet the deadline, and go over the draft with the client to make certain you're writing words he's comfortable with. Read the draft aloud to yourself before you meet. Does it measure up to the best speeches you've heard? Any clumsy expressions? Double entendres? Are the sentences of the right speaking length? Any bollixes? Any tongue twisters?

4. Revise that first draft to the client's specifications. (Remember—it's *his* speech.) Set a deadline for delivery of the final draft.

5. Meet that deadline for the final draft, and be prepared to make any final changes.

6. Be in the audience yourself when the client delivers the speech. Take notes. Rate him as a speaker, and yourself as a speechwriter. How many times did you wince as he spoke? Did the humor fly, or flop?

7. After his speech, mingle with the audience. What are they saying?

Did they like the speech? Was it too long? Did they understand it?

Having done all these things, you can consider yourself a speech-writer, provided: (a) you didn't punch out some guy who criticized the speech; and (b) it bothered you to hear it criticized. Any ghost worth his white sheet dislikes criticism as much as the speaker. A professional attitude on your part will serve to channel your determination to do it better the next time into new clients and new speeches and more freelance bucks.

Fees for Speechwriting

What to charge? Here's a rule of thumb: For local political speeches requiring little research, $300; for statewide candidates, $375-$750; and for national candidates, $1,000 and up. The fees you can expect depend upon your experience, your contacts, and your reputation. If you're a top national speechwriter, for example, you might be paid $5,000. If you're a beginner at the local level, your top might be $200. A speech for a local businessman might fall in the $125 to $300 range, while ghosting for the president of a national company should command a fee of at least $500, and probably much more. I've written them for $750, and for $900, and for $2,000—here your reputation really means money.

The Ghost's Revenge

If you follow all this advice and instruction to some avail and achieve some success as a ghost, you will undoubtedly encounter the politician whose ego and personality will not allow him to recognize your wit, your clarity, your timing, your countless hours on *his* behalf, your professionalism. He will criticize, describe your speeches as "lousy," and generally make your life miserable, thus showing himself to be unprofessional and, worse, a lout.

If that happens to you, have the courage to do as one veteran political speechwriter did a few years back. This pro, who began as a ghost for the chairman of a town board of trustees, took all the abuse he could stand from his client. Having determined he could do without this client's checks (an important consideration), he wrote a final speech. In delivering it, the politican waxed eloquent as he intoned, "And now, I will tell you ten ways we can prevent the gold flow from leaving this country and how we can end inflation...."

He turned to the next page, and it was ghostly in its stark whiteness. One line was written at the bottom: "All right, big shot. You're on your own. I quit."

Research Sources for Political Speeches

American Enterprise Institute
1150 Seventeenth St., NW
Washington DC 20036
A "publicly supported, nonpartisan research and educational organization" which provides analyses of national and international issues.

American Security Council
Box 8
Boston VA 22713
Issues a "National Security Index" keyed to its belief that "American security is best preserved by vigorous support for maintenance and development of large weapons systems."

Americans for Constitutional Action
Suite 1000
955 L'Enfant Plaza, SW
Washington DC 20024
ACA is against "the current movement of our Nation into Socialism and a regimented society"; conservative in philosophy.

Americans for Democratic Action
1411 K St., NW
Washington DC 20005
ADA is considered a liberal political organization. Its members support economic legislation designed to reduce inequality, curtail defense spending, and prevent violations of civil liberties.

Committee for the Survival of a Free Congress
721 Second St., NE
Washington DC 20002
A conservative organization which publishes in-depth research papers extolling the conservative viewpoint regardless of political party.

Congressional Research Service
Library of Congress
Washington DC 20540
A major source of definitive information for speechwriters. CRS's "Issue Briefs" contain issue identification, reports, a chronology of events, and additional reference sources for each issue.

Democratic National Committee
1625 Massachusetts Ave., NW
Washington DC 20036
DNC researchers can furnish issue papers on any subject you'll ever need. Use this same address for the Democratic Congressional Campaign Committee (candidates for the US House) and the Democratic National Senatorial Committee.

League of Conservation Voters
317 Pennsylvania Ave., SE
Washington DC 20003
For environmental information.

League of Women Voters
1730 M St., NW
Washington DC 20036
One of the most active, research-oriented groups in Washington. It can provide facts on virtually every possible issue, from campaign finance reform, which it supports, to strip mining, which it opposes.

National Associated Businessmen
1000 Connecticut Ave., NW
Washington DC 20036
NAB "believes strongly in economy in government" and can provide opinion papers on economic and business issues.

National Association of Manufacturers
1776 F St., NW
Washington DC 20006
Prepares position papers on issues affecting American industry.

Republican National Committee
310 First St., SE
Washington DC 20003

The RNC, in conjuction with the National Republican Congressional Committee, (320 First St., S.E., 20003) can supply Republican position papers on any topic.

State Capitol Librarian
Your State Capital, Your State
When working with candidates for state office, try this source on specific questions.

Teaching Creative Writing

by Betty Steele Everett

In 1965 the Eighty-ninth Congress passed major legislation which provided federal funds to schools for the improvement of education. It was called the Elementary and Secondary Education Act (ESEA) and at that time almost doubled the amount of federal aid then available to schools. In 1978, Congress passed major amendments to the Act—such as the Arts in Education Program.

Over the years the divisions (Titles) of ESEA have changed as schools have tried many plans and methods to improve education. Today Titles I and IV-C are of special interest to writers. Funds for Title I ("Financial Assistance to Meet Special Educational Needs of Children") are restricted to poverty areas, but Title IV-C ("Improvement in Local Educational Practices") does not have this restriction. Title IV-C funds are to be used for "educational improvement, resources, and support."

Both Title I and IV-C are of value to writers because they provide funds to implement in local schools proven programs and practices from around the country. That means that what has worked somewhere else can be tried in your hometown schools—and some of those proven programs and practices include classes in creative writing. See where you come in?

Creative writing programs can be set up for students on all grade and ability levels; educators are acknowledging that teaching these skills is helpful to both the slow learner and the gifted student.

So how do you, a freelance writer, get such a class to teach?

Title programs are first written as proposals to be submitted to state departments of education for approval. So ideally it would be best to have your program written into the proposal when it is prepared. But if a project has already been funded, you can still work to have a course in writing included. Some proposals offer broad goals, and your course could be one of the specific means for meeting them. [See chapter on Educational Grant Proposal Writing.]

Funds for Titles I and IV-C go to local agencies, so call your local school superintendent and ask if any such grants have been awarded to the district, or if proposals are being considered. Explain what you have in mind; many school officials are not aware that a freelance writer lives in their area and could be of help to them.

When you talk to the superintendent, ask if your state funds teacher grants. These are small grants given to individual teachers (after they have written acceptable proposals) and often include money for outside speakers—a need you can also meet on a one-time basis.

Don't limit yourself to your own school district. I worked in an adjoining county, and some writers live in areas where three or four school districts are still within easy driving distance.

Ask for an interview, and have a personal résumé ready to offer. Stress your qualifications for teaching creative writing. If you have had teacher training or experience, mention it, but even more important is the fact that you have actually written and sold material on a freelance basis, or been employed as a reporter, publicity writer, etc.

Presenting Your Case

If the people writing the proposal, or heading the approved project, have not thought about creative writing as something to be included, you will have to present your case for it. Read up on some of the writing projects that have proved helpful in other communities so you can discuss them. The *Reader's Guide* at the library will give you some sources, and almost all the educational magazines have carried something about such courses at some time. Consult the *Education Index* at the library.

Creative writing can be a help to any child, and is flexible enough that a class can be included under many different programs: those for the gifted child, curriculum improvement, slow-learning children, potential dropouts, personal projects.

Write, for submission to the project director, a brief summary of what you hope to accomplish in such a writing class and how you plan to go about it. The first part—the objectives—should be specific, although tailored to meet the needs of the group you will teach. The aims of a group of gifted, college-bound seniors, for example, will be different from those of a group of underprivileged potential dropouts.

The second part of your summary—the methods you plan to use—should be flexible. Most classes can include instruction time, reading, workshop sessions in which students read their own work for constructive criticism from the others, and personal consultations with you. You may want to try using the meeting time for actual writing, with you available for help, or you may want to spend all the scheduled time on instruction with outside writing assignments. Or a combination. It will depend on the students.

(Since the creative writing course I taught was done as an "enrichment" or "extra" course, and no academic credit was given the student, I did not need to be certified. However, if this were a course for high school credit, teacher certification might be necessary.)

The salary for this sort of job is not large, but it is part-time work that will sharpen your own writing skills while paying regularly. Salaries have nothing to do with state teachers' salaries, and are determined by each individual project center. From my experience, I would estimate that these run from $30-$50 per hour of instruction, depending on the standard of other salaries in the school system, whether additional is paid for travel, etc. The best payment you will get from working with an ESEA project is the one that comes when a slow learner shows you a short story he has actually finished by himself, or a gifted student hands you his first encouraging letter from an editor: accomplishments that could not have happened without your help.

Lay Reading

An excellent source of supplemental income for the freelance writer is lay reading. Many high school English teachers are overwhelmed by the number of themes to be read. School districts have appropriated funds to be used for just this purpose. Individuals who are proficient in grammar, spelling, and composition are much in demand. The pay is generally low, but there are intrinsic rewards: The writer makes use of valuable skills while at the same time gaining insights about young people. Also, the theme reading can be done in the home at the writer's convenience. Any writer interested in this freelance possibility should contact the offices of the local school district.

— *Cheryl Trulen*

Teaching High School Journalism

by Sue Glasco

Would you like a part-time writing-related job that could provide you with a $4,000 to $6,000 base? Would you like the job to be intellectually challenging, emotionally satisfying, and yet leave you with a major part of your day and energy available to spend at your typewriter? Perhaps you too can cash in on the trend of high schools to add journalism to their curriculums.

Today's school administrators are quick to recognize that the study of journalism is not only an effective way to teach clear thinking and writing, but that it can be an excellent enrichment program for the creative youngster with a desire to delve and to record his findings. Unfortunately for them, happily for you, the supply of teachers who know the difference between a news story and an essay has not kept pace with the demand.

Because of this shortage, I was able to teach journalism part-time at the local high school. Teaching three periods a day, I received three-fifths of the regular salary for someone with my experience and educational level.

Salaries and Certification

Teacher salaries and certification laws vary from state to state and are frequently updated. The Eighty-first General Assembly of Illinois raised minimum yearly salaries for teachers with bachelor's degrees to

$10,000, with the provision that after five years that salary must be raised at least $1,000. A minimum salary for a master's degree is $11,000, and must be raised at least $1,250 after five years. Many salary schedules start with a base higher than the minimum required by law and often give automatic raises each year, depending on the financial condition of the local school district. Your part-time starting salary would also be determined by your previous teaching experience and how many periods you were to teach daily. In Illinois, if a teacher taught part-time two periods of a five-period day, he would earn at least $4,000; three periods of daily teaching would bring a minimum of $6,000.

The journalism classes in our school were started by the managing editor of our local daily, who taught only one period a day. Increasing editorial responsibilities caused him to resign. The next year an English major with summer experience on an area newspaper took over. But the provisional certification that made it possible for someone with work experience but no professional education background to teach journalism is no longer available in Illinois, though it may be in other states. You now need a teaching certificate, plus eight semester hours in journalism and sixteen in English or eighteen semester hours in journalism and six in rhetoric and composition. You will need to check your state's requirements. The reference desk at your local library should have a volume giving certification information for your state; or consult the latest edition of *Requirements for Certification for Elementary Schools, Secondary Schools, Junior Colleges* (University of Chicago Press), which offers data on all fifty states.

If you have a degree with an English or journalism background, see your local or regional superintendent of schools to find out if you are qualified for provisional certification or what courses you'd need to take to get certification in your state.

Dr. W. Manion Rice, director of the Southern Illinois School Press Association, says that it is only the large city or suburban schools where teachers are likely to teach several journalism classes daily, sponsor newspaper and/or yearbook staffs, and possibly even handle school publicity. [See separate chapter on this specialty.] Few smaller schools can afford a teacher just for journalism, so the schools will try to assign journalism duties to teachers of English, speech, or social studies. Because smaller schools may offer only one or two periods of journalism, the field lends itself to a part-time approach.

So visit your superintendent and present your credentials. School administrators are no longer bound by tradition. They are willing to try new ideas. If your local high school offers no journalism classes at present, it might be only because no one willing and able to teach it has ever come forward.

What the Job Entails

In most high schools, teaching journalism involves putting out a publication. My three classes of students put out seventeen issues of a four-page, eight-column paper. Six- to eight-page tabloids are more common, and papers may come out weekly, biweekly, or even monthly. A few schools use a magazine format, although generally school magazines are literary publications rather than news magazines and are published as an extracurricular activity of the English department. (Advising the staff of the literary magazine might also offer someone with the right training another part-time teaching opportunity, but that's another story.)

Those of you whose initiation into writing was by way of your high school paper may question my statement that teaching teenagers could be emotionally satisfying and intellectually challenging. However, with all due apologies to my generation, today's kids are far more mature than we were in high school, and many are eager to tackle some serious writing assignments.

High school journalism has come a long way since the days when newspapers were mere mimeographed joke and gossip sheets. Any self-respecting student editor today would blanch at "Who was C.T. flirting with at Teen Town Saturday night?" Modern-day editors and their staffs not only concern themselves with responsible student government and expanding student rights, but are not afraid to delve into controversial social issues from draft registration to abortion laws. (*You'll* be afraid to, but they won't.)

Today's bright students are ready to produce stimulating, high-quality journalism. My students developed a series called "Non-Delinquent Spotlight," which featured the many kinds of volunteer work being done in the community by teenagers. A variation on this theme was a well-researched article about the number of students holding down jobs, their average hours and pay, advantages and disadvantages of working. An advanced class ran an editorial campaign to encourage clubs and groups to buy shrubbery to landscape the grounds of the new school building. For a campaign against quitting school, a reporter interviewed two local dropouts. A unit on feature stories resulted in some outstanding work, including some all-school surveys. One such survey dealt with students' attitudes toward social cliques; the article was well-written and widely read. I took tremendous satisfaction in seeing youngsters get inspired by an original idea and make something good of it.

The most difficult part of my job was teaching makeup to page editors, for my own experience was quite limited. However, help was available from students themselves who worked on the paper in previous years and also from the printers. I did some supplemental library research, and we managed. By the end of the year I felt much more confident about training next year's editors.

Another problem I had was getting students to meet deadlines. They invented excuses galore as to why they were unable to arrange an interview by deadline time, for example. This was a valuable experience for me as a writer, however. You can certainly sympathize with an editor's frustrations after working with dilatory high school students.

Your Own Writing Will Improve

A close working relationship with youngsters can be a great help to the writer who wants to write for this age group or about them.

Reviewing my old college journalism class notes and the other studying I did to prepare myself to teach had a salutary effect on my own writing. As you grade others' news and feature stories, you quickly begin to see the weaknesses in your own. After telling your students a thousand times to grab the reader with the first sentence, you are forced to ask yourself if *you* grab the reader with yours!

Certainly the writer who needs the stimulation of some contact with the world outside his study will find that part-time teaching offers great benefits. Other teachers are interesting people to work with, and, in my opinion, the students who sign up for journalism are the greatest. They are the seekers, the movers and the shakers. And your opportunities for fame are greatly multiplied, since you can take some credit if any of your students ever make it big!

Teaching Poetry in the Schools

by John D. Engle, Jr.

For years writing for me was a freelance poker game with editors in which I dealt out manuscripts and received an infinite variety of rejection slips, paper clips, and now and then an acceptance in return. Eventually I learned, even as acceptances increased, that there were variations of the writing game that would pay me as much as or more than publishing.

Among these variations are reading and speaking for community, school, and writing groups; participating in writers' conferences; conducting writing workshops; teaching adult evening courses in writing at high schools and colleges; judging contests; and editing and critiquing the work of other writers. These variations were not only profitable, but they also actually taught me to play the straight freelance game better.

It was not until a few years ago, however, that a friend of mine introduced me to the most interesting and rewarding variation of all—the Ohio Arts Council Artists-in-School and Community program. Similar programs exist in every state.

The word "artists" includes "poets." The Ohio program sponsors residencies for qualified creative people in elementary and secondary schools and in community institutions such as libraries, old people's homes, and hospitals. Its goals are to provide meaningful contact between professional artists and students/citizens; to promote creative communication and an increase in self-awareness and self-expression;

and to strengthen the commitment of school administrators, teachers, and communities to the arts. Funding comes from the school or organization involved, from the state arts council, and from the National Endowment for the Arts.

In Ohio, two types of residencies are available: short-term (two to six weeks) and long-term (nine months). For short-term residencies the local school or organization is required to pay the artist $175 per week of residency. The state arts council/endowment funding pays an additional $475 per week of residency, making a total payment of $650 per week.

For long-term residencies the local school or organization is required to pay the artist or poet $4,000. The state/NEA funding pays an additional $9,500, making a total payment of $13,500 for a nine-month residency. These conditions and fees vary widely from state to state. The only way to find out the facts is to call the arts council in your state. (It's usually in the state capital and that city's information operator could tell you the number.)

Landing the Job

Getting on the approved list of residency poets was easier than I thought. I submitted a résumé and ten of my published poems. Later I was interviewed by the arts council's literary committee and other council officials. They examined my published books, asked questions about my writing and my teaching techniques, and in a short while I was informed that I had been accepted and that my name would be added to the list distributed to schools and communities throughout the state. (Since that time there have been some revisions in the application procedures. In addition to the résumé and ten poems published in at least two established magazines or in a book brought out by a recognized publisher, the poet must also fill in and submit an official application form.)

But what happens if you don't get a call? That's where your initiative, persistence, and determination come into play. You simply call schools or organizations you'd like to work with, let them know about the program and that you are interested and available, and then arrange an interview. Before doing this, however, become thoroughly familiar with all available arts council materials, forms, and deadlines so that you can answer all the possible questions that might be posed by the school or organization. Take along a portfolio of some of your best work as well as any favorable publicity you've received for your writing or teaching, and be sure to present a neat, complete résumé that indicates where and when you may be reached by letter and by phone.

Don't try to get your foot in the door of a new school by way of the principal's office. Instead, ask to see the head of the English Department. You will probably get a sympathetic reception here, since you would be doing most of your readings, workshops, and presentations under its auspices. If the head of the English Department can convince the administration that there is a need for your services, and if application deadlines are met, you'll be in!

The rewards of the job are manifold. My first residency, for example, which was in a small city school district, brought new experiences that I never expected. In addition to my work with students in the school, which consisted of workshops, assignments, and readings of their creative work, I found myself involved in newspaper, radio, and television publicity, plus readings of my own works at an evening program conducted by the local arts council. The audience was enthusiastically receptive, and before the evening ended I had sold all the copies of my books that I'd brought with me.

I learned that this kind of celebrity reception was typical when I was invited to another small-town high school in the northwest corner of the state. In addition to working with the students at the school, I was the guest of honor at one of the largest local churches, where a one-act play I had written was presented by prominent townspeople, after which I gave a poetry reading and sold still more copies of my books. As a result of my successful term of duty at this school, I was invited back for a second residency and a similar red carpet treatment.

I don't want to imply, however, that residencies are all roses. If your experience is like mine, you will find that your schedule, in spite of specifications by the arts council, will be full and exhausting. By the time you have met with various classes on different floors of a vast, sprawling building, and often in more than one building, and have given presentations and assignments and individual consultations and criticisms, you will feel that you have earned your pay. But I think you will also feel, as I do, that the rewards are more than worth the effort; and the largest part of the rewards consists of the appreciation, enthusiasm, and talented contributions of the young people who will be the writers of the future.

Again, to find out what the opportunities and requirements are where you live, contact the state arts council. If your state council is as helpful as the Ohio Arts Council, you will be provided with all the information you need. And if you fulfill the eligibility requirements, you too will discover a pleasant and rewarding alternative to the freelance game.

Other Financial Aids

In addition to giving financial aid to the various state arts councils, the Literature Program of the National Endowment for the Arts provides assistance to individual creative writers through fellowships and through support of writers' residencies. The Endowment is concerned with supporting the highest standards of quality and with aiding the development of new creativity in the writing field.

Applications will be considered twice a year and should be submitted at least seven months before the project is scheduled to start.

Complete information about the Endowment and its literature programs, including application forms, is contained in the Endowment's "Application Guidelines for Literature" available from the Information Office, National Endowment for the Arts, 2401 E St. NW, Washington DC 20506.

Many state arts councils also allot fellowship awards and grants to deserving writers of fiction, nonfiction, and poetry. The Ohio Arts Council provides fellowship awards of up to $9,000 and mini-grants of up to $1,000 to individual creative writers. These funds may be used to increase working time for planning and creating new works, to buy supplies or materials necessary to the production or completion of new work, to pay for services or rental of facilities relative to the completion of new work, to finance research related to writing, to meet expenses incurred in the presentation, performance, reproduction, documentation, or publication of work. Funds may also be used to aid in completing work already in progress.

If you are interested in this kind of funding and think you can qualify for it, call your state arts council to find out if such funds are available and to ask what you must do to apply for them. If your state council is like the Ohio council, you will be asked to submit fifteen pages of poetry, or no less than thirty nor more than fifty pages of prose, or no less than one full act of a play. In all cases you will be asked to include examples of your most recent work, or work which relates most closely to the grant application.

Other Employment Possibilities

Poets & Writers, Inc., 201 W. 54th St., New York NY 10019, has compiled a list of 606 national organizations that sponsor programs involving fiction writers and poets. This is an important reference for any writer who wishes to make his services available to organizations throughout the country. Write for it.

Another possible employment opportunity for writers, if it is not completely cut from the federal budget, is JTPA, the Job Training Partnership Act. This is a federally funded training program designed to serve persons who are economically disadvantaged, unemployed, or underemployed. Although writing is not specifically listed as one of the areas funded by JTPA, it is not necessarily excluded. JTPA provides several types of training courses, depending on need and demand. If no writing courses can be found through JTPA in your area, there may be other courses that are related to writing and which would be valuable to you in a writing career.

JTPA also offers several supportive services free to JTPA participants who are eligible for them. These services include day care for children, transportation, health care, job placement, assessment and counseling, and job orientation programs. Call your local JTPA office for details.

And the next time you find the editors are dealing you too many rejections, look around for variations on the freelance poker game. There is more than one way to win. Good luck to you!

Technical Writing

by Harold A. Holbrook

Among the less well-known but often more profitable writing jobs is that of the technical writer or editor. Those who work full-time earn $12,000 to $24,000 and up, and there are part-time freelance opportunities as well. There's a great dearth of competent writers in this field. The properly prepared beginner is quickly advanced, with little maneuvering on his own part, to positions of senior responsibility.

It is strange that so few who like to write, and who really can write, seek technical writing jobs. One reason, perhaps, is an innate incompatibility between the objectivity needed by a scientist and the imaginative, if not visionary, mental processes of the writer. Assume, for instance, that all scientists and all popular writers go to college. When they choose their courses, the scientist will concentrate on math, physics, and subjects in his prospective specialty. The writer will probably study language, composition, psychology, and similar subjects. Those who balance these interests are rare.

In life one can find many examples of this dichotomy. I have sought on many occasions to hire technical writers. I have written ads designed to entice competent applicants. Among those who have responded have been some reasonably successful writers, and many would-be writers. As a class, they offered many welcome qualifications—a general competence in exposition, pace, readability. But as a class, they exhibited a fatal flaw: They perceived only what they chose to see. They had read an ad, had seen that writers were wanted, but ignored the further requirement that the subject matter would be highly technical. Ask such a person what *sin x* means, and you'll often draw a blank or a bluff. Ask them how, then, they could write a technical dissertation, and they will answer to the effect that the engineer will tell them what to say. To an extent, this is true. It's not the tech writer's job to do research or to design equipment. His job is to report, explain, and often sell the results of the engineer's work, so the engineer obligingly (but not always lucidly) tells him what these results are. But if the writer cannot follow and comprehend what the engineer says, how can he possibly recast into effective prose the ideas presented by the engineer? If he must ask the engineer for every word that is to be written, the engineer is then the writer, and the "writer" is no more than an amanuensis.

Technical writing, then, has two basic requirements: not just an ability to write, but a comprehension of the subject. This comprehension cannot be acquired by osmosis. I've seen people work for years in the general field of technical writing who become familiar with the words used, as may a parrot, without ever understanding them. On the other hand, I've seen people enter a particular field of technical writing with no knowledge of the field itself yet with a grasp of the fundamentals sufficient to quite readily develop competence in it. One of the prime basics is math—not just arithmetic, but the concepts of rates, integrals, graphs, algebraic formulas, statistics and probability. With these basics, the engineer can communicate his methods and his proofs to the writer; without them he cannot. Likewise, physics is essential to most technical writing. Since Hiroshima, we have all become acquainted with Einstein's formula $E = mc^2$, but exactly what is energy? What is mass? What is field? A force? A moment? A couple? Many of these words have commonplace meanings. The dictionary is hopelessly inadequate as a source for understanding their respective technical meanings. And no engineer can explain his work to a writer who needs also an explanation of such fundamentals.

It is the very fact that both the ability to write and an extensive knowledge of basic science are required that makes technical writing so rewarding financially. Furthermore, writers can learn the necessary science as well as if not better than any other group in the population, and thereby improve the odds in favor of getting a tech writing job.

Three Types of Tech Writing Jobs

The major market for technical writing is with those companies that conduct research and/or produce devices ordered to fit the special needs of a particular customer. Such a company (General Motors, RCA, General Electric) has a sales organization that ferrets out the needs of prospective customers, or even suggests to such customers a need which the customer himself had not yet recognized. These companies handle a great many research and development (R&D) contracts for government agencies and other customers. Many manufacturers of parts (e.g., transformers, photocells, radar transmitter tubes) undertake development programs to supply the special needs of these and the many other companies that act as "prime contractors" responsible to their customers for complete systems (radar, radio-relay microwave links, satellites or their major subsystems, etc.).

With interest already existing, or aroused, the company prepares a *technical proposal*. This is no mere quotation of price. It is a dissertation sometimes greater in word count than *Gone with the Wind*. Many engineers, many writers, and much management to coordinate them are involved. The engineers consider all reasonable ways to attain the customer's objective, and choose the one that seems best under the restrictions (dollars and others) governing the customer's choice. The writer is not responsible for these technical concepts, or for the decision proposed. He is, however, almost solely responsible for the effectiveness with which his company's ideas are presented to the customer. It is his job to help his company win the contract regardless of competition, which can be stiff both in technical merit and in dollars. It is challenging. The stakes are often in the million-dollar range. Success under such circumstances provides a real glow of personal satisfaction, a sense of accomplishment.

With a contract won, the customer usually requires monthly or other *periodic reports* on the progress of work. These may also be the vehicle for discussing technical problems encountered and alternative actions that may be taken to solve them. The writing is technical, but it is laced with broader considerations. The writer should build as favorable an image for his company as the progress warrants. He must foster the customer's considerateness and confidence. It's a public relations job as well as a technical job.

The third category of technical writing is *handbook and instruction material* furnished with completed equipment. Too often, employers treat this work as a necessary evil, demanded by customers but of no interest to engineers and with little profit potentiality to the company. The rationale of such an employer is (1) that his own top brass will never perform maintenance, and so need not read such books; and (2) neither will the top brass of the customer. Since quality is not appraised by those who could most effectively control it, it may be permitted to slide abysmally. This means, simply, that the reluctant writers of handbooks are dubbed technical writers. Their status in an engineering organization is unenviable.

This need not be. If engineers don't want to write handbook material (they don't!), then there's a huge field for writers who can do a good job. Such writers must have practical, screwdriver type knowledge of how to check equipment and how to fix it when it fails. Think of the customer's employee who is assigned to use the equipment and make it work. He has never met the engineers who designed it; he may not be an engineer himself. Yet his job depends on making the equipment fulfill his employer's needs. He needs help. If he gets effective help in the handbook material, he can succeed. If he succeeds, his employer at least observes that no headaches are associated with the equipment. Then the image of the supplying company is enhanced, and further orders may ensue. Otherwise, the employee is frustrated by incomplete or inaccurate instructions. He fails, and sooner or later the supplying company loses the customer.

For companies manufacturing "off the shelf" technical products—home workshop tools, toys, air conditioners—the three aspects of technical writing merge into just two: catalog information and manuals enclosed with the equipment to help buyers use the product.

Pay Scales for Freelance Tech Writers

Those who seek temporary assignments can earn $15-$24 per hour, net to themselves. The most effective way to get such work is through a "body shop"—an agency that endeavors to keep a stable of writers (and other professionals). See Employment Contractors—Temporary Help in the Yellow Pages. Such employment is generally on a per-job basis, with end date estimated but not guaranteed. Advertising agencies, independent commercial artists, and others who serve industry generally cannot handle truly technical material in-house, so they do not seek such business. Sometimes, however, they have to accept such assignments from their clients; they are then prospects for a freelancer seeking an assignment.

Another Yellow Pages category to check for prospects is Technical Manual Preparation Service. While these are often primarily design services, they could be potential sources of tech-writing jobs as well. Some technical service firms are also listed under Engineers—Consulting.

If there aren't any immediately obvious prospects in your community, you may be able to learn of some in nearby cities by writing to *Contract*

Engineer, Box A, Kenmore WA 98028 Attn: Jan Erickson. This organization produces an annual directory of technical service firms and also offers a résumé-circulating service to its list.

Editor's Note: Less remunerative than technical writing, but still another opportunity for freelance income is the job of technical typist. Communities where civil, chemical, and electrical engineers or other scientists work, or teach at local universities, are a good bet. These people have papers to give at conventions or reports to present at meetings and often their secretarial staffs do not have time for these extra jobs. Also, you can provide the services at less cost than staff employees, since your employer doesn't have to pay your fringe benefits. Try placing classified ads in local and college newspapers and watch those same papers for help-wanteds from your prospective clients. As for per page rates to charge, check the "Manuscript Typists" advertising section of the latest issue of *Writer's Digest,* upping your price accordingly for papers and reports requiring special tables, charts, etc.

Translation Jobs

by Ted Morrow

For several years I answered the phone for a local translators association from my Philadelphia home/office. During that period of time I must have had hundreds of inquiries from would-be translators: "I'm just finishing a Spanish major at Coolidge College and am looking for a position as translator." I would start by explaining that there are very few "positions" of this kind, and that our association was not a business—just a loose alliance of local translators, mostly self-employed or part time. Usually I encouraged the inquirer to consider some sort of cover job that he could work at while breaking into the translation field, and I emphasized that even the best translators may have to serve a period of apprenticeship, during which they work for rather low rates for translation agencies until they have established a reputation that attracts higher-paying customers.

Probably 75 percent of these people became discouraged after such a conversation, and I never heard from them again. But I don't apologize for being realistic. Translation is perhaps the most poorly organized and least understood profession in the United States, and innumerable business people know how to exploit that fact, whether it's the agent who pays subsistence rates to highly educated immigrants or the executive who hires a "bilingual secretary" to muddle through his foreign correspondence. And those who do hire the professional prefer the freelance relationship—and to pay by the word rather than by the hour.

What Is a Translator?

As I see it, the present-day translator (and I realize this will change over the next generation) is a special breed. First of all, you have to have an innate love for the intricacies of language, syntax, and communication. If you don't thoroughly enjoy the work, you'll never survive long enough to succeed. I can't say that *circumstances* were all that favorable to my becoming a translator: I'm a just plain WASP with no ethnic background to use as a springboard. The only language I took in high school was Latin, and I found it rather boring at that. Furthermore, I was almost forty before I ever heard of professional translating. But for about ten years now I've been turning out hundreds of written translations from sixteen languages into English, and for much of that time it was the sole means of support for a family of six.

How did I attain the necessary degree of proficiency? Most of the bread-and-butter work in a given language involves everyday words and expressions—plus technical words that are often of an international nature, borrowed or coined from Latin, Greek, or even English. While I love to read great literature, because of the aesthetic pleasure it gives me, I find that more pedestrian publications—newspapers, dime novels, school textbooks, technical journals, crossword puzzles—usually make more useful background reading for my profession. And if you share my conservative Christian background, you'll find foreign Bibles (which can be obtained at reasonable rates from the American Bible Society) are also a great help in getting the feel of the idiom and structure of a given language. Some colleges and universities are beginning to set up translator-training curricula, but this seems to be in the embryo stage so far. There's still plenty of room for the self-taught translator.

A lot of people in America understand the English language well enough to get along. It's the rare person who knows how to use the written word with power and clarity. Likewise, there are many bilingual and polylingual immigrants in this country. But although they may have learned enough language skills to function in society, just about the same percentage of these people will actually know how to write effectively. It is perhaps no accident that I was a freelance writer and that I spent more than a decade working in a publishing house before I tried my wings with commercial translation. You must be able to express yourself in your native language a lot better than the average American if you want to translate.

On one occasion I was asked by a good customer to translate some scientific paper from a Slavic language. It wasn't my best language, and I had plenty of other work to do at the time, so I tried the old referral ploy: "How about So-and-So? He's a native of that country and knows the language better than I do." "Maybe so. But you can write English, and, let's face it, your friend's *English* needs to be translated! I'd rather hire you even if I had to pay you twice as much!" It may have been crass flattery, but it helped me understand a principle, and I did the job!

To Specialize or to Diversify?

Obviously you can't be too narrow as to subject matter if you want to make it full time as a translator. Several years ago a younger colleague announced that he was not going to translate anything but Russian nuclear physics. "Let the hacks take anything that comes. I'm going to be a specialist!" But eventually his work source dried up, and my friend had to decide whether to sell Fuller Brushes or branch out into Russian medicine, pharmacology, biochemistry, and what have you. With *language* diversification it's a little tougher to decide. Although it takes me longer to translate Turkish or Finnish, and thus is less profitable per se, I could cite at least a dozen cases where my willingness to handle one of the more exotic languages has landed me a grateful customer who has rewarded me with a heavy volume of steady work in the more common European idioms where I make my real money. Usually the client has looked high and low for the rare language technician who can do his Azerbaijani or Estonian. With a sigh of relief he gives the "dilettante" a chance, and if he is impressed by the quality of the translation, he thinks to himself, "I wonder how this guy handles French?" And I have my foot in the door. There are also advantages of another kind in being a polyglot. Languages borrow from each other, and more than once I have recognized a strange-looking word in German or even Turkish that turned out to be French in disguise, for example. Knowing several languages also helps to even out the flow of assignments, since work in any given language has peaks and troughs. And I find it keeps my inquisitive mind limber to stretch from time to time, never letting myself get too complacent about present linguistic achievements.

Of course, some of my colleagues will argue just as eloquently the advantage of knowing one or two languages in a greater depth than I, with my wider frontier to maintain, can possibly reach. It's possible to work faster, for one thing, which has its economic advantages. If you feel more comfortable with this approach, then keep in mind that your language of specialty should be one in which there is heavy traffic, if you want to make a living at it. For scientific and technical work, the languages offering the most work, in descending order, would seem to be these: Russian, German, French, Japanese, Italian, Spanish. If you're courting the commercial-correspondence market, Spanish, French, and Portuguese will have increased importance.

Categories of Translation Clients

Some fields of human endeavor seem to generate more than their share of translation activity. Drug companies, for instance, have to provide evidence to the FDA that they have done their international homework when a new drug is to be marketed. This can mean whole filing cabinets full of translated research materials for just one product. Patent attorneys working in the international arena have a deep appreciation for the professional translator. The patent system works on the basis of an international treaty that requires the inventor to apply separately to each country—even though, once secured, the patent becomes retroactive to the date of application in the inventor's home country. At each stage of this process the patent attorney will have to minutely examine a few foreign patents that may just contain the patented idea. Patent litigation can also be a source of translation work.

The multinationals produce quite a bit of international correspondence, minutes, and financial reports from their subsidiaries, customer complaints, etc. Periodicals like *Atlas World Press Review* need a steady flow of translated manuscripts for their readership, and they also commission translators to monitor the foreign press for the kind of material they wish to publish. Government agencies such as the National Institutes of Health and the Environmental Protection Agency sponsor massive research projects on such subjects as air pollution, cancer research, and the environmental effects of pesticides. During the course of one year (1979) a Philadelphia firm retrieved and translated several thousand articles on pesticides as part of a contract with EPA. Translators were recruited from many parts of the country for this project. An increasingly important subject in the eighties will be energy research. Alternative sources, conservation, legislation, and various public projects such as rehabilitation of public transportation—foreign publications that address these issues will need to be translated.

The largest single employer of freelance translators is a government agency known as the Joint Publications Research Service, located in Arlington, Virginia, and operated by the Central Intelligence Agency (although it handles more than CIA work). Also keep in mind that a large percentage of CIA work is not the cloak-and-dagger variety. For instance, they have quite a number of foreign newspaper articles translated for news analysis.

Wealthy families also maintain offices for keeping track of foreign correspondence that might contain threats of kidnapping, etc., as well as tips on opportunities to engage in new humanitarian projects with their tax-shelter funds.

The Role of the Agency

When the American translation industry expanded significantly in the early sixties, the translation agency became an important phenomenon. A number of translators began attracting more business than they could handle, so they began subcontracting under pressure. There were also nonlinguistic entrepreneurs who perceived the commercial possibilities of matching up a circle of customers with a circle of translators and keeping the two happily interlocked. Other services of the translation agency include bidding on government contracts, processing translations to make them conform with customers' specifications, and generally giving counsel to the translator.

Translation agencies are always looking for the novice translator who is willing to work at a lower rate of pay, so if you don't have a reputation yet, this can be a valuable stepping-stone. But try to connect with an agency that provides you with some feedback so that you can upgrade your work. Even old-timers may not be completely independent of the agency. A good translator often has no time to engage in marketing activities, and if business is slow with his direct contacts, he'll probably call up a couple of agents and ask what's doing. Look in the Yellow Pages and you'll find them under Translations and Translators. The Philadelphia directory, for instance, has a number of listings of out-of-town agencies in addition to the local ones. It helps to live in a big city and along the East Coast, but even if you're in Appalachia it isn't hopeless, since a large amount of translating jobs go through the mail anyway. One of my most successful colleagues lives in a rural area of New York State, another in the Upper Peninsula of Michigan. There are also professional organizations to assist the translator. At the national level there is the American Translators Association, Box 129, Croton-on-Hudson NY 10520. There are also numerous local associations, which I find especially helpful, since they maintain more face-to-face relationships than the bigger groups. And not all are clustered along the Atlantic seaboard, either. There are quite vigorous organizations in places like Pittsburgh, Kansas City, and Houston.

Once you've gained a little experience, consider getting yourself listed in the Yellow Pages, and placing an ad in the nearest big-city daily. (And of course keep your eye on the help-wanted ads there, too.) My favorite way of advertising is to prepare an actual translation in a specific field—chemistry, say—then mail copies of it to chemical companies. After a while, your reputation will spread by word of mouth.

Translation Pay Rates

There are many factors that influence the rate of pay for translation work: language, subject, length of job, type of customer, and the presentation of the work. Government projects are notorious for low remuneration, but sometimes the high volume makes them worthwhile. A translation can be camera-ready copy or just a neatly typed final draft. It can also be a rough draft that the customer will reprocess, or even a cassette tape that the customer will transcribe. If you hire a transcription typist, figure on the typing bill being about 20 percent of what you receive from your customer. You may not want to dictate until you have acquired sufficient speed to make it pay.

With the above reservations, let me suggest to you some going rates for a final draft to a commercial customer in one of the more common European languages: somewhere between 5 and 10 cents per English word, the actual amount depending on the customer involved. Government work may bring you only 2.2 to 7.5 cents per word. A translation agency will extract a middleman's fee, usually amount to about a third of what he collects from the ultimate customer, although this can vary according to the amount of processing he does to the job. One friend of mine, who works for an exclusive clientele in five languages, is an unusually meticulous artisan, and has freelanced for over twenty years, is currently making 10 to 12 cents per word. But I don't advise a beginner to ask that kind of price.

The translator has to be not only a scholar and an artist but also a businessman, given the present state of affairs. But look at it this way: It's a great American frontier, so if you're the pioneer type, enjoy it while you can.

Editor's Note: Translations of literary works by US publishers come about in several ways. A foreign publisher working through an American agent may contact a US publisher. An American publisher may see a promising book at the Frankfurt Book Fair and buy the rights. An American writer with proficiency in another language may approach a US publisher with some sample chapters of a literary work. In each case the services of a literary translator are required. The rates he'll get depend on his status. An absolute minimum suggested by the P.E.N. American Center, an international organization of writers, is forty dollars per thousand words, and the average seems to be forty to sixty.

TV Documentaries

by Joseph Hanania

In 1971, the Federal Communications Commission passed a law requiring each television station to set aside at least a half hour a day to non-network programming, and a certain percentage of that, often a half hour a week, to public service programming. Many of the local stations and affiliates have fulfilled this requirement by programming talk shows, which are relatively easy to produce, can be turned out in endless succession by a relatively small group of station staffers, and do not entail any great overhead. A few stations, on the other hand—their imaginations fired by the prestige and success of "60 Minutes"—have stepped up their production of more expensive locally made documentaries. In choosing to do so, not only have they opted in favor of spending more money to improve the quality of local programming, they have also provided the freelance journalist an effective door for entering television. How so?

Television producers, film editors, cameramen, and sound men basically specialize in how to put a piece of film together. The "Six O'Clock News" reporter, who may cover three or four stories per show, rarely has time to *investigate* a story. In fact, almost the only person who has both the necessary skills and the time to dig out facts that official sources would rather not reveal is the freelance journalist.

Thus it is no coincidence that in Philadelphia, my hometown, John Guinther, one of the city's leading freelance political writers, is also one of the city's leading freelance documentary researchers. So impressively has Guinther established his credentials through a string of investigative magazine articles, in fact, that not only did Philadelphia station WCAU-TV contact him initially with a documentary proposal they wanted him to research, but several months after the piece had aired, the station requested him to research a second piece for them—at a substantially higher rate. Similarly, Ann Jarmusch, a leading Philadelphia freelance art writer, broke into TV by compiling, at the station's request, a calendar of art events scheduled around the city. After she handed in the calendar, the station asked her to research material for a one-hour special on art in Philadelphia.

Not entirely surprisingly, the station's previous experiences with the two freelancers above made it that much more receptive to my own application. Which is not to say that I had an easy time getting in. Not at all.

The Right Treatment

As an established freelance writer with major Philadelphia publications, it still took me three years of phone calls, query letters, personal interviews, and proposals galore before I finally got the go-ahead from the executive producer to *outline* a *possible* documentary project. Even that go-ahead came primarily because a government agency was sponsoring a conference on drinking-water safety, one of my areas of specialization, and the documentary unit had nobody else to send. It also helped that one of my phone calls came a day before the conference was to start.

It would take another two months of phone calls, coaxing, and cajoling before my proposed outline was approved and I was assigned to research my half-hour documentary. Another two months elapsed before we finally started filming, and the film lay in the can another month before being edited.

If you're getting the impression that even after selling my outline, I spent more effort trying to get the ball rolling than I did researching and helping produce the documentary, you're right. In all, researching and getting the documentary together would take a total of about two months; the intervals between each stage, though, totaled five months.

Unfortunately, getting a television station to give the green light for a documentary treatment after a producer has seen an initial proposal is no guarantee that the documentary will be made—even though the station has purchased your work. And even if the piece is filmed, there is no guarantee that it will be edited, a substantially more complex task than having a magazine article edited. Guinther's second documentary, for instance, never made it through the editing stage. Thus in TV, more so than in magazine writing, keeping the fires going under a project is as important a concern for the freelancer as is the actual research and writing that goes into a treatment.

Note that I do not use the word "script" here. For TV documentary writing, you first draft a proposal. When a producer has given the go-ahead, you write a "treatment"—which, for a half-hour documentary, is a fifteen- or twenty-page expansion of the proposal that blocks out the documentary as you envision it. You have done your research, conducted your interviews, and you know how this is all going to mesh before the camera. The treatment informs the producer what your interviewees are going to say, how they are going to say it, where they will be saying it, and what connecting footage you envision that will have to be covered with shots on one location or another; and it indicates where a narrator may use voice-over for necessary background information or as a transitional device to move from one point to another in your documentary.

This is done in a proselike manner and does not resemble a TV script for, say, a sitcom show. In fact, the only script that a documentary might have is a transcript—put together after the film has been researched, shot, edited, and aired. But I am getting ahead of myself.

Pitfalls and Producers

In trying to get a documentary started, and keeping it on track, the freelance journalist should avoid a couple of pitfalls along the way. Unfortunately, they are not easy to recognize at first and might even seem to be virtues.

Pitfall #1: Trying to impress the producer by giving him more information than he wants.

Unlike magazine writing, in which the length of an article is usually determined by its content, television has fixed time limitations, and the same phalanx of facts which would so impress a magazine editor becomes a smokescreen to the producers, obscuring the central core of the documentary.

I learned this lesson after discussing my first documentary proposals three years ago with a producer at another station. Having gotten the go-ahead for a written outline, I got so carried away with the possibility of having a piece on the air that, instead of turning in the usual five-page sketch, I turned in some thirty pages, every three or four pages outlining still another aspect of the same subject (which was how sports heroes viewed themselves). I envisioned the producer saying "Joe, this is ter-rific! How about if we start off by taking just two of these segments, and flesh them out? Then we'll produce a sequel from another two segments. The way you've presented this proposal, we might even do a *series* on the subject!"

Actually, I didn't hear from my producer for weeks. When I finally got him on the phone, he said: "The material is good, but my readers think your proposal has got too much in it for a single documentary. I'm afraid we just don't see any way to use it."

By the time proper communication had been reestablished, with our documentary more narrowly focused and our list of interviewees firmed up, the production company's New York headquarters had issued new orders as to just what its affiliates were allowed to do. Unfortunately, one of the things affiliates were no longer allowed to do was to produce an investigative sports documentary such as mine. The lesson: Give a producer only a narrowly focused, in-depth outline. Let him propose whatever alternatives he also wishes to pursue. Remember, you are not selling the field; you are selling a single, easily definable concept.

Pitfall #2: Don't believe even the most well-meaning producer's promises of tomorrow.

Television is an ever-fluctuating medium, where today's hotshot producer may be odd man out tomorrow. So when you finally get a producer to buy an idea, push to have it written and filmed *now*. I learned this after "selling" a documentary proposal to a producer, only to have him explain to me that, since the station was about to start summer reruns and he was thinking of taking a few weeks off anyhow, how about if we postponed moving on it until September? I wanted to take a vacation myself, and agreed. When I called the producer in September, he was clearing his desk and looking for a new job.

There is, I learned, little that a freelance journalist can do to protect himself in the ever-shifting landscape that is television. CBS's policy of drafting a written agreement of just what a freelancer is to research, when, and for how much money, is the closest thing to a safeguard a freelancer can get—but even this only ensures that he will get paid for his work and gives him no indication of how, when, or even whether his creation will ever be used.

Thus, last fall, within a few days after the station had expressed interest, I handed in a narrowly defined proposal for a documentary on sludge and drinking water. When I subsequently got the green light, I pushed to write the treatment and to start filming the piece *now*. Now happened to be amid a midwinter blizzard. "A lot of your treatment calls for outdoor shooting," my producer said. "We ought to wait until spring, when the snow melts."

"They're expecting a warm front next week," I countered.

The next week, my producer got promoted, and the new producer who inherited the project decided to go ahead. The day we started filming, Philadelphians were skiing through downtown streets, most office buildings were closed, and traffic crawled when it moved at all. But there we were, toting cameras and sound recorders over six-foot snow mounds, leaving our car parked five feet from the curb because huge snowdrifts had pre-empted the regular spaces, climbing aboard a boat to sail among ice floes, each of which looked like it would sink the ship.

Sounds crazy, no? Any sensible person would have waited until spring, right?

Wrong. While the documentary was still in the film editing stage, the producer I had started the project with accepted an offer to go to Hollywood. Two months later, his successor followed suit. Had we waited for the proper weather, the documentary might never have made it past the treatment stage.

Interviewing Tactics

The treatment itself, which took no more work to research and write than would a magazine article, included suggested sites for shooting particular scenes. (Black-and-white photos of the sites accompanied the suggestions.) To allow for commercials, the treatment was divided into four segments.

There are, however, a lot of differences between writing a magazine article and writing a documentary.

For one, at most affiliates there is no such thing as a documentary "writer." Instead, there is the researcher and there is the producer.

The researcher mostly worries about the facts and suggests the form in which they are to be presented. The producer is responsible for the final product, and concerns himself with whether the text fits in with the visuals, whether there are too many "talking heads" (straight interviews, which are considered visually boring), and how many seconds to give each part of the text.

Together the researcher and producer write the documentary, and pray that the "talent" (narrator) will read the script as it is written. As such, the freelancer has substantially less say over his material than he would in a magazine piece. There are no galleys to proofread; any change a researcher might want to make after the producer has coordinated the text and film must be able to fit into the number of available seconds and go along with available footage. Unlike magazine writing, in which an editor edits an already written piece, writing and producing a documentary is a team effort in which the freelancer has sold his research, not a finished text over which he retains final control. There are other writing problems as well.

While doing preliminary research on my documentary, I often obtained good quotes—which could be used for impact in a magazine article at once. But when you are working toward a filmed or taped version, the problem is to get the same sources to say the same impactful things on camera.

Consider how we were unable to use a good interview I had with a former director of the Environmental Protection Agency, because his answers did not make enough sense without the accompanying questions.

Me: In Philadelphia, would the water department actually know what's in the water coming out of our tap before it actually comes out?
EPA official: To some extent. They would probably be able to tell you some things about it. They would not be able to tell you, I rather suspect, a lot about it. Some basic substances, they can analyze for . . . As to whether it may be high, or relatively high, in some dangerous chemical that they may not be able to analyze for, they probably couldn't tell you that at this point.
Me: Then we may well be drinking water that is high in dangerous chemicals, and the water department is not aware of it?
EPA official: It is possible, yes. But, I think, this is also so in every other water department in this country, because analytical techniques do not exist that this water department, or the New York water department, or Pittsburgh's, can use.

We eventually got around the problem here by asking the official to restate his opinion on his own.

Finally, bringing a story together on film is also different from polishing up a story on paper. Whereas in a magazine article you can, for example, tighten quotes and string them together in such a way as to build interest and drive home the point with concision, on film you cannot move around sentences or paragraphs spoken by a long-winded interviewee, or take out the dull or obvious or irrelevant asides without visual risk. There are no ellipses on a camera that is rolling as a subject speaks. It is the researcher's job here to talk with the interviewee in advance off camera; to review with him the points raised in previous interviews when the researcher was initially investigating the topic; and to tell him that brevity and to-the-point replies are necessary for the camera, where any single shot beyond thirty or forty seconds becomes tedious for the viewer (not to mention the producer!).

Fees paid for this sort of undertaking vary from city to city. I was paid $250 for my five-page proposal outline and another $750 for my twenty-page treatment.

All of the craziness involved in making the documentary, however, finally came together and made sense for me the night the piece aired. There was the narrator, standing by the water, saying essentially what we wanted him to say. There were the officials, fudging and futzing around a bit, perhaps, but essentially saying on camera what they had said off camera. And there were the visuals driving home the points in the text, drawing the viewer in and making him almost taste the water. It was like a three-dimensional magazine article.

And, if the credit line was ephemeral, still, I got as big a charge out of seeing my name on screen for the first time as I did the first time I saw it in print.

TV Editorials

by Cookie McGee

Do any (or all) of the TV stations in your area have a station manager—or some uncomfortable equivalent—who winces into the camera and delivers editorials? If so, you might be able to put words in his mouth a few times a week—perhaps even daily. That's what I do. I'm a freelance editorialist.

When WPTF-TV in Durham, North Carolina, came under new management a few television seasons back, I sent samples of my published writing along with a note requesting an interview with the station manager. In our subsequent meeting, we talked about business, politics, religion, and media philosophies. "We are not ready to air editorials five days a week," he said. "Each one takes two hours to film, and we don't want to get stuck with something we'll have to continue until we know we can do quality work every day. But I'll look at your stuff."

Now I knew he needed my services. Posthaste I mailed nine sample editorials to him on a variety of timeless topics (fast-breaking subjects are reserved for on-site writers). He bought what he wanted—and he wanted more. (I received $35 for each editorial after it was aired—a price that pained him considerably, but which was considerably less than what it would cost for him or an assistant to do likewise.)

No special qualifications are necessary for this job, but a modicum of political savvy and an ability to write tightly on long-winded topics of the day will help.

Editorials should be kept under two minutes in reading length; the ones I write are one minute and forty-five seconds, or 250 to 300 words typed double-spaced on a single legal-size sheet.

For ideas I check with the station manager on local "must" topics, and I read *Dun's Review, Esquire, Time, Newsweek,* and the local paper. The latter, I find, occasionally presents a poorly thought-out position against which a TV editorial can react. But in general, competition with the local press is a stance that TV stations prefer to minimize.

I dictate my first draft into a cassette recorder, creating a conversational flavor that I then try to capture on paper. I speak simply, with one well-honed point in mind. Television editorials do not lend themselves to complicated concepts. Then I listen to the tape, type out a draft, and tighten to 1:45—by purging homonyms, by sidestepping sibilants, by deleting tongue twisters. Then I reread it aloud and add drama!!! or *emphasis* or pregnant . . . pauses to stage the delivery for on-camera effect.

Here are a few of my TV editorials to give you an idea of what one station bought.

On Diversified Farming

The last five years has seen big changes in economic fundamentals. The reduction in the military budget threw many in the technological trades out of work; the fuel crisis produced across-the-board inflation and made expansion, especially in construction areas, unattractive. In turn we see a lowered rate of national growth. All this demonstrates that we will need to change our lifestyles and possibly our jobs.

One of the groups of people that may not have thought about this is the farmer. American farmers are the best in the world, feeding four . . . five . . . even ten times the number of people their counterparts do elsewhere. But the fact remains that they too must be ready to adapt. It may be a status symbol in Kansas to be a big wheat farmer, or maybe even a little wheat farmer, but when you are reduced to dumping your grain in the middle of the town square it's time to rethink. There's no profit from dumped wheat and no status, either.

The same thing can be said of tobacco. While wheat farmers consider growing tobacco, maybe tobacco farmers can consider growing wheat . . . or lettuce, or carrots, or whatever. As it is, our economy would be considerably helped if we could realize more diversified farming within smaller geographical areas. The cost of fuel to transport prepared and raw foodstuffs is high as it is; but when gasoline costs a dollar per gallon, we in North Carolina aren't going to want to ship in foods grown elsewhere when we could be doing it here.

When we develop a broader agricultural base, our farmers and our consumers are all going to be happier, healthier, and richer for it.

On Welfare Reform

It is with a sigh of relief that we learn that the so-called welfare reform bill has bitten the dust. The bill's official title was "Better Jobs and Income Act," but no real lasting jobs were involved. Once again the scheme was to require work from able-bodied recipients and then create a government job for them to fill.

This is no solution. Already one out of five people works for the government. The job-creation programs would have put millions to work in nonskilled toil, such as highway tree-planting, where no skills are required or ever learned.

These temporary jobs, ranging in length from eighteen months to two years, would offer the laborer no way to make the transition from public dole to private enterprise. There was no vacation pay, no Medicaid, no workman's compensation, and no competitive standards to meet. In other words, nothing that makes the job real employment to begin with. Just more "emperor's new clothes" while increasing the number of public employees by $2^{1}/_{2}$ million.

Although demagogues have tried to make voters believe otherwise, government has no power to create jobs. Profit is the *only* source of truly new employment; government spends money made by others, other people's profits. The creation of jobs is like buying stock on credit; it produces a false economy undergirded by paper money, leading first to inflation and then to depression.

We at WRDU suggest tax credits for private business and industry to provide real jobs with actual opportunity, both in the long and short run. Business needs all the encouragement it can get.

On the Sheriff

You may not be noticing it right now, but you will later on. This is an election year ... and many eyes will be focused on the state-wide senatorial race or the general assembly races.

We would like to say something about the office of sheriff. Few people realize just how powerful a sheriff really is compared to other law-enforcement people. In fact, in terms of our daily living, all county officials exert, and will increasingly exert, a greater influence over our lives if current trends continue. It has been our experience anyway that those people with the least media visibility are the ones who can pack the biggest personal punch in terms of tangible influence ... for good or ill.

The history of the office of sheriff is not a happy one. It began in England, when the landed gentry hired henchmen to guard their properties. The "shire-reeves," as they were called, were a bloody lot. The story of Robin Hood may be fiction, but the personality-type of the Sheriff of Nottingham was all too true.

In more recent years, with the rise of big-city professional police forces, apprehensions about the sheriff have waned, but the potential power in this office has diminished not at all.

We have no endorsement for this race of sheriff in any of the counties our TV station covers. We simply tell you all this in hopes that you will take this race every bit as seriously as you do the others.

TV News and Features

by Dave Derkacy

Writers with cameras will be delighted to learn that they can film action stories of careening cars and roadblocks, and curvaceous blondes in bikinis; possibly wind up in a boat, plane, helicopter, or car filming fast-breaking stories; and earn substantial sums doing it. The method: freelance news and feature stringing for local TV markets.

Most television news departments simply do not have enough personnel to film all the stories they need. These stories are usually divided into two categories: *hard news* (fires, accidents, riots—headline-type events) and *feature news* (concerts, fund drives, personality profiles, festivals—essentially undated news stories). The latter area is where they can use a stringer's services.

Breaking In

Gaining entrée to the field of TV stringing is not that difficult. Present yourself to the news director or assignment editor at a station in a medium-size metropolitan area with the idea that you would like to shoot film for them on a freelance basis.

Most of the prospects for successful news stringing exist with medium metro-area stations (those that reach a population of 100,000 to 1 million). But don't fret if you're located in an out-of-the-way place. This may actually be an advantage, since there will be less competition. Small towns of 50,000 to 100,000 and college towns near large cities are untapped reservoirs of features and news items.

Breaking into the field requires a minimum investment. As it is best to bring in some sample stories suitable for the station's usual news coverage, you will have to buy a roll of film and process it (about twenty dollars), using a borrowed or rented camera. You might film a human-interest feature, a sporting event, or a news story, all of which should demonstrate your capabilities. If the film shows promise, the news director will offer suggestions for improvement and give you a couple of rolls of film to try out on further sample stories.

A stringer submits freelance material to TV stations on speculation, much as writers send out manuscripts to editors. Payment is per story used *on the air,* unless the station assigns a story and later changes its mind about using it — in which case you are usually reimbursed for your effort. This type of work requires exceptional writing, filming, and editing skills to distill the crucial information about a dramatic event or interesting person into an average of sixty seconds. The key to success in this field is selling your ideas to a station news director, then shooting good film that sells itself.

You won't have to do much selling if you happen to get exclusive footage of a disaster such as a flood, plane crash, or hurricane. If you are the only photographer on the scene, call the network directly and ask for the assignment editor. Tell him what you have and ask if he is interested. You may be asked to deliver the film to the nearest network affiliate. Be sure to negotiate for a price before delivery.

What You Need Besides the Filmed Feature

Whether you sell to a network or a local station, you will need to prepare an identification list, a shot list, and a chronological story line, to be sent to the assignment editor in a single package. An ID list includes the names of people shown in close-ups who contribute to the story. A shot list looks like this (LS = long shot; MS = medium shot; CU = close-up; EXCU = extra-close-up):

1. General coverage	LS crowd milling about, overturned cars, police on scene
2. MS	Police car and people interacting with officers
3. CU	Officers arguing with protester [don't forget names]
4. CU	Protester
5. EXCU	Night stick
6. Cutaway	Anxious crowd watching the action

7. MS	Cop and protester still arguing
8. MS	Other officers arriving
9. LS	Crowd starting to disperse
10. MS	Protester being arrested
11. CU	Protester
12. LS	Re-establish the scene: crowd, police cars, etc.

The assignment editor also needs accurate facts, dates, places, and circumstances. Don't try to write the story in on-the-air lingo. It will usually be rewritten to suit the on-air personality and/or accompanying visuals. Feature material, however, is more flexible, and the editor may be receptive to your polished prose if it is well integrated to the visual story line. Type your copy double-spaced, and be sure to follow the chronology of the film.

Still photographs are sometimes used on television, but only if they are of unusual events and coverage is exclusive. Smaller stations with low budgets may use more still photos of strong local appeal. In most cases they are ID shots of public officials or others in the news limelight.

Tips for Professional Filming

If your pictures are to appear on TV, they must look professional. Happily, a person familiar with still-picture techniques already understands the basic principles of good movies. Both still and movie cameras are operated in the same manner by setting the focus, f-stop, and shutter speed. Additional skills of camera movement and subject sequences can be acquired with a reasonable amount of practice.

One mark of the amateur photographer is his inability to hold a camera in one position; he is usually panning, trucking, dollying, zooming, or shooting a succession of short quick shots. A professional TV stringer will hold the camera *steady,* provide ample *establishing* shots, and use shots of varying duration. The professional pans sparingly—only to follow action, or to establish a relationship (such as that between a wrecked auto and a stop sign). Pros also avoid shooting a subject in front of an open door or window; the bright light drives the video machine into a frenzy. And remember, filming is basically the same as shooting still pictures: exposure, focus, composition. Let the subject do the acting, not the camera. Think in story and sequence terms, not in a series of unrelated shots.

Getting Ready

Your initial equipment is not likely to cost more than the outlay for

35mm still equipment. Basically, you need a 16mm film camera, preferably one with through-the-lens focusing and the ability to accept various focal-length lenses. Such additions as variable frames per second, automatic f-stop control, variable shutter speeds, and electric drives are nice to have but expensive to acquire. More important than these frills is a zoom lens for sports action, since it's important to show wide views of plays as well as close-ups of individuals—and there is little time for changing or racking lenses.

For starters, a set of three fixed focal length lenses should serve nicely for general use: a 16mm wide-angle, a 25mm normal, and a 50mm mild telephoto lens. A good beginning outfit will cost around four or five hundred dollars, used. Such equipment can be located through ads in film magazines or the used-equipment section of camera stores.

I began with an outfit purchased through an ad in the paper. I got a vintage 1930 Bolex, three lenses, a 16mm film editor, and eight rolls of black-and-white film for two hundred dollars. It wasn't long before I was making fifteen to twenty dollars per film clip by stringing for an Indianapolis TV station. The camera has paid for itself many times, and I've used the extra income to shoot experimental short films.

One stringer I know began with a Kodak Cine Special and only a 25mm normal lens (total cost: seventy-five dollars). He had to use a great deal of imagination with such limited equipment, but found he could move backward for a wide-angle effect and forward for a telephoto effect.

Other equipment needed includes a light meter—a must—and possibly a tripod. Any cadmium-sulfide meter (the ones with batteries), such as Luna-Pro or Sekonic, should suffice, especially in poorly lit areas. Although a tripod is awkward in fast-breaking news, it has its uses in sports coverage from high up in the press box. You will also need to know your movie camera's shutter speed, which a competent camera repair service can determine if the instruction manual doesn't provide the information. Use this shutter speed as a fixed point of reference. On the Bolex it is 1/80, so after taking the meter reading, you merely match the f-stop to that shutter speed. With a movie camera you need only focus, set the f-stop, and begin shooting.

You will also need film. Most TV stations now use VNF (video news film), and all stations will furnish it or another type and tell you how to use it, once you are established as a stringer for them.

Getting the Story

What kinds of stories can be filmed with this equipment? A bluegrass music festival, an all-star football game, a Ku Klux Klan arrest, a Soap Box Derby, an NCAA swim meet—the range is limitless. And there's the occasional assignment that's a dream come true. A station fifty miles distant once phoned me to see if I'd like to cover a story on the *Playboy* photographer who was shooting pictures of campus beauties for a feature on the girls of the Big Ten. Would I? I hurriedly got my gear together, arrived on time with camera in hand—and *they* were impressed! I got the story, along with a nice check for the footage.

News stories may also cause you to be awakened at 5 a.m. to cover an apartment complex explosion, only to discover that you have to wait for it to become light enough for you to shoot!

One way way to overcome the darkness is with portable movie lights. These range in price from $100 to $400 and are well worth it, as they could increase your story coverage in dim-light situations (offices, jails, twilight). Typical units are the Frezzi, the Cine-60, and the Smith-Victor. Movie equipment of this type is available from Com-Quip, 630 Ninth Ave., New York NY 10036. Ask for their Cine-Shopper catalog.

Another method is to use the natural light of the fire as a light source. Shoot wide open and silhouette the firemen and people scurrying about against the background of the flames. Try a reverse angle and use the fire as a main light to capture close-ups of faces and equipment. Or use the light from the fire truck spotlights as they are focused on men climbing ladders or chopping holes in roofs.

Techniques That Sell

Fortunately, most stories have a formulalike format, beginning with an establishing shot. This is usually a wide-angle shot that shows locale, people, or surroundings. Its purpose is to visually orient the viewer; it generally lasts from six to ten seconds.

Next, move in close to show the details of the scene, or film the scene from different angles for variety. Close-ups of people, small objects, and signs give the viewer a sense of being there—they're like adjectives in writing. These shots may last from three to seven seconds apiece.

After the opener, details, and relationships, the final shot reorients the viewer to the beginning and completes the cycle. If there is action, pan with it, but avoid panning and zooming for effect.

Buddy McAtee, a former stringer for WRTV-6 News in Indianapolis, who later became a staff photographer, strongly advises a stringer to "build sequences that help tell the story, because the longer the story is on the air the more you will be paid." Stations pay either by footage used or by seconds on the air: ten dollars for thirty seconds, fifteen dollars for sixty seconds, twenty dollars for sixty-plus seconds is not uncommon. Thus, striving for better news reports adds directly to your income.

For example, suppose you are asked to cover an art fair. Instead of shooting general shots of milling crowds, you would do better to concentrate on, say, one particular craftsman and an interesting customer—in this case, a cute nine-year-old girl. The shooting might look like this:

Shot	Seconds	Action
LS	:06	wide angle of several craftspeople practicing their skills, and the passing crowd
MS	:03	a silversmith
MS	:03	a young girl approaches
CU	:04	skilled hands making a pair of earrings
CU	:03	girl's look of anticipation
CU	:03	artist's face
MS	:05	girl and artist
CU	:05	montage of several other types of jewelry made by the artist
MS	:02	another angle of girl and artist
CU	:02	artist's hands
MS	:04	he presents her with earrings
LS	:05	re-establishes the fair
Total	:45	

Now you have a sequenced story that an editor would be reluctant to cut, thereby adding more income for your effort. (It is advisable to hold all shots at *least* three seconds so the editor has *some* leeway with your material.)

Buddy McAtee also suggests studying local news shows and the way that staff photographers approach their stories. Thus you can lock in to the personality of the station you intend to approach with your freelance proposal. But knowing how to capture a story on film is only half the freelancer's work. The other half is digging up stories and selling them to a station news director, who may be tough to convince.

Stories That Sell

Again, McAtee has helpful advice: "You really have to sell the station on your story idea. It's a real hustle, but you have to sell your product." McAtee is not easily discouraged. He once called to see if a station wanted coverage of a football game. Told they were getting the videotape from another station, he asked "Why not use some isolation coverage, say profiles of particular players as they run, pass, or block? It would be good for a sports highlight piece on different players." The station liked the idea—and bought it.

Because local sports schedules are often heavy, few stations can cover all the games all the time. This is a gap the freelancer can drive his camera through. Nearly half of Buddy McAtee's freelance sales were on sports topics. Therefore, it would benefit a stringer to brush up on football, indoor track, tennis, handball, soccer, and other athletic endeavors that can turn into a fast sale. We are a sports-minded nation, and most station news managers know it!

An active imagination is vital to stringing, as stations are always looking for new ideas. For instance, I once suggested that it would be fun to show what Indiana University students do on spring break in Florida. The station gave the okay and I was soon in Daytona, filming students in a variety of beach attire. I filmed license plates from the home state as well as T-shirts with the university emblem for a local tie-in, then hurried home with my story. (In addition to a plump check, I picked up a tan on this assignment.)

But you don't have to travel very far for most stories. Many ideas are initiated by items in city or college newspapers. A university news bureau also acts as a public relations department, and you can get good human-interest story ideas here: scientists at work, students at play, etc. Hospitals often have public relations people, too, who will feed you leads. Spread the word that you are actively stringing, and keep your ears open.

It also helps to check in with the local police and fire departments. Identify yourself and tell them the types of stories you want to cover. They may even escort you, as they did me, to a million-dollar, two-ton marijuana bust and the burning of the "tangible" evidence. Other sources of stories may include historical societies, libraries, local sports clubs, and newspaper ads (for unusual businesses). Don't overlook calendar events: Halloween or Friday the 13th, for example. Columbus Day is widely celebrated, but how about a tie-in with a local hobbyist who has built replicas of the *Niña, Pinta,* and *Santa Maria.* Float them in a pond and, for a special effect, move the water to create a turbulent "sea." Filmed in close-up, it could be an effective visual.

Once you are accepted as a stringer in your area, the ideas and assignments will come your way as regularly as the news at six. From this point on, it is important that you follow up on each story and make sure that your film gets to the station ahead of the deadline. Remember, it has to be developed and edited before the newscast. Therefore, you should know bus schedules, plane delivery services—and be prepared to drive the film to the station if it's an important story (stations usually pay mileage).

Many stringers earn $3,000 to $7,000 per year for their efforts. One enterprising stringer, who covered the southern portion of Indiana for several stations, raked in over $10,000 a year as a freelancer before one station hired him full-time to save money!

Freelancing news and features for local TV markets may not be for every writer, but if you have the stirrings of a scriptwriter, and the restless urge to compose behind the camera as well as at the keyboard—you'll find this a creatively satisfying occupation.

Glossary

blurb—the selling copy on the cover of a magazine or the jacket of a book that tells what's inside.

cold type—type set by a photocomposition method for offset printing as opposed to the hot-metal type used in letterpress typesetting machines.

collateral materials—brochures, annual reports, etc., prepared by an advertising agency in addition to the advertisements themselves for print or broadcast media.

copyestimating—estimating the amount of typeset copy that will be produced from a manuscript given a certain typeface size, line width, etc.

copyfitting—fitting a given amount of copy into an assigned space by specifying a certain type size, design, etc.

cut—an illustration (formerly a woodcut), which might be a photo-engraving for letterpress, or a photoprint for offset printing.

cutline—the caption for an illustration.

cut point—the beginning of a portion of a cassette tape recording that is to be edited out.

filmstrip—a continuous strip of 35mm film containing separate pictures or frames that is projected one image at a time, without producing any simulation of motion.

galleys—originally, the shallow metal trays containing composed type; now usually a shortened form of "galley proofs," the first version of typeset copy sent to the editor for correction.

mechanicals—artists' "boards" (sheets of heavy white cardboard) on which artwork and/or camera-ready text is pasted for photographing before printing.

offprint—a copy of an article or other section of a magazine or journal, frequently from extra unbound pages of the publication.

outcue—the notation of that point in a transcript of a recording where the closing portion of the program begins.

pop-on sound effect—a sound effect that does not fade in but rather is heard at full volume as soon as the audio tape starts.

PUP—pickup point; notation which indicates that place in a tape recording you want to use when editing the tape for broadcast.

racking—focusing a lens.

stringer—a term that derives from a practice in the old newspaper days: Editors used a piece of string to measure the amount of type set from a correspondent's copy in order to pay him according to the number of column inches he had written. Now used to refer to a correspondent in the field for a newspaper or magazine.

slide film—an audiovisual program consisting of separate images, usually 35mm frames within 2x2″ mounts projected separately or in combination with slides from one or more other projectors.

slide/tape—a slide film synchronized with an audio tape or record or other means of sound reproduction.

sound/slide film—see slide/tape.

tearsheet—literally a page torn from a magazine or newspaper containing an author's article, story, etc.

videotape—a ribbon of tape in various widths that can be magnetized by electronically generated methods to record and reproduce an audio signal and a visual image.

Bibliography

Advertising

Advertising. John S. Wright et al, 4th ed. McGraw-Hill, 1977.

Advertising Manager's Handbook. Richard H. Stansfield. Dartnell, 1977.

Cases in Advertising and Communications Management. Stephen A. Greyser. Prentice-Hall, 1972.

Confessions of an Advertising Man. David Ogilvy. Atheneum, 1963.

*From Those Wonderful Folks Who Gave You Pearl Harbor. Jerry Della Femina. Simon & Schuster, 1970.

"A Guide to Careers in Advertising" and "What Advertising Agencies Are—What They Do and How They Do It." Available from the American Association of Advertising Agencies, 200 Park Ave., New York, NY 10017. Price: 60c each.

Handbook of Advertising Management. Roger Barton, ed. McGraw-Hill, 1970.

How to be a Successful Copywriter. Betsy Anne Schellhase. Arco, 1965.

Madison Avenue Handbook [an annual directory]. Peter Glenn, ed. Peter Glenn Publications.

* *The Permissible Lie: The Inside Truth About Advertising.* Samm Sinclair Baker. Beacon, 1968.
* *Promise Them Anything.* Edward Buxton. Stein & Day, 1972.
Retail Advertising Copy: The How, the What, the Why. Judy Y. Oiko. National Retail Merchants Association, 1977.

Association Administration

Lesly's Public Relations Handbook. Philip Lesly. 2d ed. Prentice-Hall, 1978.
Principles of Association Management. United States Chamber of Commerce and the American Society of Association Executives, 1975.
Tested Advertising Methods. J. Caples. Prentice-Hall, 1974.

Audiovisual Writing

Audiovisual Script Writing. Norton S. Parker. Rutgers University Press, 1974.
Creative Film-Making. Kirk Smallman. Macmillan, 1969.
* *Film and Its Techniques.* Raymond Spottiswoode. University of California Press, 1951.
Guide to Film Making. Edward Pincus. New American Library, 1969.
* *Independent Filmmaking.* Lenny Lipton. Simon & Schuster, 1972.
Movie-Making: A Guide to Film Production. Sumner Glimcher and Warren Johnson. Washington Square Press, 1975.
The Screenwriter's Handbook: What to Write, How to Write It, Where to Sell It. Constance Nash and Virginia Oakey. Barnes & Noble, 1978.
Screenplay: The Foundations of Screenwriting. Syd Field. Dell, 1979.
Script Models: A Handbook for the Media Writer. Robert Lee and Robert Misiorowski. Hastings House, 1978.
Scriptwriting for the Audio-Visual Media. Robert Edmonds. Teachers College Press, 1978.

Periodicals

Audio-Visual Communications and *Industrial Photography;* both monthly; both from United Business Publications, 475 Park Ave. S., New York NY 10017.

Book Publishing

The Careful Writer: A Modern Guide to English Usage. Theodore M. Bernstein. Atheneum, 1965.
The Complete Guide to Editorial Freelancing. Carol L. O'Neill and Avima Ruder. 2d ed. Barnes & Noble, 1978.

Guide to Book Publishing Courses: Academic and Professional Programs. Susan E. Shaffer, ed. Peterson's Guides, 1978.

*"How to Make an Index," in *Leacock Roundabout.* Stephen Leacock. Dodd, Mead, 1946.

*"Index: There Is No Index," in *My Remarkable Uncle.* Stephen Leacock. Dodd, 1942.

Indexes and Indexing, Robert L. Collison. John DeGraf, 1969.

Indexing Your Book: A Practical Guide for Authors. Sina K. Spiker. 2d ed. University of Wisconsin Press, 1963.

A Manual of Style. 12th ed. University of Chicago Press, 1969.

Publication Manual. 2d ed. American Psychological Association, 1974.

Style Manual. rev. ed. US Government Printing Office, 1973.

Webster's New Collegiate Dictionary. 8th ed. G. & C. Merriam, 1979.

Webster's Third New International Dictionary, Unabridged: The Great Library of the English Language. G. & C. Merriam, 1976.

Words into Type. Marjorie E. Skillin and Robert M. Gay. 3d ed. Prentice-Hall, 1974.

Business Writing

Associated Business Writers of America and Professional Freelance Writers Directory [annual]. National Writers Club, 1450 S. Havana, Aurora CO 80012.

Communicating with Professional Investors. Phyllis S. McGrath. The Conference Board, 1974.

The Company Editor. Charles B. Moore and William F. Blue, Jr. Ink Art Publications, 1979.

Do-It-Yourself Marketing Research. George E. Breen. McGraw-Hill, 1977.

The Encyclopedia of Management. Carl Heyel, ed. 2d ed. Van Nostrand Reinhold, 1973.

"For Better Business Writing." John S. Fielden. *Harvard Business Review,* January-February 1965.

Historical Anniversaries of Notable People, 1980, 1981, 1982. Etna M. Kelley. Available from Philip Murphy Co., 60 E. 42nd St., New York NY 10017.

Motivating Human Behavior. Ernest Dichter. McGraw-Hill, 1971.

Writing for Business. Mary C. Bromage. University of Michigan Press, 1965.

Periodicals

The Anniversary Newsletter [monthly]. Lawrence Ragan Communications, 407 S. Dearborn St., Chicago IL 60605.

Editor's Newsletter: Trends and Techniques in Business Communications [monthly]. Box 243, Lenox Hill Station, New York NY 10021.

IABC News [monthly]. International Association of Business Communicators, 870 Market St. No. 928, San Francisco CA 94102.

Journal of Organizational Communication [quarterly]. IABC.

Ragan Report: A Weekly Survey of Ideas and Methods for Communication Executives. Lawrence Ragan Communications.

Educational Grant Proposal Writing

The Art of Winning Foundation Grants. Howard Hillman and Karin Abarbanel. Vanguard Press, 1975.

Basic Guide for the Preparation and Submission of Proposals for Research Support. Foster S. Buchtel. Available from Western's Campus Bookstore, University Student Center, Western Michigan University, Kalamazoo MI 49008. Price: $1.50 plus $1 postage.

How to Get Government Grants. Philip Des Marais. Public Service Materials Center.

How to Prepare a Research Proposal. David Krathwohl. Available from the Syracuse University Bookstore, 303 University Pl., Syracuse NY 13210. Price: $2.95 plus $1 postage.

Periodicals

Federal Grants and Contracts Weekly. Capitol Publications, 2430 Pennsylvania Ave., NW, Washington DC 20037.

Foundation News [bimonthly]. Council on Foundations, 888 Seventh Ave., New York NY 10019.

Grantsmanship Center News [bimonthly]. 1031 S. Grand Ave., Los Angeles CA 90015.

How to Evaluate Education Programs [monthly]. Capitol Publications.

Fund Raising

The Art of Fund Raising. Irving R. Warner. Harper & Row, 1975.

Genealogy

American Origins: Sources for Genealogical Research and Records Abroad. Leslie Pine. Genealogical Publishing, repr. of 1960 ed.

Finding Your Roots. Jeane E. Westin. Ballantine, 1978.

Genealogy as Pastime and Profession. Donald L. Jacobus. 2d ed. Genealogical Publishing, 1978.

Searching for Your Ancestors. Gilbert H. Doane. Bantam, 1974.

Opinion Research Interviewing
Professional Interviewing. Cal W. Downs et al. Harper & Row, 1980.

Programmed Instruction
*Developing Programmed Instructional Materials. James E. Espich and Bill Williams. Fearon-Pitman, 1967.
Good Frames and Bad: A Grammar of Frame Writing. Susan M. Markle. 2d ed. John Wiley, 1969.
Preparing Instructional Objectives. Robert F. Mager. 2d ed. Fearon-Pitman, 1975.

Public Broadcasting
A Public Trust: The Report of the Carnegie Commission on the Future of Public Broadcasting. Bantam, 1979.
To Serve the Public Interest: Educational Broadcasting in the United States. Robert J. Blakely. Syracuse University Press, 1979.
Available from the Corporation for Public Broadcasting (1111 Sixteenth St., NW, Washington DC 20036):
CPB-Qualified Radio Stations.
Handbook of Information Sources for United States Public Television.
1979 Annual Report.
Available from Public Telecommunications Press (National Association of Educational Broadcasters, 1346 Connecticut Ave., NW, Washington DC 20036):
Learning from Television. Wilbur Schramm and Godwin C. Chu.
The Nixon Administration Public Broadcasting Papers: A Summary.
People in Public Telecommunications [NAEB annual directory].
The Politics of Interconnection: A History of Public Television at the National Level. Robert K. Avery and Robert Pepper.
Program Decisions in Public Television. Nathan Katzman.
Public Broadcasting Act of 1967.

Public Relations
Bibliography [updated annually]. Available free from the Public Relations Society of America, 845 Third Ave., 12th floor, New York NY 10022.
Effective Public Relations. Allen Center and Scott Cutlip. 5th ed. Prentice-Hall, 1978.
The Library Public Relations Recipe Book. Irene E. Moran, ed. Includes a ten-page annotated bibliography. Available from the Library Ad-

ministration and Management Association, c/o American Library Association, 50 E. Huron St., Chicago IL 60611. Price: $4 postpaid.

Public Relations Careers: In Business and the Community. Patrick Monaghan. Fairchild, 1972.

Public Relations for Public Libraries. Betty Rice. H.W. Wilson, 1972.

Public Relations Information Sources. Alice Norton, ed. Gale Research Co., 1970.

Radio

Advertising. Kenneth A. Longman. Harcourt Brace Jovanovich, 1971.

Air Time. Ronald Seidle, Holbrook Press, 1977.

Chases' Calendar of Annual Events: Special Days, Weeks and Months in 198- [issued annually]. Apple Tree Press.

The Craft of Interviewing. John Brady. Writer's Digest Books, 1976.

Mass Media: An Introduction to Modern Communication. Ray Eldon Hiebert et al. Longman, 1979.

Television and Radio. Giraud Chester et al. 5th ed. Prentice-Hall, 1978.

Understanding Broadcasting. Eugene S. Foster. Addison-Wesley, 1978.

Speechwriting

Public Speaking as Listeners Like It. Richard C. Borden. Harper & Row, 1935.

Teaching High School Journalism

Journalism. William Hartman. Laidlaw, 1968.

Journalism in the Mass Media. Norman B. Moyes and David Manning White. Ginn, 1974.

The Mass Media and the School Newspaper. De Witt C. Reddick. Wadsworth, 1976.

Press Time. Julian Adams and Kenneth Stratton. Prentice-Hall, 1975.

Scholastic Journalism. Earl English and Clarence Hach. 6th ed. Iowa State University Press, 1978.

Translation

After Babel: Aspects of Language and Translation. George Steiner. Oxford University Press, 1975.

The Nature of Translation: Essays on the Theory and Practice of Literary Translation. James S. Holmes et al. Mouton, 1970.

Proteus: His Lies, His Truth. Robert M. Adams. Norton, 1973.

The Theory and Practice of Translation. Eugene Nida and Charles R. Taber. United Bible Societies, 1969.

Toward a Science of Translating. Eugene Nida. Heinman, 1964.

Translation and Translators: An International Directory and Guide. Stefan Congrat-Butlar. ed. Bowker, 1979.

Translation: Applications and Research. Richard W. Brislin, ed. Halsted, 1976.

TV

American Cinematographer Manual. Charles G. Clarke and Walter Strenge. 4th ed. American Society of Cinematographers.

*Filming TV News and Documentaries. Jim Atkins, Jr., and Leo Willette. Chilton, 1965.

The Five C's of Cinematography. Joseph V. Mascelli. 8th ed. Cine-Graphic, 1979.

Independent Filmmaking. Lenny Lipton. Simon & Schuster, 1972.

Practical Motion Picture Photography. Russell Campbell, ed. A.S. Barnes, 1971.

Professional 16/35mm Cameraman's Handbook. Verne and Sylvia Carlson. 2d ed. Amphoto, 1974.

Television News: Writing, Filming, Editing, Broadcasting. Irving E. Fang. 2d rev. ed. Hastings House, 1972.

Periodicals

American Cinematographer. 1782 N. Orange Dr., Hollywood CA 90028.

General

The Art of Readable Writing: 25th Anniversary Edition. Rudolf Flesch. rev. and enl. ed. Harper & Row, 1974.

*Finding Facts: Interviewing, Observing, Using Reference Sources. William L. Rivers. Prentice-Hall, 1975.

How to Be a Successful Housewife/Writer. Elaine Fantle Shimberg. Writer's Digest Books, 1979.

How You Can Make $20,000 a Year Writing (No Matter Where You Live). Nancy Edmonds Hanson. Writer's Digest Books, 1980.

Information Sources: The 198- Membership Directory [updated anually]. Information Industry Association, Suite 904, 4720 Montgomery Lane, Bethesda MD 20014.

Law and the Writer. Kirk Polking and Leonard S. Meranus, eds. Writer's Digest Books, 1978.

Sell Copy. Webster Kuswa. Writer's Digest Books, 1979.

The Technique of Clear Writing. Robert Gunning. rev. ed. McGraw-Hill, 1968.

The Writer's Resource Guide. William Brohaugh, ed. Writer's Digest Books, 1979.

You, Inc.: A Detailed Escape Route to Being Your Own Boss. Peter A. Weaver. Doubleday, 1975.

Periodicals

Freelancer's Newsletter [semimonthly]. Box 89, Skaneateles NY 13152.

About the Authors

Allan Amenta, coordinator of Instructional Development Services at California State University in Long Beach, has written and produced motion pictures, video programs, sound/slide films, and filmstrips for educational, corporate, commercial, government, and other clients, and has written articles for numerous magazines and journals, including *Playboy, American Home, Writer's Digest, The Writer,* and *Audio-Visual Communications.* His AV programs have won many honors and awards, most recently the Silver Medal of the International Film and Television Festival of New York for a synchronized slide/tape about black studies at Cal State, Long Beach.

Alan R. Blackburn of Billings, Montana, did his fund-raising writing in Cleveland, and in so doing raised some sizable sums for his own exchequer. Besides bulletins and newsletters, he wrote 600 ninety-second radio scripts for the program "Salute to Business" and scripts for B.F. Goodrich documentaries.

Virginia Blankenship supplements her PR work by selling features and book reviews to the small-national-magazine market, and has completed a historical novel.

James Boeringer is chairman of the Music Department at Susquehanna University in Selinsgrove, Pennsylvania. He freelances reviews and features to many English and American music magazines, and his three-volume study of British organs, *Organa Britannica,* is to be published by Bucknell University Press. He is also a composer and organ recitalist.

Michael S. Bucki is the Peabody-award-winning news and public affairs director at WABE-FM, Atlanta. He frequently contributes features and short documentaries to National Public Radio's "Morning Edition" and "All Things Considered."

Robert Cassidy, a member of the National Book Critics Circle, is the author of *Livable Cities* (Holt, Rinehart & Winston), as well as managing editor and book review editor of *Planning,* an urban affairs magazine published in Chicago.

Dave Derkacy is currently a communications specialist with the Agency for Instructional Television, the largest distributor of classroom video series in the US. His articles and photographs have been published in the *New York Times, PhotoGraphic Magazine,* the *Louisville Courier-Journal,* and other publications. His photographs illustrate two college textbooks published by Macmillan and Houghton Mifflin. He has filmed hundreds of news and feature stories for WRTV-6 Indianapolis and has also freelanced for WISH-8 of Indianapolis. Other efforts include TV commercials, documentaries, and educational films.

Mary A. De Vries, managing editor of Editorial Services in Bull Shoals, Arkansas, has written, edited, and produced a full range of association literature, has had twenty fiction and nonfiction books published, and has ghosted numerous biographies and autobiographies. Currently she is writing a spy thriller and a guide to business writing, editing, and production.

Elizabeth L. Dugger notes that considering she started writing free press releases in the lowlands of New Jersey, moved on to composition editing in the hills, and now edits and proofreads texts in the mountains of Vermont, her career has gone steadily uphill. Freelance editing supplies the regular income that supplements the checks for writing original material, published in the *New York Times, Cat Fancy,* the *Feminist Art Journal,* and numerous trade and local publications. Her first novel is thus far unpublished, so she is eagerly seeking more editing to keep her critical faculties in practice.

Al Eason of Overton, Texas, has sold hundreds of articles, and thousands of columns, to such publications as *Outdoor Life, Sports Afield, Southwestern Angler,* and *American Hunter.* In addition, he has authored two books, *How Pro Guides Find and Catch Fish,* published by the Cordovan Corporation of Houston, and *Boom Town: Kilgore, Texas,* published by that town's chamber of commerce.

Gloria Emison, a former editorial associate of *Writer's Digest,* has, as a freelancer, indexed textbooks, cookbooks, historical books, and books for other freelancers. Her greatest ambition is to gather all the debris of daily life into the definitive index and consider it dealt with once and for all.

John D. Engle, Jr., has published more than 1,000 poems in various magazines and newspapers, including *Good Housekeeping,* the *Saturday Evening Post,* the *Christian Science Monitor,* the *Kansas City Star,* the *Denver Post* and others. He's also published three books of poetry.

Betty Steele Everett has taught writing in high school and adult education programs in Ohio, and at the Black Mountain Christian Writers' Conference. She has been a freelance writer for some twenty years; in that time she's sold more than 1,200 articles and short stories.

Leon Fletcher, a former college administrator and speech instructor, freelances from Monterey, California, writing during the mornings, sailing most afternoons. Most of his articles are about boating, travel, and education. His college text, *How to Design & Deliver a Speech,* published by Harper & Row, is now in its second edition. While writing educational proposals as described in his article he raised more than seven million dollars. The diversity of topics an educational writer may encounter is illustrated by some of the more than fifty projects on which Fletcher wrote: they included educational television, welding, dyslexia, computer-assisted instruction, astronomy, multimedia lectures, art, teacher training, typing, and foreign languages.

Sue Glasco majored in journalism at Southern Illinois University and later earned an M.S. in speech there. She was a debate coach and taught English and speech full time at a Chicago suburban high school for one year before her marriage. During her children's growing-up years, writing and teaching have been part-time pursuits. As a columnist and freelancer she has been published in a number of religious, family, and juvenile magazines and newspapers.

Joseph Hanania has worked for NBC-TV as a freelance story analyst; currently he is story editor for a Styloform Films documentary on hoboes. He also contributes freelance articles about film to the *Los Angeles Times* and has published articles in the *Village Voice, Philadelphia Magazine,* and elsewhere. In addition, he serves as vice-president of public relations for the California Water Resources Association.

Robert E. Heinemann is founder and president of a corporate communications firm in Glastonbury, Connecticut. Writing and editing for his national clientele keeps him quite busy, but, he says, "I'll also admit to an occasional freelance assignment, and a never-ending effort to conclude a lesser American novel."

Harold A. Holbrook has thirty years' experience in the technical-writing field. He headed the proposal-writing section of Raytheon's Wayland Laboratory in Massachusetts until he reached their mandatory retirement age; since then he has been working steadily at long-term, full-time freelance assignments, most recently at Computer Systems Engineering.

Connie Howard worked for six years as the advertising manager of Regency Mall in Indiana, Pennsylvania. She is now the radio & TV co-ordinator for Indiana University of Pennsylvania's Center for Community Affairs, where her writing has led to moderating work on a number of KDKA-TV (Pittsburgh) public affairs programs as well as producing programs for WJAC-TV, Johnstown, and WTAJ-TV, Altoona.

Bob Jacobs is an associate professor of radio-TV-film at the University of Wisconsin-Oshkosh. He entered the teaching profession out of what he calls a "fit of conscience" after working in Hollywood as a writer and director for fifteen years. He remains a freelance writer and filmmaker, and has a small TV commercial production company, in which his students get practical experience. He just completed his first novel, a horror-fantasy called *Season of the Beast,* and is working on a full-length feature film script dealing with pro football.

Dave Kaiser is currently editor of *Saudi Report,* a weekly newsletter published by Saudi Research and Marketing, Inc., of Houston. He is also responsible for all copy that goes from the United States to several daily newspapers and several weekly magazines published by the same firm. As a freelance writer and editor, he has prepared weekly publications for over a dozen years and written for a number of national and international publications.

Etna M. Kelley, a freelance writer specializing in anniversary articles and services, is the author of *The Business Founding Date Directory,* which lists 10,000 companies founded between 1687 and 1915. She also produced lists of city and town birthdays and milestones; 1981 and 1982 lists are now in preparation. Her *Bibliography of Anniversary Articles* comprises 240 titles, many with brief synopses that give information on how anniversaries were celebrated. Miss Kelley also edits an anniversary newsletter which appears frequently as a supplement to the *Ragan Report.*

Michael H. Ketcher is research editor and assistant marketing director, on a freelance basis, for the journal *Taxing & Spending,* published by the Institute for Contemporary Studies. As a writer he specializes in business, economics, and consumer topics.

Mike McCarville, whose non-ghostly byline has appeared in *Friends, Corvette*

News, Columbia, Our Sunday Visitor, Kansas City, Oklahoma Today, and other publications, has written over 400 speeches for politicians and businessmen.

Cookie McGee is business editor of *The Leader,* the newspaper that serves the Research Triangle Park in North Carolina. Her freelance social and political commentary has appeared in Raleigh newspapers as well as in TV editorials.

James McLendon was a newspaperman for years, and a stringer for the UPI in Central America. He is the author of more than 300 magazine articles, and for some years now has devoted himself to writing novels. His first novel, *Death-work,* was a bestseller and was translated into all the world's major languages. His most recent novel, *Eddie Macon's Run,* is having similar sales. Recently he signed a three-novel contract with Doubleday. McLendon is also the author of a nonfiction book on the Great Depression in Florida. He recently completed his first original motion picture screenplay.

Arnall Mohre works as a private investigator in Metairie, Louisiana. He has published a book, *Be a Private Investigator,* which comes with a packet of secondary information; it deals with how to set yourself up in the business.

Anne Montague is an assistant editor at Writer's Digest Books.

Ted Morrow has been a full-time freelance translator for eight years, in German, Russian, French, Spanish, Italian, Portuguese, Dutch, Danish, Norwegian, Swedish, Finnish, Hungarian, Romanian, Czech, Polish, Estonian, Latvian, and Azerbaijani.

Jan A. Noble, Sr. is a full-time freelance writer in Bristol, Indiana. He has written a booklet entitled "Power Résumés for Broadcasters," and a résumé-writing "kit" entitled "Writing Your Résumé—Professionally—Effectively — For RESULTS," which he sells for ten dollars primarily to those clients who can't afford going through the full résumé process. Noble has written over a thousand résumés since 1972. He also writes résumés on a nationwide basis by mail. Other freelance writing includes magazine articles, working with ad agencies, writing and producing audiovisual slide sales presentations for companies, and editing an in-house company publication.

Ted Oglesby, Jr., is associate editor of the Gainesville, Georgia, *Times* and has won several state newspaper awards. He teaches advanced investigative reporting and international relations at Brenau College. He freelances in his spare time.

Eugene Perret's recent credits include a five-year writing stint with "The Carol Burnett Show," for which he won three Emmys and a Writers Guild Award. With Bill Richmond he has produced "Welcome Back, Kotter," "Three's Company," and "The Tim Conway Variety Show." J.P. Tarcher will soon publish his *Hit or Miss Management,* a comedy how-to book for executives.

Ted Schwarz is a full-time Arizona freelancer who has written some thirty books on subjects ranging from photography to history. He has also written for NBC and Westinghouse radio affiliates, Storer Broadcasting, and radio station WIXY in Cleveland.

J. Stouder Sweet works in the public information office of a university, and is listed in the Directory of American Scholars. Many years ago he was in charge of the genealogy room in the Library of Congress. He copied the names of the books in the room and published them in a guide to genealogy and local history, now out of print. He once thought of writing a study of "mug" books, but despaired of ever identifying them all.

Linda Trainor, a communications consultant for an international brokerage firm, is also the author of the *Lawyers' Advertising Handbook.* In addition to her freelance copywriting background she also has co-written and produced five educational films; recently she received a first-place award from *Business Insurance* magazine for a slide show and booklet on employee benefit communications.

Wanda Voncannon served as press relations officer for the Longview (Texas) Independent School District, then freelanced features to the local paper. She has received first-place awards from the Texas Press Women's Association in several categories, including "Publicity or Promotion—Newspaper."

DeForest Walton freelanced as a business writer for ten years, and then, with Tom Kleene, established a company to provide editorial services in Detroit and the Midwest. Presently Walton & Kleene has expanded with an office in Houston. The major area of service is still "writing for business." Says Walton, "All our staff employees are writers, and we contract additional freelancers who have special backgrounds in business writing. We feel that the written word is the starting point for all communication."

C.G. Welton founded his own PR firm in Hartford, Connecticut. His work for the local printer earned him the Printing Industries of America's Ben Franklin Award.

Bill Williams was a technical writer and editor of a monthly company magazine before becoming interested in programmed instruction. He is now president of The Wordshop, which produces a wide variety of materials, including PI texts, workbook/cassettes, and videotapes. "I still find time (occasionally) to write an article or story and am working—albeit slowly and sporadically—on a novel."

Nancy Abbott Young is an editorial assistant on the *Public Telecommunications Review* and *Current,* an industry newsletter, at the National Association of Educational Broadcasters, and serves as a freelance editor for *NewsWaves,* the new national publication of the Coast Alliance, an environmental protection coalition. She has written several plays and collections of poems and lyrics. Her narrative poem "Food Stamps, USDA" was dramatized on WMAR-TV, Baltimore.

Lloyd Zimpel has edited *Man Against Work* and *The Disadvantaged Worker.* The San Francisco-based writer has published a novel, *Meeting the Bear,* and is coauthor of *Business and the Hardcore Unemployed.* He has contributed fiction and nonfiction to many periodicals, including the *Nation, Transatlantic Review,* the *New Republic,* and *Commonweal.*

Index

B

C

S

T

U

Other Writer's Digest Books

General Writing Books

    Beginning Writer's Answer Book, edited by Polking and Bloss, $14.95

    Getting the Words Right: How to Revise, Edit and Rewrite, by Theodore A. Rees Cheney $13.95

    How to Become a Bestselling Author, by Stan Corwin, $14.95

    How to Get Started in Writing, by Peggy Teeters $10.95

    International Writers' & Artists' Yearbook, (paper) $10.95

    Law and the Writer, edited by Polking and Meranus (paper) $7.95

    Make Every Word Count, by Gary Provost (paper) $7.95

    Teach Yourself to Write, by Evelyn A. Stenbock $12.95

    Treasury of Tips for Writers, edited by Marvin Weisbord (paper) $6.95

    Writer's Encyclopedia, edited by Kirk Polking $19.95

    Writer's Market, edited by Bernadine Clark $18.95

    Writer's Resource Guide, edited by Bernadine Clark $16.95

    Writing for the Joy of It, by Leonard Knott $11.95

    Writing From the Inside Out, by Charlotte Edwards (paper) $9.95

Magazine/News Writing

    Complete Guide to Marketing Magazine Articles, by Duane Newcomb $9.95

    Complete Guide to Writing Nonfiction, by the American Society of Journalists & Authors, edited by Glen Evans $24.95

    Craft of Interviewing, by John Brady $9.95

    Magazine Writing: The Inside Angle, by Art Spikol $12.95

    Magazine Writing Today, by Jerome E. Kelley $10.95

    Newsthinking: The Secret of Great Newswriting, by Bob Baker $11.95

    1001 Article Ideas, by Frank A. Dickson $10.95

    Stalking the Feature Story, by William Ruehlmann $9.95

    Write On Target, by Connie Emerson $12.95

    Writing and Selling Non-Fiction, by Hayes B. Jacobs $12.95

Fiction Writing

    Creating Short Fiction, by Damon Knight $11.95

    Fiction Is Folks: How to Create Unforgettable Characters, by Robert Newton Peck $1.95

    Fiction Writer's Help Book, by Maxine Rock $12.95

    Fiction Writer's Market, edited by Jean Fredette $17.95

    Handbook of Short Story Writing, by Dickson and Smythe (paper) $6.95

    How to Write Best-Selling Fiction, by Dean R. Koontzgght $11.95

    Fiction Is Folks: How to Create Unforgettable Characters, by Robert Newton Peck $11.95

    Fiction Writer's Help Book, by Maxine Rock $12.95

    Fiction Writer's Market, edited by Jean Fredette $17.95

    Handbook of Short Story Writing, by Dickson and Smythe (paper) $6.95

    How to Write Best-Selling Fiction, by Dean R. Koontz $13.95

    How to Write Short Stories that Sell, by Louise Boggess (paper) $7.95

One Way to Write Your Novel, by Dick Perry (paper) $6.95

Secrets of Successful Fiction, by Robert Newton Peck $8.95

Writing Romance Fiction—For Love And Money, by Helene Schellenberg Barnhart $14.95

Writing the Novel: From Plot to Print, by Lawrence Block $10.95

Special Interest Writing Books

Cartoonist's & Gag Writer's Handbook, by Jack Markow (paper) $9.95

The Children's Picture Book: How to Write It, How to Sell It, by Ellen E. M. Roberts $17.95

Complete Book of Scriptwriting, by J. Michael Straczynski $14.95

Complete Guide to Greeting Card Writing, edited by Larry Sandman (paper) $7.95

Complete Guide to Writing Software User Manuals, by Brad McGehee (paper) $14.95

Confession Writer's Handbook, by Florence K. Palmer. Revised by Marguerite McClain $9.95

Guide to Greeting Card Writing, edited by Larry Sandman $10.95

How to Make Money Writing . . . Fillers, by Connie Emerson $12.95

How to Write a Cookbook and Get It Published, by Sara Pitzer, $15.95

How to Write a Play, by Raymond Hull $13.95

How to Write and Sell Your Personal Experiences, by Lois Duncan $10.95

How to Write and Sell (Your Sense of) Humor, by Gene Perret $12.95

How to Write "How-To" Books and Articles, by Raymond Hull (paper) $8.95

Mystery Writer's Handbook, edited by Lawrence Treat (paper) $8.95

Poet and the Poem, revised edition by Judson Jerome $13.95

Poet's Handbook, by Judson Jerome $11.95

Programmer's Market, edited by Brad McGehee (paper) $16.95

Sell Copy, by Webster Kuswa $11.95

Successful Outdoor Writing, by Jack Samson $11.95 **(paper) $8.95**

Mystery Writer's Handbook, edited by Lawrence Treat (paper) $8.95

Poet and the Poem, revised edition by Judson Jerome $13.95

Poet's Handbook, by Judson Jerome $11.95

Programmer's Market, edited by Brad McGehee (paper) $16.95

Sell Copy, by Webster Kuswa $11.95

Successful Outdoor Writing, by Jack Samson $11.95

Travel Writer's Handbook, by Louise Zobel (paper) $8.95

TV Scriptwriter's Handbook, by Alfred Brenner $12.95

Writing and Selling Science Fiction, by Science Fiction Writers of America (paper) $7.95

Writing for Children & Teenagers, by Lee Wyndham. Revised by Arnold Madison $11.95

Writing for Regional Publications, by Brian Vachon $11.95

Writing to Inspire, by Gentz, Roddy, et al $14.95

The Writing Business

Complete Handbook for Freelance Writers, by Kay Cassill $14.95

Freelance Jobs for Writers, edited by Kirk Polking (paper) $7.95

How to Be a Successful Housewife/Writer, by Elaine Fantle Shimberg $10.95

How You Can Make $20,000 a Year Writing, by Nancy Hanson (paper) $6.95

Profitable Part-time/Full-time Freelancing, by Clair Rees $10.95

The Writer's Survival Guide: How to Cope with Rejection, Success and 99 Other Hang-Ups of the Writing Life, by Jean and Veryl Rosenbaum $12.95

To order directly from the publisher, include $1.50 postage and handling for 1 book and 50¢ for each additional book. Allow 30 days for delivery.

Writer's Digest Books, Department B

9933 Alliance Road, Cincinnati OH 45242

Prices subject to change without notice.